THE SUNDANCE KID

THE

SUNDANCE

KID

AN UNAUTHORIZED
BIOGRAPHY OF

ROBERT
REDFORD

LAWRENCE J. QUIRK AND WILLIAM SCHOELL

TAYLOR TRADE PUBLISHING
Lanham • New York • Boulder • Toronto • Oxford

Published by Taylor Trade Publishing
An imprint of The Rowman & Littlefield Publishing Group, Inc.
4501 Forbes Boulevard, Suite 200, Lanham, Maryland 20706

Distributed by NATIONAL BOOK NETWORK

Library of Congress Cataloging-in-Publication Data

Quirk, Lawrence J.
   The Sundance Kid : an unauthorized biography of Robert Redford / Lawrence J. Quirk and William Schoell.
      p.   cm.
   Filmography: p.
   Includes bibliographical references and index.
   ISBN-13: 978-1-58979-297-5 (cloth : alk. paper)
   ISBN-10: 1-58979-297-1 (cloth : alk. paper)
   1. Redford, Robert.   2. Motion picture actors and actresses—United States—Biography.   I. Schoell, William.   II. Title.
   PN2287.R283Q57   2006
   791.4302'8092—dc22   2006000845

∞ ™ The paper used in this publication meets the minimum requirements of American National Standard for Information Sciences—Permanence of Paper for Printed Library Materials, ANSI/NISO Z39.48-1992.

Manufactured in the United States of America.

To Robert Dahdah, the Truest of Friends

All my life I've been dogged with guilt because I feel there is this difference between the way I look and the way I feel inside.

—*Robert Redford*

CONTENTS

Acknowledgments

The authors tender their appreciation to Rick Rinehart, Ross Plotkin, Janice Braunstein, Chris Thillen, and everyone at Taylor Trade Publishing/Rowman & Littlefield. We also thank the many people who shared their thoughts and memories of Robert Redford with us, those prominently named in the text, and those who gave confidential interviews.

INTRODUCTION

Movie stars are not normal people.

It's not just that most people don't spend their lives being endlessly scrutinized by the media; most people aren't *idolized* beyond all reason or logic by people who not only don't know them, but will probably never even meet them. When the celebrity is considered a sex symbol on top of that, the level of curiosity, indeed obsession, reaches a fanatical level. For at least half of his life, if not more, Robert Redford has been viewed with a microscope, although he hasn't made it easy for observers to bring him into focus.

Redford is often fanatical himself—about his privacy. He has given many interviews over the years, but he is reticent to talk about his personal life. His family is off-limits, and he lets it be known that he doesn't like people talking about him. Because of this, even some people who had only positive and admiring things to say about him, especially those who work for or with him, spoke to the authors of this book only on condition of anonymity. As a leading man Redford may have stepped aside for the likes of Brad Pitt, Tom Cruise, and George Clooney; but he is still perceived as a formidable figure in Hollywood, largely because of Sundance and his reinvention of himself as a director of undeniable ability.

Critics have always been divided over Redford's acting skill, with some seeing him as a master of understatement and others thinking of him as wooden. He has been more warmly embraced as the director of such superior films as *Ordinary People* and *Quiz Show*. His interest in a variety of causes has earned him new fans and made him enemies, and even his fellow liberals think he sometimes goes too far.

But Redford can never be dismissed as just a pretty-boy actor of limited ability who got his day in the sun due to a certain romantic magnetism. Redford was no comparative flash in the pan like, say, Troy Donahue or fill-in-the-blank. It takes a certain degree of smarts to have a career that lasts as long as Redford's. His creation of the Sundance workshops for independent films and his essentially overseeing the Sundance Festival, not to mention his work as executive producer on many different movies, have kept him a decided player for many more years than those of most actors his age.

Redford's career is thus worthy of serious study. In this biography we look not only at his personal life but also at his films, his acting style, his directorial approach, and his political and environmental causes, not to mention various aspects of his work at Sundance.

This is the story of a major movie star, how he became that star, and how and why he has lasted.

His father was a milkman named Charles and his mother was the former Martha Hart, a housewife. They lived in Santa Monica, California, where Charles Robert Redford Jr. came into the world on August 18, 1937. He was blond and blue-eyed, a perfect little boy, and the Redfords were happy, although a little uncertain how they would keep up with the bills. As a young boy Redford didn't see too much of his father, who was up at dawn to deliver the milk and didn't return from his rounds until after his son returned home from school. Redford always remembered his father as a hard worker and a good provider for his family. His mother was the very model of positive thinking, always happy and always looking out for ways to make life better for her son and husband. But Redford felt there was more to them than met the eye.

"My family had a dark, cold side," he remembered many years later. "My father's background was Celtic, Irish; he was a transplant from New England. Then there were the Scots on my mother's side, from Texas. It was a great storytelling family—not at all affectionate—yet they didn't talk much about themselves, so there was a lot about their lives that I didn't know." When Redford was a small boy his father took him for a visit to his old neighborhood, an "Italian ghetto," as Redford described it, in New London, Connecticut. Redford was shocked when a friendly Italian woman actually picked him up and gave him a hug. "Nobody ever lifted me in the air in my family; I was lucky to get a handshake." Years later Redford would have a problem being affectionate and physical with other people, and because of it would never quite get past what some critics saw as a certain stoicism in his acting.

In the post–World War Two period when Redford was around

ten, his father got employment at Standard Oil as an accountant, which meant higher pay and shorter hours. The family was then able to afford a larger and nicer home in the tonier community of Van Nuys. Describing the difference between Los Angeles and Van Nuys, Redford recalled, "those mountains were much more of a demarcation point as a kid in the fifties. Once you came to the [San Fernando] Valley, it was just a wasteland, there was nothing there, and at night there were no lights out there. People spilled into the Valley, so it drew a polyglot, an eclectic mix of mostly immigrant families who could afford to live out there because it was now cheap . . . but the trade-off, for me, was horrendous: sterile, flat, boring, cookie-cutter homes in neighborhoods that had no character."

One of his favorite activities during this period was going to the library on Wednesday night with his parents. "It was such a big deal, to go in and get my own book. I dove into mythology, and that was the most important thing I ever did, for it was full of all these larger-than-life things, windows into greater possibilities, other realms." Unfortunately, as Redford got older his interest in reading would be supplanted by other, less beneficial activities. In any case, his childhood hero was no literary figure but rather baseball player Ted Williams.

Already Redford, despite his love for his parents and vice versa, was developing a horror of typical middle-class life and the workaday world where the Puritan work ethic ruled. Already fairly arrogant, as well as a budding nonconformist of sorts, he resented that he was automatically supposed to be eternally grateful because his parents *worked* and *sacrificed* to provide him a good life and should feel eternally guilty if he wasn't. It wasn't that he didn't appreciate what his parents did for him; he just didn't want to have it held over his head all the time. It made him feel suffocated, trapped, as if in order to show his gratitude he would have to do whatever his parents wanted. Redford at that point had no idea what he wanted to do with his life, but it was going to be *his life* and no one else's.

Redford had always had issues with his father. "Things were pretty rough because he was angry and upset with his life. He should have been a sportswriter but was too afraid to take a chance. My father was imprisoned by his work ethic which told him that work and earning was everything and that a man shouldn't throw around compliments or emotions." According to Redford, his father had actually had him thrown out of his Boy Scout troop when the elder Redford was scoutmaster. (One could say about Redford that he "wasn't exactly a Boy Scout," except that apparently he *was*—literally—although not for very long.) Despite his father's having what Redford perceived as a hard and cold nature, the younger Redford deemed his father a liberal due to the influence of being raised by an aunt who was an ardent follower of Emma Goldman.

In 1952, when he was fifteen, Redford attended Van Nuys High. "I was a total goof ball in school, just a worthless student, always looking for a way out of going to class or a way to have more fun than I was having, or to *escape*—to hooky out. That was my chief modus operandi." He later described Van Nuys as "a cultural mud sea" and said he detested school. "You sat in your little rows with your little inkwells and pledged allegiance to the flag and bells rang to let you in and out. I hated it." He also found that most of his schoolmates seemed like spoon-fed nonentities who just soaked up what they were told and taught and came up with nothing new or original on their own.

A serious problem for Redford—not to mention his perplexed and disappointed parents—and a motivating factor in his life—was his envy of the wealthier kids he knew and the lifestyle and homes they enjoyed. He couldn't understand why he had to live in a comparatively modest home when people who were no better than he was were sitting in luxury. He wanted desperately to go inside one of these fancy houses and see what they were like, to see what he was missing, and spent much of his time in dreaming up ways of getting invitations from one of his richer acquaintances. Most of the guys Redford hung out with were no better off than he was.

Redford did not at that time think of himself as good-looking. "My hair was too wild, I could never comb it, it was all cowlicks. Hippies were always making fun of my hair. And I had freckles. So it was 'Hey, Freckles!' I didn't hear a lot of 'Gee, isn't he cute.' That came later and I got confused and flattered by it." Redford would always say that he didn't get into the movies because of his looks. "I had this early image of myself as not being acceptable in terms of looks and personality," he recalled.

Typical of Hollywood types in their youth—despite the trips to the library when he was very young—as he became a teen, Redford was not academically inclined and was no longer much attracted to books. To him reading about something was dull compared to experiencing it in real life. But his distaste for reading made him, like Steven Spielberg and so many others in the film business, semiliterate throughout his life—or at least a far cry from an intellectual. Redford learned to read and eventually would read scripts and even the books they were based on, but to him reading was never fundamental. He found more enjoyment in playing tennis, which he did until he was sixteen when he "got tired of it." He also began climbing in Yosemite and in the Sierras.

With a friend, Redford decided to try some things that were more stimulating than reading and writing. The two young men took up climbing buildings as a hobby, shinnying up the Bank of America or the Fox Village Theatre, whereupon they would unscrew the lightbulbs and smash them on the sidewalk below. In typical bored highschooler fashion, Redford thought this was really cool. The two also stole car hubcaps and sold them for twenty bucks apiece.

A potentially more productive activity was when the two friends went to either Warner Brothers or Universal studios—even Redford doesn't remember for sure—and applied for jobs as stunt men. Actors were "sissy-boys," but stunt men were real men, and Redford and his buddy were convinced that they had what it takes. The casting director, however, felt differently. He listened to them politely, took down their info and phone numbers, and essentially told them "don't call us, we'll call you." They never heard back from the studio. Angered by this lack of a reaction, Redford and his buddy broke into the studio warehouse, where instead of exploring or even stealing, they simply threw things around and made a mess. On another occasion he "wasted a place" in Newport, California, and found himself in jail.

When Redford first told these stories of his "aimless youth"— often exaggerated to make it sound like his childhood was a lot rougher than it really was, thereby making his huge success seem more deserved, as if in compensation—he would say that the fellow bad boy he hung around with was a "friend" named Billy Coomber. Many years later, Redford would attribute these same adventures to himself and his "half brother." It has been established that Redford's mother had a son by another man, but everything else about this boy and his origin has been deliberately kept in the dark by Redford, who rarely mentions his half brother, William Coomber. Some accounts have this mysterious half brother dying in "the war"; but that was actually Redford's paternal uncle, who, according to Redford, was a Rhodes scholar who died during the Battle of the Bulge. Whatever the case, Redford and his brother grew apart after their youthful misadventures. Redford stays mum about his brother's fate. Redford did reveal, however, that his mother had twin daughters who died at birth.

Redford also hung out with girls; his good looks meant that he had little trouble attracting many. Like most young, good-looking guys, he was rather heartless with the women, admitting years later that he and his buddies never related to the girls they went with as people. Redford and his friends would cruise the boulevard and motion girls over to their car; quite a few of them would hop inside for a spin, a necking session, and occasionally more. On dates Redford preferred to take girls to the beach for a romantic walk rather than to the drive-in to make out. He wasn't completely devoid of sensitivity when it came to the opposite sex.

A woman who was known as "Jessie" at this time knew Redford and remembered him well. "At first I thought he was as dumb as a post, and I thought it was a shame that his good looks had to be wasted on someone so stupid. I also thought that some of the other guys were much better looking. I never got to know Redford real well, but well enough to think that he sort of put on an act. He had to act like a meat head because all of his friends were meat heads and he wanted to fit in. I thought he was more intelligent than he let on. I never thought he would amount to anything."

Like many boys who aren't academically inclined, Redford was interested in sports. He found, as such men do, that it was easier to hit a ball or run across a field than to read a page full of unfamiliar words. He spent much of his time excelling at baseball and football, playing tennis and swimming, until he was known as one of the high school's sports stars. His artistic leanings were not nurtured in the drama club, but rather in the art club, where he did many sketches of friends, teachers, and other people and things that he observed. Some of these sketches made their way into the high school yearbook.

One of them shows three sexy, flirtatious women measuring a red-faced centurion for a new outfit. It is undeniably crude, but also shows a certain flair and talent. Redford's first love would always be art.

When he was a senior, Redford was one of a bunch of ballplayers who were told they could get out of registration day, having to listen to dull indoctrination speeches, if they served as ushers and made sure students were seated in the right section according to their last names. He admits he was "a complete jerk" when one "little girl, a tiny thing" came running down the hall outside the auditorium. Redford gave the girl a hard time, asking her what her name was and refusing to let her pass by. Finally she said her name was Wood, and Redford told her she had to sit with the *W*'s all the way around on the other side. Another usher kept making signals to Redford, trying to catch his eye, but Redford was having too much fun and ignored him. Redford told the girl that if her name was Wood, she had to go around to the other entrance, and that was that. "Nobody gave you permission to change your name," he told the girl. Finally Miss Wood lost her temper and called him a son of a bitch before she dashed around to the hallway on the other side. Redford's buddy said, "Don't you know who that *was*? That was *Natalie Wood*. She's in *the movies*." Redford recalled, "And then I was glad I had pushed her around . . . because I had a dim view of movie people." Redford had probably enjoyed teasing her because she was so pretty, although he hadn't recognized her. Little did he dream that years later he would appear in two Hollywood movies with not-so-little Miss Wood, who would fall passionately in love with him.

A pivotal moment in Redford's life took place when he was eighteen; his mother passed away at age forty from a "rare blood disease." Her death devastated him, especially because he finally realized that his attitudes and some of his behavior must have been deeply disappointing to her. His relationship with his father was not as close, and Redford thought nothing of leaving home despite the loneliness and desperate grief his father must have been feeling. His father's very neediness made Redford nervous, impinged upon his free spirit, made him fear that his life would not be his own but someone else's. Redford was not one to be beholden to anyone; he would do as he wanted, justifying all actions regardless of consequences as part of his credo that it was *his life*. He chose to get far away from California and his father by accepting a baseball scholarship to the University of Colorado. He thought it was time to get away from the beaches and breathe the clean mountain air of Colorado, where he could climb mountains instead of banks and movie theaters. His move to Colorado also marked the start of his lifelong love of skiing.

Although Redford should have been happy that his college career would emphasize sports, he still had to take some courses. He discovered that he was just as ill-prepared as ever for anything that might stretch his intellect. The only class that interested him was art, but he was more interested in doing sketches than he was in learning about the great painters of the past. Smug and arrogant, convinced that no one had anything important to teach him, he soon gave up trying to achieve good grades and stopped reading and studying. What's worse, he became disillusioned with the mindlessness, what he called the "one-dimensional life," of the athlete. He loved playing sports and could be as competitive as the next fellow, but he discovered that virtually nothing mattered but winning. "If you didn't win you were made to feel like shit, like you were worthless," he once said. Sports were supposed to be fun, but they weren't fun for him anymore. It all seemed like much ado about nothing. He had no desire to be what he called a "test tube jock."

Redford found one occupation he enjoyed, and that was getting plastered, although he would later claim that his drinking problem was exaggerated and "distorted over the years" (mostly by Redford himself, in another attempt to romanticize and "macho up" his early life). He thought about going to baseball practice, or having a few drinks, and the drinking began to win out. It took away a need to make heavy decisions, as well as the nagging fear that he was fucking up his life, disappointing his dead mother, letting his father down. When he was drunk the world seemed infinitely promising, and it didn't really matter which path he chose. Nothing mattered but having a good time, feeling good, occasionally getting laid, beating back the demons of doubt and insecurity with a few beers and a couple of shots.

Of course, he lost his scholarship. He had missed practice way too often and had been spotted drunk, staggering, more than once. Even if they could raise the money for tuition, neither he nor his father saw any reason for him to continue at the university. Redford packed up, said good-bye to some mates—drinking buddies and a few weepy girls—and then headed home to his father.

He would not stay home for long.

For Redford, staying home in Van Nuys with his father was not an option. He neither wanted nor required anyone's approval, but he knew that the way he'd flunked out of college did not sit well with his father. Redford still wanted to live his own life, although he wasn't certain what that life should be. Sports had not turned out the way he'd expected, so he couldn't see a career as an athlete. He loved doodling, sketching, and cartooning, but he couldn't see making a living at it. Nearby Los Angeles held no appeal for him. "I grew up in a film industry community," he remembered, "and it didn't have that Holy Grail appeal that it has for some people. I was there and I was not impressed." His chief memory of this period was of being full of anger and impatience for something *to happen*. "There was something seething in me to get out."

Redford decided to take off, hitchhiking across the country, taking the odd job here and there. Nothing serious, nothing permanent: a carpenter's apprentice; a cashier at a supermarket. He got fired from one position for falling asleep on the job, and from the supermarket because he couldn't figure out—or more likely didn't care to learn—how to pack groceries into a paper bag. He managed to save some money he earned from working at the Standard Oil Refinery, where his father got him a job as roustabout. He saw the country and hoped things would just fall in line. He spoke fondly of these days, how he would always run into interesting people and have new experiences. Eventually he made his way to New York City, which he found overwhelming. Unequipped to deal with the hectic pace of Manhattan, so different from lazy California, he decided to leave not only New York, but the country as well. With a certain amount of dumb courage, he decided it was time to see the world. He left New York and headed for Europe on a freighter.

In Europe he carried on in much the same fashion as he had back home, hitchhiking, getting odd jobs, sleeping in youth hostels. He traveled to Greece, spent some time in Germany, and wound up in Paris, where he decided to settle for awhile. He managed to grab fruit and vegetables from the markets so he wouldn't starve. In a much more sophisticated move, he turned to hanging around Harry's bar, where Americans who were charmed by the young California boy with the striking good looks bought him drinks and dinner and sometimes made proposals. When he wasn't trying to cadge a meal from some rich tourist, Redford put on a beret, hung out in Montmartre, made dozens of sketches, and tried to look like a French artist. Occasionally—or so he claimed—some tourist would think he was an honest-to-goodness Parisian until he spoke. He was so anxious to soak up life and experience that he got involved in student demonstrations, even though he had no idea what the shouting was about and got clubbed by cops for his trouble. Although eventually he would get behind many causes, for most of his life Redford has remained staunchly apolitical.

Redford left Paris and headed for Florence, where he decided to study art at the Montparnasse Academy and try to turn his preoccupation into a serious career. Years later he would remember that he was always hungry, lonely, and broke; living in a rat's nest of a room; wearing the same clothing until it was practically in rags; drinking and smoking incessantly, hallucinating, and indulging in fantasies of suicide; unable to talk to anyone he knew about his problems. His life fit the stereotypical, romantic notion of the "starving artist" and then some—everything but the proverbial bloodhounds sniffing at his rear end, to paraphrase *All About Eve*. Some of his acquaintances during this period had no idea how he survived. They wondered if he were either a gigolo or a male prostitute servicing the wealthy older men or women of Florence. He claimed to be depressed, nearly desolate, because a teacher he admired wasn't quite as admiring of his painting as Redford expected him to be. When this teacher told him bluntly that he was merely imitating other artists and making no progress of his own, Redford decided that the world of art would not be the salvation that he'd hoped for. Although he may have had some talent and could have developed a career as a commercial artist, he was in no way a budding Rembrandt. When he left the world of art, that world did not lose a prospective genius.

It is also true that this "dark" period of Redford's life did not last very long. His privation seemed more acute to him because he had grown up in a loving home where—even if his parents weren't rich—he never wanted for anything. Hardly an actor or artist alive doesn't recall some early days when money was tight and meals were scarce compared to when they were living at home. But it is all part of the Romantic Redford Legend. Of his days in Europe, Redford would later say: "I came and got my teeth kicked in. I was too young and inexperienced, and a lot of rough stuff happened." Redford refuses to elaborate on this "rough stuff"—perhaps indicating that it is another attempt to romanticize his younger days, or that he indulged in behavior which nowadays he would find unseemly.

Redford remembered that a "nice guy" put on an exhibition of his work and paid him $75 for it. He left Italy and returned to hitchhiking across the Continent. Eventually he made his way back to Los Angeles, where his friends seemed dull compared to his acquaintances in Europe. He felt as if he had traveled a vast distance just to wind up back where he started, with nothing to show for it. He drank heavily, seeking release and oblivion in alcohol. "I was dying a little bit each day," he remembered. He was living—with his father's help—in an apartment complex, where one of his neighbors was a pretty young Mormon woman named Lola von Wagenen. Lola was instantly impressed by Redford, and he felt the same. Even better, Lola really listened to him and seemed to understand what he was going through. This was probably no more than a smitten girl hanging onto every word of the boy she had a crush on, but to Redford it seemed as if Lola could see inside his soul. While in Europe he had felt insignificant, like a nobody; he needed someone to *listen* to him, to make him feel important and worthwhile. The adoring young Lola served that function, as she would for many years. The two spent long hours walking and talking their way through the streets, sometimes until the sun came up, and they were astonished at how quickly the time had flown. Lola recalled that the two didn't actually date for quite some time, so they never went through that awful awkwardness of the first date, the need to impress that often makes people act differently from the way they are. Redford and Lola really knew each other from the first; there were no airs, no pretensions.

Lola encouraged Redford to pursue his art studies, and he decided to enroll in the Pratt Institute of Art and Design in New York. Marriage did not seem to be in the cards right away, and Lola was unable to go with Redford to Manhattan because her parents insisted she go to college out west. Instructors at the institute were less than bowled over by Redford's work, and he drifted into a course on theatrical scenic design. "I kept being questioned about what I wanted to do," he recalled. "I hated to be asked about things I didn't think I had to have answers to at such a young age, so I made up an answer. 'I'm going to be an art director.'"

It was also true that Redford had an artistic itch that just had to be scratched, and something about the theater appealed to him. He claimed not to like actors, to have no interest in acting, but a friend suggested that he audition at the American Academy of Dramatic Arts to see if he had any aptitude for acting. He had often been told that he looked like an actor and had "movie-star good looks," so he figured it was worth a try. He wasn't especially nervous before his audition, because he really didn't care if he made a good impression. The fever to be a thespian was not burning in him.

He described his audition in this way: "I had to deliver two monologues; one for comedy and one for tragedy. I really made a mess of the comic scene and one of the teachers at the audition made some remarks that I felt were uncalled for. I never liked being made fun of and this guy really made me mad. Luckily, I was *supposed* to be angry for the second scene so I managed to do a pretty good job of that one. At least the teacher seemed to like it."

The review board at the academy saw enough in Redford, rough-hewn though he was, to offer him membership. It may not have been his acting ability so much as his charm and looks and his potential for achieving stardom that impressed the teachers. "The teachers at the academy were just as susceptible to a good-looking face or an ingratiating manner as anyone else," remembers Estelle Pierce, who attended the academy at the same time as Redford. "If he had been as stiff as a board, if he'd exhibited not a trace of ability, then of course it wouldn't have helped him. But despite their vaunted reputation, the academy took on quite a few students because they had 'star appeal' or sex appeal, not because they were great actors. The ability to be at ease in front of the group, any group, was important. And 'presence' was *extremely* important." To be fair, the teachers may have thought Redford could be developed into a major talent despite his inadequacies, which included a lack of projection, an underlying shyness (which he covered up with cockiness), and a tendency to slouch in a "California" fashion.

Another problem was Redford's admitted arrogance. "[I] behaved as most young actors did," he said, "meaning that there was no such thing as a good actor, 'cause you yourself hadn't shown up yet. I'd go see John Gielgud appearing in *Ages of Man* and I'd say 'Yeah, well, it was okay, but . . .' I enjoyed nothing."

Redford did not learn much at the academy, mostly because of his still extant chip-on-the-shoulder attitude, the feeling that no one could teach him anything. He went through the motions during classes, coming to feel, as he has all his life, that acting can't really be taught. "The best thing an actor has is his instincts," he said once, "and I don't think you can learn them." He did feel that lessons at the academy taught him not to be afraid to let go in front of people. This breakthrough occurred when he and the other students in class were assigned to choreograph a poem, to move around the room in a creative and freeing way while reciting it. Redford wondered what the hell this nonsense had to do with acting; he had no interest in making a damned fool of himself. But when his turn came, he jumped out of his seat and began reciting Poe's *The Raven*, matching the lines to vivid motions as he swept through the room, grabbed people up out of their seats, and dashed in and out of the corridor outside, jumping and shouting with glee and energy. It was a surprisingly exhilarating experience. He felt suddenly freed of self-consciousness and inhibition, as if there were nothing he couldn't do in front of an audience if he had to. Whether Redford really appreciated Poe's ode to unending grief is debatable.

Another experience that stuck in his mind occurred when he performed a scene from Arthur Miller's *All My Sons*. He noticed that the other actor in the scene, rather than listening to Redford in character, was mouthing Redford's lines as he, Redford, spoke them; it annoyed Redford no end. From the very beginning, Redford always carefully listened to and watched his fellow actors in a scene—a positive aspect of his technique that lasts to this day. As director Sydney Pollack put it years later: "It's money in the bank to cut to Bob listening 'cause he's really listening. Very few actors do. They'll act that they're listening; they'll decoratively listen. But he's quite content to just hang on whatever [they're] saying. And there's a reality created by that that's wonderful."

In retrospect, his instructors were right when they saw leading-man potential in Redford, although at first they may have over-praised his abilities because he seemed to have more talent—of a sort—than you would expect in a young man with no acting experience who'd never been in a drama class. Yet, there are indications that Redford *did* have great potential, that he continually impressed his instructors with his expressiveness, his use of feelings, his interpretation of character, and his creative approach to acting. His teachers felt that he hid his love of acting behind a blasé demeanor, when the truth may have been that he barely disguised his benign contempt for the "teaching" of something that he felt was inbred.

Redford had a horror of doing the classics. His appeal has always been contemporary, and in his work he has generally avoided period films. The classics tend to be the province of highly talented character actors who can really lose themselves in characters that come from an entirely different time and place, not of leading men with lesser abilities who feel more comfortable in a place not too far away from themselves. Cast in Chekhov's *The Seagull*, Redford confessed he had never heard of Chekhov, let alone *The Seagull*.

One of his instructors noted a "deep anger" in Redford that the young man was able to use in constructive ways. Many of the instructors' notes on Redford, however, read like a lot of pretentious gobble-dygook; one senses they simply liked Redford—in whatever way—and wanted to help him achieve whatever he could; some, perhaps, wanted to get to know the handsome young man socially, or to make him somehow beholden to them. Many of the notes read as if the instructors were trying to cobble up something positive to say to justify Redford's continued enrollment in an academy whose lessons he neither enjoyed nor respected, although in later years he would say nice things about the AADA when he visited and spoke to students.

"They liked him, all right," remembers Estelle Pierce. "He had a lot of contempt and anger in him but his basic good nature came through." Another classmate recalls that "Bob was cocky and knew he was attractive. He used to joke that maybe one or two of the teachers were attracted to him. Whether they were or not I don't know. Although it was widely thought that one of the women faculty members was completely smitten with him. There was a married male teacher who seemed very warm and friendly toward Bob, he seemed to want to know him better, mentor him, and it may have been just a father and son thing, but frankly I always wondered. Redford was very good-looking and was well aware of it."

Many straight actors are perfectly willing to foster platonic (as far as *they're* concerned) friendships with older women or gay men who may or may not have romantic feelings toward them in order to use them as contacts. It is not known if Redford ever did that to the extent of, say, Warren Beatty, who had such early mentors as gay playwrights Tennessee Williams and William Inge. "I never heard any gay rumors about Redford," says this former AADA classmate, "though he undoubtedly had acquaintances who were gay, whether he was aware of it or not."

In spite of—or because of—his resistance to classic drama, the AADA often cast him in such works, such as *Antigone*, in which he got high marks for his performance as Creon, especially from one supportive instructor, Francis Lettin. Lettin felt that Redford was a great actor but would never be acknowledged as such, because great actors were seen as being larger than life and flamboyant; Redford's work was seen as too subtle to be recognized as great except by those who worked in the business. (This theme would be taken up by Redford proponents in later years, when he was sharply criticized for being careful, dull and wooden.) Throughout his career the critics would be divided between those who felt Redford was a brilliant master of subtle underplaying to those who simply thought he was overly cold, stiff, and not all that talented. In truth, Redford and his proponents would never quite understand that it was possible to be convincingly emotional in a scene without having to chew the scenery.

Redford was always to have contempt for "the method" and those who studied with Strasberg, feeling that the principles they espoused created "mechanical people" instead of real actors. However, he swore by the AADA's own method of "stepping outside of yourself," which had helped him feel comfortable emoting, acting out, acting crazy, doing whatever he had to do, in front of large groups of people. But fundamentally Redford never really believed in acting schools and was unhappy at the AADA.

Another problem with studying at the academy was that Redford, although he made some friends, was lonely for his soul mate. He had made a mental and physical commitment to Lola, and having her on the other side of the country was much too difficult to bear; later, many would insist that Lola missed him more, and it was her often verbalized need for him that finally got him to propose. They spoke on the telephone as often as they could and exchanged many letters, but that was not enough for Lola, who was deeply in love. Redford also had strong feelings for Lola—although like most handsome, self-absorbed young actors, it was true that he let himself be loved. One of the main reasons he got married was to make a point to his father and friends. "They feared that I was going to go off the deep end, or that I would never amount to anything, or die at an early age. I wanted to prove them wrong."

Redford went back to California in September of 1958, and on the twelfth of the month he and Lola were married. Lola's parents were not thrilled; they worried whether an "actor" could possibly be capable of taking good care of their daughter and any children they might have. They were even less thrilled when they learned that the newlyweds were going to hitchhike their way back to Manhattan. The couple found a small apartment on Columbus Avenue on the Upper West Side of the city, and Lola went to work at a bank for $55 a week while Redford continued his classes at the academy. They were so strapped for cash that they had to sell most of their wedding gifts and live on homemade bread while Redford cobbled together some furniture. It wasn't long before Lola was pregnant, adding to their feelings of financial insecurity.

Redford made his Broadway debut because of a connection at the AADA, an instructor named Mike Thoma, who was also the stage manager for the hit comedy *Tall Story*. They needed a group of actors to play high school basketball players for a crowd scene. Redford threw on a sweater of the type favored by high schoolers of the period, went down to the theater, and dribbled a ball across the stage with some other fellows. Because that was all that was required of him except for one quickly shouted line, he was cast. The director of *Tall Story*, Herman Shumlin, recalled years later that Redford had stood out because of his looks and his stage presence. "You either have it or you don't and Redford had it," he remembered. "There was something in the way he walked, some confidence or charismatic air that made you think he was one of the ones who was going to make it. I was never surprised when good things began to happen to him."

And good things would begin to happen to Redford in spades.

But there would be tragedy as well.

I nstrumental in helping Redford move out of a crowd of extras and into the professional rank of actors was an agent at MCA (originally Music Corporation of America) with the unlikely moniker of Stark Hesseltine. American Academy of Dramatic Arts (AADA) instructor Mike Thoma had wanted to see what Hesseltine thought of Redford's chances, and sneaked him into a couple of performances at the academy, including *Antigone*. After watching Redford perform, Hesseltine turned to Thoma and told him: "I have to have him!" Thoma reminded Hesseltine that agents weren't actually allowed to see AADA students until after graduation, as the academy was afraid overeager theatrical representatives might spirit their students away before they'd completed the necessary training. After all, it wasn't about creating stars but rather great actors.

"That was the theory, yes," recalls Estelle Pierce, "but don't let anybody kid you. If they spotted somebody with star quality they'd give them the full treatment. It was good for business. If an AADA graduate went on to become famous, the academy could take credit for it. And many of the teachers had—let us say, their *favorites*—and would use all their industry contacts to help them to the exclusion of others."

Another classmate recalls that "Hollywood types, movie star types, didn't necessarily receive preferential treatment at the academy. My experience was that the faculty fussed more over those who were seen as having an extra-special talent. But I'm sure there were cases where a faculty member might particularly like a student—and I'm making no insinuations, mind you—and give them some extra help in getting along in the outside world if they could."

Thoma told Hesseltine that he could get into trouble if it got out that he'd let an agent attend an academy performance, so he would have to wait until after Redford graduated to offer the student representation. Which is what Hesseltine did when he invited Redford up to his office. He was then astonished that instead of eagerly accepting his offer, Redford sat in his chair and asked him, "What do I need an agent for?" Hesseltine later recalled that "it was possibly the only time that a struggling actor had to be convinced by me that he needed representation. I think he was just very wary. The academy was great for teaching acting but it fell short, perhaps, in explaining the *business* of the business to its students."

One of the first things Hesseltine did for his new client was set up an audition for him for a new play by Dore Schary called *The Highest Tree*. Schary was originally a screenwriter and producer who had taken over MGM after Louis B. Mayer was ousted in the early fifties, but was himself fired in 1956. He then returned to his first love, playwriting, and came up with the Tony-winning *Sunrise at Campobello*. Schary had often been fond of messages in the films he made, and this characteristic transferred itself to his plays, especially *The Highest Tree*. In this play, a nuclear physicist who has helped create atomic bombs tries to rectify what he has come to feel is a mistake when he learns he has a terminal illness.

Redford was told to go to the theater and do a scene from the play for the casting director, who was, incredibly, named Ruth Frankenstein. Frankenstein watched and listened as he emoted, and then had him wait outside in Schubert Alley while she spoke to Hesseltine. Finally the agent emerged to tell his client that Frankenstein had been impressed with his work—or more likely, had felt he couldn't do much harm to the all of six lines he would be required to speak in the very small role of Frederick "Buzz" Ashe Jr.

The Highest Tree was directed by its author, Dore Schary. Natalie Schafer—"Lovey," or Mrs. Howell, of *Gilligan's Island* fame—played Redford's mother in the play, and she remembered that Schary was barely able to direct the veteran cast members, let alone a relative newcomer like Redford. "I don't think he thought much of poor Bob," Schafer told Lawrence Quirk in an interview many years later. "He kept telling him 'project, project, we can't hear you.' And criticizing how he stood, what he did with his hands, and he only had a few lines. Most of it was just standing there and listening, which I recall he did perfectly well. That's part of an actor's job, too, listening." An actress named Elizabeth Cole was cast as Redford's sister. She would work with Redford again after changing her name to Elizabeth Ashley.

The Highest Tree went out of town for tryouts in different cities. The pregnant Lola was almost due, and an anxious Redford was on the phone with her getting daily reports. Natalie Schafer recalled: "He was like all expectant fathers, happy, proud, kind of nervous. I think the whole company was sharing his joy. And then of course . . . it was just awful." The child—a boy they named Scott Redford—was born while Redford was still out of town. Redford and his wife were overjoyed and life seemed good, with Redford in a Broadway show, however small his part, a new baby at home, and Lola busy playing mother and loving it; she had no acting ambitions of her own. Money was tight, but they had every reason to expect that things would improve. But then one morning two months after Scott's birth, Lola discovered that their baby son wasn't moving. Hurried phone calls were made, but it was too late. For reasons unknown, the boy had succumbed to crib death. The cast of *The Highest Tree* took up a collection for the young, emotionally devastated parents, and Redford left the show for a week to be with his heartbroken wife. They took off for a weekend drive through Pennsylvania just to get out of town and to get away from the apartment where their beloved son had died.

Years later Lola Redford would recall that both parents felt terribly guilty after their little boy's death. "I had this notion that when you come from strong Mormon stock, you just don't have children who die," Lola said. After her other children were born, Lola was never able to hire a babysitter to look after them; she spent all of her energy "guarding" them from harm. "For almost nine years, I gave those children my undivided 100% neurotic attention," she said. "I was so afraid they would die."

As many people do to work through their grief, Redford threw himself back into his acting, determined to finally earn Schary's approval and prove that he could do the job. *The Highest Tree* opened in November of 1959, and Redford and his fellow cast members were hopeful, although privately Redford had never thought much of the play or of Schary, its writer/director. Redford was depressed that in the cheery opening-night notes he received from fellow cast members, no one ever described him as being a good actor. However, at Sardi's restaurant afterward, where casts traditionally waited for the reviews, Redford nearly convinced himself that he was in a hit due to all the happy, smiling people who came up and congratulated him and the others. His good mood abruptly dissolved when someone walked in with the reviews, which were mostly negative. Redford recalled that he had barely taken a bite of the sandwich he'd ordered when he saw that just about everyone in the party—now a wake—had fled into the night. *The Highest Tree* closed after only twenty-one performances.

Hesseltine was unable to get Redford new theater work immediately, and the Redfords were strapped for cash. Redford tried to add to his income by doing TV advertisements and having commercial agent Jean Thomas send him out to audition after audition. The response was underwhelming, with the consensus being that Redford was good-looking and competent but nothing special, just another handsome blond actor in a city full of the same. Redford never did a single commercial until many, many years later. It may be that as a "theater actor" he was too intense, or at least the advertisers saw him that way. In any case, his financial situation only became more desperate. Ironically, when Redford became famous, the advertising agencies asked Jean Thomas and every other TV commercial agent to send over a "Robert Redford" *type*.

This was the time of the popular television quiz shows, most of which were telecast from New York. Desperate for income of some kind, Redford decided to become a contestant on a show called *Play Your Hunch*. Merv Griffin, later to become a talk-show host and creator of *Jeopardy*, hosted the show. "The largest prize was about $25," recalled Griffin, so *Play Your Hunch* was a far cry from such big-money shows as *Twenty-One*, which later become the subject of one of Redford's finest movies. Redford remembered that his stint on *Play Your Hunch*—his first television appearance—was more like an acting job than anything else.

"Two other guys and myself stood silhouetted behind three screens while in front of them stood one of these other guys' twin brother," recalled Redford. "The contestants had to guess which one of us was the twin. I only did it because they promised me $75." There was no cheating or coaching of contestants, but Redford had to pretend he was something other than an actor from LA. The director had him say that he was an artist, so that Merv Griffin could tell some hastily scripted jokes about painters and the like. Redford got caught up in the hype, with everyone raising their voices excitedly as the show began in a highly exaggerated fashion, but he also found the experience hokey and pretty awful. At the end of the show, when the prizes were announced for the "subjects"—as opposed to the contestants—Redford learned that he had become the proud possessor of a fishing rod from Abercrombie and Fitch. Afterward, when he reminded everyone that he'd been promised $75, he was told that was the value of the fishing rod. He was furious.

Stark Hesseltine suggested that Redford temporarily go back to California, where he would have better chances of getting television work via another MCA agent named Monique James. First he appeared on an NBC western called *The Deputy* with Henry Fonda—it was the first time he worked with a major movie star. Next he was cast in "Captain Brassbound's Conversion" on NBC's *Hallmark Hall of Fame*. This adaptation of a comedy by George Bernard Shaw starred Greer Garson as a woman determined to explore Morocco despite the dangers. She is accompanied by Captain Brassbound (Christopher Plummer) and his sailors. George Rose played a sheik, and Redford was cast in the small role of a sailor. Rose recalled that "Bob was a handsome young man, likable, but he didn't stand out in any particular way, though he seemed eager to learn and in awe of Garson."

Monique James then wanted to get Redford a more substantial part—playing a Nazi soldier on CBS network's *Playhouse 90*, the main dramatic competition for Hallmark's show. Unfortunately, the casting agent for the episode, which was entitled "In the Presence of Mine Enemies," insisted on another James client: the better-known George Peppard, whose debut film, *Home from the Hill*, had just been released that year. James knew that Redford needed the break more than Peppard did, and she felt that Redford would be more appropriate for the part. She told *Playhouse 90* that Peppard wasn't interested, but she had another actor who'd be perfect—Redford.

CBS countered that Redford might be fine, but they needed a star. James pestered them until they agreed to let Redford read for the part; but when he was through he was told that, yes, he was fine, but they *still* needed a star—too bad. CBS finally relented after realizing that Redford would work for next to nothing. James didn't care, because she knew this part could really get her client major attention.

"In the Presence of Mine Enemies" was written by Rod Serling of *Twilight Zone* fame. It takes place in the Warsaw Ghetto, where the Rabbi Adam Heller does his best to give his people hope and spiritual leadership during a living nightmare in which many members of his congregation are regularly taken away to be murdered. Sgt. Lott, the part played by Redford, was a German officer who must see that order is upheld in brutal fashion but whose own instincts tend more to the compassionate. The star of "In the Presence of Mine Enemies" was the formidable Charles Laughton as Rabbi Heller. Nearing the end of his life and career, Laughton did not have the luxury of long rehearsals nor the time to prepare for a live performance of a difficult role. Although he was a brilliant actor, Laughton was not always at his best. It was noted at the time that for much of the teleplay he underplayed "to the point of catatonia," giving his less experienced costars, including Redford, a chance to shine. Laughton's accent came and went with the tides.

Laughton's biographer, Simon Callow, wrote of Laughton and Redford that "the comparison in the two actors' styles is instructive. Redford is impeccably 'truthful': he follows all the Method prescriptions [this is ironic, considering what Redford thought of the method], his action is clear, his inner life ticking nicely over. Laughton, meanwhile, appears to be asleep for most of their scenes together. Then he talks of the dignity of his people, and of the superiority of love to hate, and a huge ocean of feeling is released, and the whole absurd farrago suddenly matters, because he becomes the voice of his tribe, and love's advocate. Redford (who is by no means unskilful in the role) seems, at these moments, to be made of cardboard." But no one has ever seriously suggested that Redford was ever in the great Laughton's class as an actor.

There was a problem with a scene in which Redford as the Nazi was to give an outraged and resistant Rabbi Laughton a hard slap across the face. During rehearsals Redford only pretended to slap Laughton, and the night of the live on-air performance Laughton asked Redford how he was going to handle the slap. Laughton was

a bit taken aback when he realized that Redford the neophyte had
no idea how to give another actor a "stage slap" without actually
hitting him, and Laughton had no time to teach him. Redford told
Laughton he'd just slap him very lightly and quickly on the cheek
but Laughton vetoed this action with vehemence. "You can't actually
slap me, my boy!" Laughton told him. "I hate to be touched. You'll
have to work it out somehow; I can't help you." Redford asked the
director, Fielder Cook, what he could do; but it was almost air time.
If Laughton didn't want to be slapped . . . When the sequence came
and the cameras were rolling, transmitting the teleplay to millions of
homes in glorious black and white, Redford just went with his instincts and hauled off in his best Nazi sociopathic manner and
whacked Laughton in the face, inadvertently giving Laughton, with
his priceless reaction, one of his best moments. After the broadcast,
Redford was horrified and rushed to Laughton to apologize to him.
Laughton held up a hand and told him an apology was not necessary,
that he had done what he had to do to make the scene true and
believable and dramatically effective. Laughton, in fact, was so nice
about it that Redford would tell writer James Spada that this was the
end of his being in awe of his better-known costars and letting it get
the better of him.

Redford got such good notices for his appearance on *Playhouse 90*
that Monique James no longer found him a hard sell. In 1960 he
quickly had appearances on an NBC show called *Tate*, in an episode
called "The Bounty Hunter" that starred Robert Culp and a pre–*One
Flew Over the Cuckoo's Nest* Louise Fletcher. On another episode of
Tate, "Comanche Scalps," Redford played a young man whose
brother tries to murder him after he has married his brother's ex-
fiancé. Also in that episode, Leonard Nimoy of *Star Trek* fame played
a Comanche Indian. On an episode of the suspense series *Moment of
Fear* entitled "The Golden Deed," Redford looked positively smashing as a charming wolf in sheep's clothing who saves a child from
drowning but turns out to be a smooth and dangerous criminal type.

In "The Case of the Treacherous Toupee" on *Perry Mason*, he had
a supporting role as a handsome roué involved in a murder plot. The
star of the show, Raymond Burr, recalled years later that a lot of
good-looking young actors had guest-starred on the show, which ran
for years, but few had the memorable presence of Robert Redford.

Redford also played an army captain in a fictionalization of the life of Andrew Jackson in "Born a Giant" on *Our American Heritage*. Bill Travers played Jackson, and others in the cast were Barbara Rush, Walter Matthau, and Farley Granger. This assignment gave Redford a break from the "bad boys" he'd been playing on most of these other shows. While he didn't want to be seen as just the "all-American blond and blue-eyed boy" stereotype, neither was he anxious to be typecast as the dark and sinister neurotic or psychotic.

Redford got an important if smaller role in November 1960 for a TV adaptation of one of Eugene O Neill's most famous works on *Play of the Week* (in two parts). *The Iceman Cometh* deals with the defeated, alcoholic inhabitants of a boarding house who hang out in the back room of the downstairs bar and tell themselves that one day they'll sober up and fulfill their true destinies. Hickey (Jason Robards Jr.) is a traveling salesman who drops in to expose their deceptions, supposedly "freeing" them of foolish false hopes; but he turns out to be the most delusional of all. Not on the level of O'Neill's masterpiece, *Long Day's Journey into Night*, the often compelling parts of *The Iceman Cometh* never quite add up to a cohesive whole, although it offers insights into the human condition. There are powerful moments in the long and talky play, however, and O'Neill gave his actors some terrific chances to show their mettle. *The Iceman Cometh* set the standard for plays in which desperate, drunken characters pour out their pathetic hopes and fears while sinking into alcoholic oblivion. The play, which takes place in 1912, was ahead of its time in presenting a proud black character who refuses to be patronized by the whites. The title refers to a story a character tells about a wife running off with the iceman—those men who brought ice to homes and bars in the days before refrigeration.

Redford was thrown into a cast of some powerhouse older actors when Sidney Lumet directed him in the television adaptation of the drama. First there was Jason Robards Jr. in the part of Hickey. Although Robards isn't necessarily brilliant in the part, he does have some very fine moments. Farrell Pelly gives perhaps the finest performance of the evening as Harry Hope, the old Irish widower who owns the establishment and hasn't gone outside since his wife died.

James Broderick (father of Matthew) is excellent as Willie Dean, the former law student; so is Myron McCormick as Larry Slade.

Redford plays Don Parritt, a young man who comes to the boarding house to see Larry, whom he sees as a father figure. Larry was once involved with Parritt's mother, a radical who has been arrested for a bombing incident. As the play progresses, we eventually learn that Parritt turned his own mother in for money and seeks absolution from Larry. Although at this point in his game, if ever, Redford certainly did not have the consummate skill of the veterans in the cast, he manages to hold his own in scenes with McCormick and even Robards. Redford does a fine job of getting across Parritt's loneliness, confusion, and vulnerability. It's not necessarily great acting, but it is effective and sufficient. He is particularly good in the scene when he tells Larry how much his mother once loved him.

Redford learned this part while rehearsing for his next and more substantial Broadway role, in *Little Moon of Alban*. James Costigan's play had originally been broadcast on television before being revised and expanded and given its Broadway debut (in those days television dramas, such as *Marty*, were often turned into feature films as well as legitimate plays). The story concerned a young lady named Brigid (Julie Harris) whose lover, Dennis (Redford), is killed by a British soldier (John Justin) during the Irish Revolution. Later on, Brigid winds up falling in love with this same British soldier. Herman Shumlin, the director of *Tall Story*, was also directing *Little Moon of Alban* and hired Redford for the role of Dennis Walsh after one audition. Shumlin and others associated with the production insisted that Redford was a fine actor, but he was never as good in his scenes with Julie Harris as he was without her. Shumlin felt that Redford was too in awe of Harris; others simply noted that Redford, whatever his abilities, was simply not in her class as an actor. It wasn't that Redford was holding back, but that Harris's superior abilities made him seem much less impressive.

Julie Harris remembered that Redford seemed rather timid in the love scenes, and she had to do all the work, worrying that she might have overdone the affectionate gestures to compensate for her costar's typical underplaying. Redford felt the trouble was that he found Harris intimidating because she already had the whole role worked out in her head on the first day of rehearsal, and her responses remained the same ever after; there was nothing new to play against, no room for "chemical interaction" between the two actors. Harris had worked out her finely honed performance to an infinite degree, and Redford had to fit himself inside of it. While this may be true, it is also true that Harris might have adapted her responses and reactions more readily and naturally to an actor who was more experienced and accomplished, more on her level of expertise.

Shumlin, however, merely thought that Redford wasn't performing to his potential and was very rough on him. It got to the point where the director often felt he had to instruct the actor in many line readings and even simple gestures. The ever-arrogant Redford did not react well to Shumlin's stern attitude and got angry with him. The irony was that Redford had complained to his MCA agents that he got little if any direction on television, but when this experienced Broadway director wanted to help him give the strong performance he felt he was capable of, Redford rebelled.

Redford recalled that "it seemed I was either being over-directed or under-directed at this point. Someone who did nothing with me made me nervous. I thought, well, why aren't they directing me? I should be getting direction because I'm new. If I got too much I hated it and if I got too little I'd get paranoid. It was very contradictory." His agents, especially Stark Hesseltine, tried to reassure him that many directors did not feel they had to say anything to him because he was doing all the right things on his own. Redford was afraid that some directors simply thought he wasn't that good and had to make the best of him—no amount of direction could turn him into a great actor, especially in the short rehearsal time for a TV show—and in this he was right as well.

But Shumlin really thought Redford had something. He wasn't about to give up, despite Redford's obvious contempt for him and his methods, which the actor later deemed "old-fashioned." Eventually Shumlin broke through with Redford and was pleased with his performance, which many critics also admired. The *New York Post* called him "splendid," and the *Newsday* critic bemoaned the fact that Redford was "done away with too soon." Some critics felt that when Costigan expanded the play, it lost its focus on the love story. *Little Moon of Alban* opened in December of 1960 and closed barely three weeks later.

A brighter note was the birth of Redford and Lola's second child and first daughter, Shauna. Again, Redford was out of town when the baby arrived—*Little Moon of Alban* was having a post-Broadway run in Washington, D.C. His stand-in took over as Redford returned to New York to see his wife and baby girl. Julie Harris remembers that Redford, who was torn between running to his wife and doing the work he was hired to do, hesitated to leave rehearsals. Harris told him that he must be present at his first child's birth (she was unaware of the first baby's death) and asked that he please go. "He was a very nice man and a good actor," recalls Harris.

There are indications that many people who knew Redford early in his career saw him as being not just talented, but *extremely* talented, with unlimited potential that has never quite been tapped in most people's eyes. Several people, including Howard Shumlin and Garson Kanin, compared Redford to Spencer Tracy; although most people, if pressed, would clearly feel that Tracy, a character actor as well as a star, was a much better actor. Certainly there was no physical resemblance between the two. Perhaps if Redford had stayed on the stage longer and endured the overdirecting he hated, he might have developed more solid acting chops, although it has to be said that he was to give many solid performances in films in the years to come.

With a new mouth to feed, Redford was doubly disappointed by the failure of *Little Moon of Alban*, so in 1961, he accepted several more television assignments to pay the bills. He did another *Play of the Week* in January. It was the premiere of a project, "Black Monday," that writer Reginald Rose had originally hoped to see on Broadway. In 1961 the play was probably much more controversial for television, because it dealt with the situation of a black child being admitted to an all-white school in the southern town of Bethlehem. David Susskind, who was interested in the topical subject of integration, asked Rose for the rights to present it on television, and Ralph Nelson directed. Redford was cast along with Ruby Dee, Pat Hingle, Andrew Prine, and a pre–*Lou Grant* Edward Asner. Redford played a near-psychotic racist.

Redford also appeared on ABC's *Naked City* as one of a group of young men who murder a derelict, and he followed this up with the title role of "The Coward" on the historical NBC series *The Ameri-*

cans. In this he was cast as George Harrod, who faces a firing squad for showing cowardice during combat. Jackie Coogan and a pre–*All in the Family* Carroll O'Connor were among the cast. Redford appeared in another NBC western show, *Whispering Smith*, as Johnny Gates, the son of a woman who plans to kill Smith (Audie Murphy) because years before he had locked up her now-dead husband. This role was followed by guest spots in two contemporary dramas: on the popular "road" show *Route 66*, he played Janosh, who's suspected of murdering the daughter of his father's partner in a steel mill. On *Bus Stop*, he was given yet another bad-boy role as Art Ellison, who fusses over his wife and baby but is much more interested in a couple who have just won a sweepstakes.

Redford later claimed that he got tired of doing all these intense mini-dramas for television and wanted to be back on Broadway, which was considered much more prestigious. He asked Hesseltine to get him into a comedy. Hesseltine felt this might be a problem, because Redford had appeared in nothing but dramatic parts to date. He said it would be easier to find Bob a role in a drama because many of the Broadway directors would probably have caught him in one of those television shows or another. Hessletine suggested that comedy might not be Redford's forte in any case. But Redford felt that "acting was acting" and insisted that he wanted to do a comedy. Hesseltine shrugged and said he'd see what he could do.

Redford was anxious to prove himself in the lead in a big Broadway show, one that might last more than a couple of weeks. He was anxious to feel the excitement of a live audience not somewhere out in the dark in their living rooms, but in front of him in the theater itself.

For Redford, that excitement of live theater would not last long.

Redford wound up playing the part of "Mike Mitchell" in a play by Norman Krasna entitled *Sunday in New York*. Producer David Merrick had not at first thought that Redford was right for the part, so he told Stark Hesseltine that if his client wanted to read for Mike Mitchell he would have to pay for his own airfare from California to New York. Redford agreed that it was worth a shot—and the cost of the tickets—and he auditioned for the play's director, Garson Kanin. Kanin thought Redford showed real comedic flair and gave him the part. As noted earlier, Kanin not only thought Redford's acting style reminded him of Spencer Tracy but also—inexplicably—thought he resembled him! Redford always wondered if he got the part primarily because Kanin and Tracy were good friends.

Sunday in New York was about a newspaperman who falls for a zany and virginal young lady (Pat Stanley) who has just arrived in New York full of a lot of energy and breathless anticipation. Conrad Janis and the quirky Sondra Lee were also in the cast. The play opened on November 29, 1961, and while it lasted longer than Redford's first two Broadway efforts, it was gone from Broadway within a few short months. The play's notices were very mixed, but Redford came in for quite a bit of praise. Redford was particularly gratified by a review in *Theatre Arts*, stating that "Robert Redford, as an amiable part-time critic on the make, is winning, witty and enormously resourceful; he now proves that the comic mask fits him as snugly as the tragic one always did, and enters the tiny band of young actors who are as versatile as they are prepossessing." Influential *New York Herald Tribune* critic Walter Kerr wrote that Redford was appealing and "first-rate no matter what the evening is doing."

Redford was always annoyed at the audience members who put on their coats and rushed out of the theater after the play instead of applauding with everyone else. Stark Hesseltine was worried that one night the angry young man would actually shout out something to start a fight. Enlisting the aid of his wife, Redford decided to play an April fool's joke on Hesseltine. He had Lola call the agent and say that her husband had gone ballistic during curtain call, punched out a patron, and wound up in jail. Hesseltine was staggered—this was in the days before tabloids routinely ran stories of Stars Behaving Badly—and had a few bad moments of planning damage control until Lola finally told him she was joking.

One night Redford had a glamorous backstage visitor—Natalie Wood, who was all smiles, all "Hollywood," and wanted to congratulate him on his performance. Clearly she did not recognize him as the high school boy who'd bullied her on registration day when she tried to get to her seat in the auditorium. Wood would remember him after this encounter, however; in fact, he would stick in her mind—and her heart—for quite some time. Her date for that occasion came backstage with her; he was Warren Beatty, who would soon see Redford as a lifelong rival.

After *Sunday in New York* closed, Redford made his way west again to do another round of TV shows and appear in his first movie. Some shows he had done before appearing in *Sunday in New York* aired during the play's run. These included a guest shot on *Alfred Hitchcock Presents* in the teleplay, "The Right Kind of Medicine." In this he played Charlie Pugh, who is shot by police when they try to arrest him for burglary and must spend the rest of the episode finding someone to attend to his serious wound. In later months he did two additional episodes of *Alfred Hitchcock Presents*. The first, "A Piece of the Action," had him caught up in a gambling melodrama with Gig Young and Martha Hyer. In the second, entitled "A Tangled Web," he played a rich woman's son who—to his mother's absolute horror—is determined to marry the maid (Zohra Lampert).

Redford also appeared in the almost-classic *Twilight Zone* episode, "Nothing in the Dark." In this he was teamed with the great British character actress Gladys Cooper, who plays an old woman living in a condemned tenement that is about to be torn down. But the old woman refuses to leave or even unlock the door. She hears a shot outside her door and a cry for help. A policeman, played by Redford, has been shot in the street. Moved to compassion, the old woman lets him in. She dresses his wound and nurses him, and the two talk. When she grew older, she explains, she began to see the Angel of Death; and she is afraid he is now coming to get her. The foreman of the demolition team comes to tell her she has just a short while to leave before the building is destroyed. When it sinks into her mind that the foreman can't see the policeman, the woman realizes that *he* is the Angel of Death. He assures her that there is nothing in the dark to fear and that it is time for her to move onward with him at her side, unafraid.

George Clayton Johnson's script for "Nothing in the Dark" is simplistic but moving. Cooper is superb, as usual, and Redford is fine as the handsome angel of death. He plays with the same boyish earnestness he exhibited in *Iceman Cometh*, but in a somewhat more commanding (and center stage) part he registers much more star quality and presence and looks terrific. Redford underplays nicely, giving his character some degree of otherworldly dignity without going so far as to give away the game—although it was unlikely any viewer of the show was actually surprised by the outcome. As a young man interacting with a very old woman, he is compassionate ("How can you live like this?" he asks her) and just a bit patronizing.

Director Lamont Johnson said of Redford that "he required very little direction and had the right instinct for the role." Interviewed about her long career and the many famous people she worked with by Lawrence Quirk in London in 1971, Gladys Cooper said, "I wasn't surprised that [Redford] became a major star, because he clearly had star quality, something innate. And he was *so* good-looking."

On "The Last of the Big Spenders" on *Dick Powell Theater*, Redford played the son of Dana Andrews, a dying novelist who hasn't seen his son in twenty years. Redford also appeared on such shows as the compelling legal drama *The Defenders*, *Rescue 8*, the popular western *Maverick*, and the pilot episode of what was to become the extremely popular *Dr. Kildare*, starring Richard Chamberlain. He also appeared on the *Kildare* episode, "The Burning Sky," as a medical assistant who refuses to help Kildare operate on a fire victim during a crisis; in this episode, Redford worked with Carroll O'Connor again. Years later, when asked, Chamberlain did not recall that the famous Robert Redford had ever appeared on his show until reminded of it. This was also true of Robert Stack, who had no memory of even meeting Redford when he guest-starred in an episode of *The Untouchables* as a recent college graduate who tries to hook up with a mobster to help him sell bootleg whiskey to students.

Redford got a lot of attention for one of his bad-boy roles in "Bird and Snake" on the TV dramatic show *The Breaking Point*, in which he played an intelligent thug who takes out his sadistic tendencies on the other members of his therapy group. But it was a "good-guy" role that earned Redford an Emmy nomination for Best Supporting Actor. In "The Voice of Charlie Pont" on *Alcoa Premier*, he played George Laurents, who is happily married to Lisa (Diana Hyland). Then an old pal named Charlie (Bradford Dillman) shows up, still carrying the torch for Lisa and determined to make trouble. Redford has some strong scenes during which he realizes what's up and questions his wife's love for him. (Dillman was also nominated for an Emmy in the Best Actor category.)

Bradford Dillman remembers: "In 1963 I did an Alcoa program that earned me an Emmy nomination. Playing a lesser role, that of my best friend, was a relative unknown named Robert Redford. Ten years later we worked together again, in the popular film *The Way We Were*, and this time I was HIS best friend. The opportunities he has created for young filmmakers are well-documented. He is a remarkable man who has enjoyed a remarkable career, and I am proud to tell people that I know him."

Monique Stevens had no problems in getting guest spots for Redford, but she was hoping to sign him up as the star of a series, the dream of most actors in television. An offer came in for a new western called *The Virginian*: if Redford agreed to star in the series for five years, the network would pay him $150,000 a year. Although by today's standards that amount is small, for the early sixties it was quite a deal. Stevens was stunned when Redford considered it and then turned it down. A graduate of the American Academy of Dramatic Arts (AADA), Redford still saw himself as a New York Theater Actor, and at that time he genuinely loved the excitement of performing in front of an audience. It energized him and kept him on his toes. Being on live TV gave him the same "edgy" feeling, to a lesser degree, but *The Virginian* would be shot on sets and outdoors, not in a studio. And in general, live television was quickly becoming a thing of the past. Redford saw his TV work as a "good training ground" but not the real deal, which was Broadway. Stevens argued that he was throwing away the chance to make it big on TV and possibly wind up in the movies, every actor's goal. Redford was unmoved. It was the theater for him, and that was that. *His* goal was to be seen as a major dramatic actor, a Tracy or Olivier, someone who would be seen as a standard bearer, a Great American Actor. Everyone had told him how wonderful he was; there was no way he couldn't believe it himself.

The irony is that Redford wound up in the movies anyway. New York producers were not as anxious to sign up an actor who'd been in three flops. Perhaps anxious to prove that he didn't need to do *The Virginian* to wind up in movies—and needing the money—Redford signed a three-picture deal with the young brother team of Denis and Terry Sanders; Denis, 33, directed while his brother, 29, produced. The first and last of the three films was *War Hunt* (1962). *War Hunt* was not an auspicious debut for Redford. The actual star of the film was John Saxon; Redford was "introduced" in the film and played the role of a Korean War soldier, Ray Loomis. His costars included Gavin MacLeod, who later played Murray on *The Mary Tyler Moore Show*; Tom Skerritt, who went on to star in TV's *Picket Fences* and the Hollywood movie *Alien* (not to mention Redford's film version of *A River Runs Through It*); and Sydney Pollack, who later became a director who worked with Redford on many different occasions. MacLeod and Skerritt's characters in *War Hunt* are nothing like the personalities for which they would later become famous.

Redford's acting in this movie is okay, but nothing special; neither are his looks—due to the austere, low-budget, black-and-white filming—although his face is expressive. Stanford Whitmore's underwritten screenplay gives Redford virtually no powerful scenes to show off with; he's just one of a group of soldiers in Korea in May 1953. Saxon, as Raymond Endore, sneaks behind enemy lines at night in blackface for reconnaissance and slits the throats of as many enemy soldiers as he can find. During the day the troops listen to enemy broadcasts by the Dragon Lady, saying things like "how many of you will die for somebody's dividends?" Endore has taken under his wing an orphaned Korean boy named Charlie. Redford/Loomis tries to convince Endore that the boy must be told he will have to go to an orphanage (the possibility of adoption is never suggested). The commanding officer tells Loomis to stay away from the spunky little Charlie because "he belongs to Endore." Nowadays the spectre of pedophilia might enter the picture, but that doesn't seem to have been the point of this film from the early sixties. The best scene is an argument over Charlie that leads to violence between Saxon and Redford. At the end of the movie, after a cease-fire, Endore goes crazy, enters enemy territory, and has to be shot. Charlie runs off in horror. Directed by Denis Sanders, *War Hunt* has a once-removed quality to it that does nothing to add to its veracity. It is low-key and unmemorable. The Hollywood *Reporter* found Redford's performance to be "translucent."

When Redford first read the script of *War Hunt*, he mistakenly thought that he was going to play Endore and was disappointed about it. He had just played a psychotic role on *Black Monday* on TV and was afraid he was getting typecast. "But when I got to the studio, I discovered, to my joy, that John Saxon would do that part." Once filming began, however, he realized that of the two biggest parts, he was stuck with the least interesting. The film, shot over a period of three weeks in California's Topanga Canyon, was made for a quarter of a million dollars—distinctly low-budget, even for the 1960s. "It was like a bunch of film students together," Redford recalled. "It really was a good feeling—but it wasn't a feeling of Hollywood." He naturally bonded with the one other actor who had as little ties to Hollywood as he did—Sydney Pollack, who also had Broadway origins. The two would commiserate about how out of place they felt on a movie set, where there was no rehearsal as on Broadway and scenes were shot and reshot endlessly.

The premiere of *War Hunt*, which Redford rarely thought about as he was filming it, was eclipsed by the birth of his second child, David James, or Jamie. Redford did not go to see the film in the theater, because he was afraid someone in the audience might yell out some "killing comment" that would devastate him. He may have had some trepidation about how he would look on the giant screen, as most actors do, good-looking or not. The film got surprisingly good reviews, although its attempts to be hard-hitting fell flat. Redford also got mostly positive notices.

John Saxon, who is excellent in *War Hunt*, remembers that "Very shortly after we had finished filming *War Hunt*, Robert Redford asked to get together and came to my house. He spoke very clearly as if to air it to someone, or himself, that he had no intentions to stay in Los Angeles and try to get to do TV shows. He was going to go to New York. And work in the theater. I admired the confidence in this regard, as I didn't think it was something I would take the risk to do. The next time I saw Redford was in New York when he was working on Broadway in *Barefoot in the Park* with Elizabeth Ashley."

The Sanders Brothers expected Redford to do two more films for them to satisfy his contract, but Redford hated the scripts they kept sending him. Part of the problem was also that Redford's pay was skimpy, and he knew he could make much more money elsewhere. But when he suddenly broke his contract and returned to New York to do a play, the Sanders boys wasted no time in filing suit. The litigation dragged on for months, preventing Redford from doing another film until the whole business was settled. Frustrated, he concentrated on his Broadway work and simply bided his time until he was free.

In the meantime, the film version of *Sunday in New York* came out—minus the Broadway leads, Redford and Pat Stanley. Stanley was replaced by Jane Fonda, who would work with Redford in the future. Redford's part went to an actor who was better known at that time—Rod Taylor, who starred in Alfred Hitchcock's *The Birds*. Redford was bitter about this, but even his TV work had not put him on the same level of recognition. There was also the problem of the contract with the Sanders Brothers, although a major studio could probably have taken care of *that* had they really wanted Redford. Eventually Redford's career would easily eclipse Rod Taylor's.

The play that Redford returned to New York to do was Neil Simon's *Barefoot in the Park*, a comedy of young newlyweds going through growing pains. Elizabeth Ashley was set to play the bride, and Mike Nichols was going to direct. Nichols had just seen Redford on TV in the part that nearly got him an Emmy, knew of his theater background, however limited, and thought he would be wonderful as the husband. In fact, the story goes that Nichols would commit to directing the play only if he had Redford in the cast. Elizabeth Ashley had seen Redford in *Sunday in New York* and knew he could play comedy, so she concurred. Neil Simon registered no objections, so Redford was hired.

By that time Redford had brought some property in his wife's hometown of Provo, Utah—a two-acre plot that he bought for $500 in 1961 that would eventually swell into the Sundance Resort—and was busy building his house. "It was kind of secret, off the map, and that's why I chose it," he recalled. "It was remote enough from civilization to feel you were part of nature, part of the way it was. Part of that pioneering spirit that established this state." Flying from the wide open spaces back to the *theatuh* provided him with a bit of culture shock. During early rehearsals he was still on West Coast time, still full of thoughts of his own home, while the others chatted about Things of Theater and concentrated on their lines. Redford did not make much of an impression on the rest of the cast; he seemed like someone who wasn't happy anywhere—on TV, in films, Broadway, Utah, or New York—he emitted a constant dissatisfaction when he should have been overjoyed just to find the work that eluded so many other, often more talented, actors. He was starring in what might well turn out to be a big hit Broadway show, and he was blowing it.

Redford felt he was very bad in the part, and during out-of-town tryouts Nichols had to talk him into staying. Nichols seemed determined to help Redford in spite of himself. Nichols told Redford that he wasn't going to fire him no matter how bad he was, but he thought he could help him fix the problem. Redford played to the rest of the cast while Liz Ashley played to the audience. Redford was sulking because she got the big laughs—the audience just loved her, and she was hip and sexy—and he barely got a snort or two.

Even early in her career the talented Ashley had a diva-like, larger-than-life quality that especially sparkled in front of a live audience. Some found her riveting, others thought her overblown, but they couldn't take their eyes off her. Nichols took Redford to dinner and told him he'd had a similar problem when he was partnered on stage with the pretty Elaine May. Redford wouldn't get anywhere until he saw and acknowledged that there was always a kind of competition—often friendly, sometimes not—between actors on the

stage. The trick was in getting attention for yourself without compromising the play, your performance, or the performances of the
other actors, even the one who was stealing the scenes. Gradually,
Redford began increasing his effects, the size of his performance—
sometimes overpowering Ashley, sometimes not, as Nichols helped
them achieve a balance that worked best for both actors and for the
play.

Elizabeth Ashley wasn't just a diva; she was a self-described bitch,
as she would recall years later. At the time, she was dealing with
assorted personal problems and the pressure of suddenly finding a
leading man who was not as easy to overwhelm on stage as she had
hoped. Some actors are content to be one consummate piece of a consummate cast, and others need to be the "best thing" in the show;
even better, of course, is to be the best thing in a great cast. Ashley
was no longer the best thing—although she had competition from
the supporting players as well—and she worried that Redford was
getting too much attention and help from director Nichols, to the
detriment of her performance. Before long, it got out that Ashley
and Redford were involved in a bitter, flat-out "feud." While this
information was vastly overstated, the two did have their difficult
moments.

Part of the problem was simple miscommunication. Someone
would pass along to Ashley something that Redford had allegedly
said, but it might have been out of context, exaggerated, or completely misinterpreted. Ashley might respond to this, and her comments would get back to Redford. Before long the two were speaking
only onstage, dissing each other behind their backs. Ashley complained on a talk show about how terribly Redford had treated her
and what awful things he said. The irony was that both actors actually liked and respected one another, or would have had they been
left to their own devices. Redford later claimed that he liked Ashley
and found her sympathetic. According to someone close to the production, "Mike Nichols was the one who kept those two at odds because he thought it added to the sexual energy of their performances,
an off-stage antagonism that kept them on their toes while they were
on-stage. It worked."

Redford did enjoy working with costars Mildred Natwick and
Herb Edelman. During a scene when Redford was supposed to be

drunk and would laugh and open the door to rush out of the apartment, one or the other would be waiting outside to see if they could
really get him to crack up with a silly pose or costume. Even Liz
Ashley got into the act: on Redford's birthday she hired a stripper to
stand outside the door stark naked, causing the actor to laugh for so
long that the audience, who could not see the lady in the wings, wondered what the hell was happening.

Barefoot in the Park opened in October 1963 to mostly admiring if
not universally positive notices. Some critics enjoyed it as the light,
frothy concoction it was meant to be; others noted that as the *Village
Voice* put it, the play was "peopled not by characters but by general-
izations of characters." *Women's Wear Daily* opined that Redford was
"the 'great big lug' type" and found him professional but, surprisingly, "not very charming," which may have been their perception of
the character and not the man who played him. Many people thought
that Redford had the makings of a fine comic actor. "I was convinced
he was going to be the next Jack Lemmon," noted William Goldman.
Redford's friend from theater circles, a man named Gene Hackman,
briefly played a supporting part in *Barefoot* before getting his own
leading role in *Any Wednesday*.

During the play's run, Redford was reunited with *War Hunt* star
John Saxon when the latter was visiting New York. "I'd just finished
working in Boston on *The Cardinal*, a film directed by Otto Preminger," recalls Saxon, "and I told Bob at lunch at the Russian Tea
Room that working with Preminger was definitely an experience that
could dent an actor's esteem. *Barefoot in the Park* was sold out, so
Redford had the Stage Manager place a seat in the wings so I could
see the show."

Neil Simon felt that Redford and, improbably, Richard Dreyfuss
were two of "the sexiest leading men I ever wrote for." Simon would
have a recurring nightmare in which one of his plays would suddenly
be transformed into a dreadful musical in which "George C. Scott is
doing a tap dance, Al Pacino is playing a saxophone, and Robert
Redford is singing like Ezio Pinza in *South Pacific*."

Years later, Mike Nichols wanted Redford to take the role eventually played by George Segal in his adaptation of Edward Albee's play,
Who's Afraid of Virginia Woolf? Nichols visited him on the set of *Inside Daisy Clover* and tried to build up Redford's ego and interest by

telling him how people who'd seen footage from *Daisy* said he positively jumped off the screen. The problem was that at the time of Nichols's visit, Redford had yet to appear before a camera—not one of his scenes had been shot. Redford was amused by this, but he nixed the idea of his appearing in *Who's Afraid of Virginia Woolf?* He just didn't like the play and was probably uncomfortable with its allegedly homosexual subtexts and references.

When it became clear that *Barefoot in the Park* was going to have a long run, Redford had Lola and the children come to New York from Utah. As much as he enjoyed starring in a hit show and having his family at his side, he became restless again rather quickly. The show ran for four years, but Redford left *Barefoot* before a year was up. Saying the same lines, doing the same thing night after night after night became wearying. Even the ongoing gags the cast pulled on him, and vice versa, could no longer keep it fresh. He needed new challenges, new projects.

He had done what he'd set out to do: conquer Broadway. He left the show; it did not leave him. Having made a major success on the Great White Way, Redford would turn his back on the theater and never appear on a stage—on Broadway or anywhere—ever again.

He had new worlds to conquer now.

When asked by writer James Spada why he'd turned his back on Broadway, Redford came back with a borderline haughty reply. He thought the theater was becoming too commercial—in this he was certainly correct—and explained that he "was looking for something with some literary quality and there wasn't anything for me in that revolution. Nothing has come along in the theater since then that has interested me enough to attract me." While the commercialization of Broadway has by now been well established—sitcom stars doing Shakespeare, Disney movies turned into musicals—it seems incredible for Redford never to have found some project that would ignite his passion. Redford may not have had much interest in doing frothy, mindless comedies like *Sunday in New York* or *Barefoot in the Park*, but serious plays were also being written and produced in that period and after. And many of the films he was to appear in were not exactly intellectual—*The Hot Rock*, *Sneakers*, and so forth.

Redford turned his back on Broadway because the money was chump change compared to what he could make in Hollywood, and because the thrill of performing before a live audience quickly faded when he had to say the same lines night after night. After a couple of months in a play, he would feel like coming onstage in his underwear just to relieve the monotony. The New York Theater Actor also had a family to support; the movies beckoned. But he did not establish himself in Hollywood overnight. *War Hunt* did not make much of a ripple.

In his second film, *Situation Hopeless . . . But Not Serious* (1965), Redford was cast as Hank, one of two American fliers in World War Two who are shot down and hidden by Frick (Alec Guinness), a friendly German shopkeeper who convinces them that it is safer to stay hidden than to go outside. Years go by; the war ends; and still Frick keeps the two men in his basement, never telling them that the fighting is over. When the two men are released, still without knowing the truth, they are shocked to discover that they have needlessly been kept prisoner. Still, the three men remain friends, and in the end the lonely Frick goes to work as a butler for the other flier, Lucky (Michael Connors). Perhaps because the actual situation was more grotesque and tragic than amusing, it led one critic to snipe that the movie "could more aptly be titled *Situation Hopeless—and Not Funny.*"

Redford made the film in Munich, where he lived in the same apartment he had occupied during his early European trip. The movie was based on a novel entitled *The Hiding Place* by actor-writer Robert Shaw, best known for his roles in *Jaws* (as Quint, the shark fighter) and *The Sting*, in which he costarred with Redford. The novel had already been presented in England as a made-for-TV special. Redford enjoyed working with Alec Guinness, who warned him that it wasn't an easy—or amusing—job to make a screen comedy. He explained that it was hard to sustain a fine comic performance when it was broken up into tiny little pieces of film, with many separate shots. Redford would make very few comedies in his future.

Redford also greatly liked his younger costar Michael Connors, who had already appeared in several movies. Often billed as "Touch," Connors later came to national prominence as the star of the popular private-eye series *Mannix*, although he was never a big star on the order of Redford. Redford did not particularly care for the director, Gottfried Reinhardt, whom he found too heavy-handed and Germanic in his approach. With only his second film, Redford was already becoming critical of his directors' techniques, feeling that he "could do better." He would prove his directing ability with his own projects many years in the future.

Redford was often bored during the shooting, so he drew sketches that appeared in the film as Hank's artwork. He was delighted when Lola flew over for a visit, bringing the two children along. Shauna and Jamie were adorable and attractive children, and they had fun as the whole family explored Munich together, often accompanied by Connors and his wife.

Redford later claimed that it didn't faze him when the film was screened by executives at Paramount and deemed "unreleasable." The film was excoriated at press screenings, rarely getting any favorable comments, although there was some admiration for the actors and Redford's youthful appeal. Redford had mixed emotions: he had worked hard on a film that would never see the light of day. On the other hand, he might be spared the embarrassment of being widely seen in an obvious stinker. He was not surprised by the reaction to the movie. As with *War Hunt*, which he later liked when he saw it, he had the feeling during filming that *Situation Hopeless* would truly turn out hopeless. The picture would eventually see the light of day, however.

"Incredible as it seems, I'm going to make something out of you," a studio head of the 1930s tells his latest star in *Inside Daisy Clover* (1965), Redford's first big Hollywood film. The movie was based on a novel by Gavin Lambert, who also wrote the screenplay. The actual stars of the film were Christopher Plummer and Natalie Wood— who personally asked for Redford in the supporting role of Wade Lewis. Daisy Clover (Wood) is a precocious sixteen-year-old whose singing voice improbably nets her a Hollywood contract. Turned into a kind of older Shirley Temple, she is taken under the wing of studio head Raymond Swan (Plummer) and his wife Melora (Katharine Bard). Daisy is romantically pursued by the older movie star, Wade Lewis (Redford), who marries her but abruptly leaves her in the lurch. She learns that Wade has not only slept with Melora and many other ladies but also has a penchant for other men. Then the much older Swan makes a play for her. Suffering a nervous breakdown, Daisy is cajoled into returning to the set of her latest movie, but instead blows up her house and walks happily away from Hollywood before ever reaching her eighteenth birthday.

Wade Lewis is another in a long line of portraits of casual, sardonic sensualists who figure if it feels good, do it, regardless of the emotional cost to the people they sleep with. Swan says of Lewis, "They take him to heart; he takes them to bed." Redford is quite good as the glib, amoral movie star; he explains that his real name is Lewis Wade, but the studio felt that "Wade Lewis" sounded sexier—which it does. Redford's excellent line readings, which capture the character's depth-free and negatively insouciant attitude toward life and people—his object is not to hurt people, but to please himself—betray his background in the New York theater. He gives a particularly nice reading of the line "Poor rich lovely lonely lady," putting just the right emphasis on each word while making the line flow effortlessly and naturally. Talking about Lewis, Swan goes on about the thousands of women who go home to their dark bedrooms and dream about him, a scenario that certainly came true for the real Redford in the years that followed.

Inside Daisy Clover was meant to be a trenchant, powerful, and cutting satire of Hollywood; but despite some good moments—Daisy having her hysterical nervous breakdown in a soundproof booth while recording songs for her movie, for instance—and good performances, it just doesn't work. The script is a hodgepodge of Hollywood fact and folklore; like Marilyn Monroe's mother, Daisy's mother winds up in an institution. A big production number, *You're Gonna Hear from Me*, is kitsch from start to finish, featuring a parody of a stereotypical Broadway song (at least we hope it was meant to be a parody). A late sequence, when a disgusted and disillusioned Daisy tries to commit suicide but is constantly interrupted, is played for laughs. This mixture of the serious with the comedic results in a schizoid movie whose under-written characters fail to grip. The story seems clichéd instead of mesmerizing, arch and superficial instead of true and human.

Although Lambert's book was heavily sanitized for public consumption, the film still has borderline unacceptable moments. Lewis's pursuit of a fifteen-year-old would never have passed muster in the days of the Hays office, and Melora's line after she phones Wade's hotel room—"Your husband never could resist a charming boy," she tells Daisy after another man answers—would have been excised at the early script stage. (For years, when the film was shown on television, that line was always cut.) In saying "boy," we assume that Melora is simply dividing the world into boys and girls, although Wade's penchant for underage girls might also literally apply to boys. No movie, even in the sixties, would have dared to delve into that regrettable aspect of human sexuality. Several scenes were cut before the film's release. When Daisy first encounters Wade in the bedroom after she is presented to the public, they already seem to know one another; Daisy does not react the way a starstruck teenage girl would react to meeting a handsome matinee idol.

Redford was brought into the movie at the request of Natalie Wood, who remembered him from *Sunday in New York*. Wood truly believed that the role of Daisy Clover might give her the opportunity to win an Academy Award. She had appeared in dozens of movies as a child, and was one of the few youngsters to make a successful transition to adult acting roles, although her career eventually faded out after a few years of stardom (*West Side Story, Gypsy, Sex and the Single Girl, Love with the Proper Stranger,* etc.) and much promise. She saw something in Redford when he appeared on stage, found him quite attractive, and wanted him for her leading man. Although Christopher Plummer got top billing with Wood and had the bigger part, Redford was the love interest.

Redford was advised against taking the part of Wade Lewis because the character was "homosexual" (although he is clearly also attracted to women). He suggested that he would prefer to play—would *only* play—the character as "narcissistic, constantly on the take, never on the give . . . someone who bats ten different ways: children, women, dogs, cats, men, anything that salves his ego. Total narcissism." This is exactly how the character of Wade Lewis comes off in the film, but Redford has always felt his performance was compromised by the inclusion of the aforementioned phone sequence in which the character's homosexuality is definitely revealed. According to Redford, he had explained to the film's producer, Alan J. Pakula, what he wanted to do with the role, and Pakula had agreed; but after filming was completed, the new sequence was inserted without his knowledge and "knocked hell out of . . . the interpretation. It isn't fair to an actor to direct him and agree on a concept and play it all the way through and have the film finished and then come around from behind without telling him and put something in that reinterprets the role." Redford was so disgusted and disillusioned—and unaccountably embarrassed—that he wanted to take off from Hollywood.

Alan J. Pakula had a different take on this, of course. According to Pakula, Redford was simply embarrassed to play a gay character. "This was the 1960s after all. Long before Gay Lib. Good-looking

actors always fear the stigma of being labeled a homosexual. After-
wards, actors often sought the challenge of playing gay roles, but this
was a much earlier period." Pakula and many others agree that Redford's narcissistic interpretation is not at all compromised by one sequence revealing that his character sleeps with men as well as
women—that he "bats ten different ways," as Redford himself put
it. It is much more likely that Redford was undergoing a kind of
typical homophobia of the period—not a hatred of homosexuals, but
a dread fear of being *perceived* as a homosexual—that has plagued
pretty boys and actors, and especially pretty-boy actors, since time
immemorial. Even in today's much more enlightened era, many
actors are scared to "play gay," and gay actors are scared of being
"outed."

Redford also felt that the powers that be weren't taking his input
seriously, that he had been betrayed by them. According to Redford,
he had agreed to take the part only if he could do it his way. It may
not have occurred to the young actor, in only his third movie, that
it was somewhat outrageous for a supporting player to make such
demands and that it was fairly commonplace for more experienced
producers and directors to listen politely to the suggestions of comparative neophytes and then do what they felt was best. Pakula and
his director, Robert Mulligan, felt the film needed an added punch—
"something shocking to juice it up," as Redford put it—and they had
the right to do so; after all, it was their film. But we can also sympa-
thize with Redford, who must have been mortified to play a more or
less gay role in an intolerant era when gays—and those who played
gays—were mercilessly lampooned. Would he ever live it down? The
irony is that most reasonable people would agree that Wade Lewis's
sexual interest in minors was *far worse* than his interest in men.

Redford was actually very savvy in recognizing that Wade Lewis
was an essential narcissist who chose bed partners to assuage and
build his own ego. This type of person, so common in Hollywood,
was undoubtedly a sort that Redford had encountered in real life,
even in the sacred theaters on and off Broadway.

Although her performance as Daisy isn't bad, Natalie Wood is
simply too old to be convincing as a sixteen-year-old. Ruth Gordon,
who plays her mother, seems just as unreal in this film as she does

in any other. Katharine Bard is more on the mark as Melora, and Christopher Plummer gives a ferocious, outstanding performance— one of the best of his career—as Raymond Swan. Despite that kitschy "Broadway" number, the score by Andre Previn is also an asset.

Natalie Wood and Redford got along very well during filming, as expected, and would remain friends until Wood's untimely death many years later. A grimly ironic incident occurred when the two actors filmed a scene in a sailboat. The camera crew was in another, larger boat a few yards away, attached to the smaller boat with cables. When a sudden swell arose, the two boats were pulled apart and Natalie began to panic. Finally the cables snapped, and the sailboat was set adrift in choppy water. Although Redford kind of enjoyed it, Natalie had always been frightened by the water, so he held her in his arms to quell her fear. His sense of humor about the whole incident also helped to keep Natalie's mind off any danger until they were reunited with the crew and could finish the scene.

One afternoon Natalie confided in Redford that when she was a child, her mother got her ready for her screen test by tearing the wings off of a butterfly right in front of her. This created such a hysterical reaction in the girl that her mother practically shoved her in front of the camera, shouting, "She's ready!" Natalie liked and enjoyed working with Redford much more than she had enjoyed working with Warren Beatty in *Splendor in the Grass*. She came to despise Beatty, although she later revised her opinion of him. Natalie was engaged at that time, and Redford was happily married to Lola. But as many of her colleagues and Hollywood insiders knew at the time, it did not prevent Wood from developing an infatuation and then an intense love for Redford. No one thought that Natalie was truly attracted to Ladi Blatnik, her fiancé. If Robert Wagner, whom Wood married twice, was the grand passion of her life, then Redford was a close second.

Wood often liked to play parts that she identified with. The scene when Daisy learns that her husband is bisexual must have certainly resonated with her. According to her biographer Suzanne Finstad, Natalie told her friends and relatives that she divorced Wagner after their first marriage because she "found him in a compromising position with another man." Finstad also added, however, that "[Wagner], through representatives, denies this version of events and any allegations of bisexuality."

Roddy McDowall played the small role of Baines, Swan's assistant. About Wood and Redford's relationship, he observed, "It was clear that Natalie was falling hopelessly in love with Bob—although I think it got more intense on their second film together—and just as clear that Bob thought of her as a sweet younger sister. Maybe if he hadn't been married there might have been more on his end. I think she found him a very sympathetic listener, a kind man—he was grateful for her help with his career." Others have suggested that what Wood really felt for Redford was the adoration of a sympathetic and protective older brother.

As for the film itself? "That one certainly didn't turn out the way anyone hoped," McDowall remembered. "It was too much of one thing and not enough of another—or maybe the other way around." Redford himself always felt the picture "had a stiffness to it." He did, however, receive a Golden Globe award as the year's "Star of the Future" for his work in the film.

The Chase was always Marlon Brando's picture. Or maybe it was producer Sam Spiegel's. Brando was the only actor whose name appeared above the title. But he and director Arthur Penn always blamed Spiegel for ruining the movie. Penn had hoped to edit the movie while working on a Broadway play in New York, but Spiegel grabbed the footage and cut it his own way in England. "What happened was that the center of the film moved out of my hands and clearly into Sam Spiegel's hands," Penn remembered. "I was a babe in the woods. I didn't know from fancy Hollywood fucking."

But while shooting was going on, it was Brando who was in control. "He'd move this here and that there, and pretty soon it was *his* place, his environment," Penn remembered. "The other actors—actors of no small accomplishment themselves—stood around literally in awe while he worked." When Brando realized that Spiegel was rewriting the script, inserting scenes intended to up the box office but only diminishing the drama, he figured what the hell—and began causing one delay after another, just to irritate Spiegel. Realizing that he could not prevent the film from being compromised,

Brando decided just to take the money and run. Brando pursued numerous women while making the film, and he bonded with Jane Fonda due to their mutual political interests. This same bonding did not occur between Brando and Redford, however. Many years later, in the seventies, both men would get involved in the Leonard Peltier case. Redford would spend a decade trying to get Peltier pardoned; but Brando, scared off by the FBI, would not remain on Peltier's support team.

Although Redford had scenes with Jane Fonda, who played his wife in *The Chase*, the two did not bond while making the picture. Fonda tended to keep to herself, and whatever free time she had was taken up by her fascination with Brando and his ideals. She didn't find out that she and Redford also had a lot in common, including certain political attitudes, until they starred together in the film version of *Barefoot in the Park*.

In *The Chase*, Redford plays "Bubber" Reeves, a bad boy whom we're told—but not shown—isn't really so bad, after all. Redford, who hardly looks like a Bubber, breaks out of jail with another inmate. When they try to steal money from a man driving by, the other inmate murders the fellow and runs off. Now Bubber is wanted for a much more serious crime. He returns to his hometown and finds it's a regular Peyton Place, where middle-aged people sleep around, get drunk, and carry on like college kids. The sheriff (Marlon Brando) is determined to find Bubber and bring him in before a lynch mob can string him up. Bubber's wife (Jane Fonda) is having an affair with the son of one of the town's more prominent citizens. Bubber and his wife are briefly reunited in a junkyard, where the young scion is accidentally killed. Bubber winds up dead, despite the sheriff's efforts.

Based on a novel and play by Horton Foote and with a screenplay by Lillian Hellman, everyone expected *The Chase* to be great. But despite the busy goings-on in the film, including a bravura beating of Brando in the courthouse by some thugs, *The Chase* emerged as tawdry, superficial, and even a little dull. It's very hard to care about Bubber, the sheriff, or anyone else; they all seem like under-written types instead of genuine characters. Redford's perfunctory performance doesn't much help. When he says the line, "It's been a long day, a long two years," he shows hardly any feeling. He looks quite athletic as he crawls and jumps over the roof of a train. Brando mumbles; Miriam Hopkins, as Bubber's mother, chews the scenery; and Jane Fonda is, at least, vivid. *The Chase* is an almost-comical mess.

Many people did not think Redford was a wise casting choice in *The Chase*. "Casting overshot the mark," wrote Paul Buhle and Dave Wagner in *Hide in Plain Sight*. "Robert Redford, for the best political but all the worst cinematic reasons, served as the returning non-hero 'Bubber.'" Actually, Redford was originally supposed to play Fonda's new boyfriend, the rich man's polished and well-mannered son played by James Fox in the film. Redford would have been far more appropriate in that role, but he insisted that he understood Bubber Reeves and wanted to play him. Penn let him do so. "I got in trouble with the law when I was just a kid myself," Redford recalled to on-set reporters, "so I understand where Bubber is coming from. I feel closer to him than I do to the character I was supposed to play." As originally scripted, Bubber may have been the smaller of the two parts—and in the finished film, Fox may have had more dialogue—but Redford was shrewd enough to realize that everything centered on Bubber, who was one of the four major characters. The rich man's son was just a supporting part.

At first Redford worked sporadically on the film. "I had to keep introducing myself when I went on the set, but I was on salary all that time so I wasn't unhappy." Most of the time Redford worked with the second unit, which filmed him running through woods and fields trying to keep one step ahead of the law, and he saw little of director Arthur Penn, who was busy with the other actors in Hollywood. Redford ultimately blamed Penn for letting things get out of control, for putting up with the "unspeakable conditions" imposed on him by producer Spiegel. Redford felt Penn should have fought harder to change things, or simply walked off the picture. When Redford became a big name, he would try to avoid these unpleasant situations by "walking off" a picture before it even started if he felt the conditions would not be right. Redford criticized Penn for his "retroactive criticism," which did not sit well with Penn.

Redford later claimed he had never been that crazy about the script to begin with. He thought it included way too many characters and tried too hard to be all things to all people, bouncing around liberal ideas about civil rights without the solid framework to back them up.

The picture, jeered at its first screening, opened to mostly negative reviews. Bosley Crowther of the *New York Times* damned it as a "picture to leave you cold . . . phony, tasteless." The *New York Morning Telegraph* found it "a witless and preposterous hunk of drivel," and *Life* deemed it "a disaster of awesome proportions." Judith Crist in the *New York Herald Tribune* and Archer Winston of the *New York Post* praised Redford's performance as Bubber; but the best notices for the actor came from *Variety*, whose critic, seemingly smitten, opined that Redford gave the best performance in the film and the best of his short career. The critic waxed enthusiastically about Redford's "economy of dialogue delivery" (which others simply saw as a lack of emotion) and how he made his presence felt throughout the picture even though he was off the screen for much of the running time. Leo Mishkin of the *New York Morning Telegraph* was a little more on the mark, and put *Variety*'s comments in the proper perspective, when he noted that "Robert Redford makes a handsome, if unconvincing, escaped convict." It was not the first time that Redford's looks and undeniable on-screen charisma had fooled some observers into thinking he was better than he really was.

Redford had been filming *Inside Daisy Clover* with Natalie Wood when she asked him to be the leading man in her next film, *This Property Is Condemned* (1966). The movie was very loosely based on a one-act play by Tennessee Williams; the play became the film's prologue. The rest of the movie was the product of several screenwriters, who seemed to be working against one another to fabricate a superficial soap opera that was a far cry from anything by Williams. Yet Wood and others connected with the film kept thinking they were making a "Tennessee Williams" movie, and Wood thought of her character, Alva, as a Tennessee Williams heroine. She said, "It's the closest I'll ever get to playing Blanche DuBois [of *Streetcar Named Desire*]," which was her dream role.

Originally the film was to be directed by John Huston, and there was serious talk of Natalie's idol Vivien Leigh (who'd portrayed Blanche DuBois on film) playing Natalie's mother, Hazel. When that fell through, Liz Taylor and Montgomery Clift were penciled in as the leads. Eventually the assignment was turned over to Wood, who, smitten with Redford, insisted on his doing the picture with her. Her wedding to fiancé Ladi Blatnik, who was considered a playboy anxious to snare a movie star and all the perks that came with her, was put on hold. The nuptials were rescheduled for Christmastime, but Wood canceled only a month or so before they were to take place. "Better a long engagement than a short marriage," she said. She saw her therapist daily.

No one wanted to direct *This Property Is Condemned*, which was seen as a sure stinker. It was Tennessee Williams filtered through Hollywood hacks, who used some of his ideas and developed ersatz characterizations, but the script was devoid of his special genius (Williams himself had absolutely nothing to do with the film). Francis Ford Coppola was one of the credited screenwriters, but it's impossible to tell how much he wrote actually made it into the finished film. One top director after another turned the picture down. "I started to panic," Redford remembered, "because I wanted to do the film, and I wanted to work with [Natalie] again, but it was a mess, it needed somebody to straighten it out." Then Redford got what he thought was a great idea. His costar in *War Hunt*, Sydney Pollack, with whom he'd remained friends, had directed a few TV shows and plays in the past few years, as well as the low-budget film *The Slender Thread* with Anne Bancroft, and he needed a good break. Although, like Redford, Pollack saw himself as a vaunted "theater person," he could not resist the clarion call of Hollywood.

Redford knew Pollack would be a tough sell as director. In Hollywood, he was a complete unknown. Redford told Wood, who had to approve the director, that Pollack was "red hot" and it would be a real coup if they could get him. After Wood gave a startled Pollack a call, he came out to Hollywood to meet her. The two clicked and Pollack got the assignment—the second of many, many films he would direct, often with Redford as his star.

The film was shot partly in Mississippi, for some genuine Southern atmosphere, and partly in studios back in Hollywood. Pollack, who worked well with actors because he was an actor himself, was a lifeline for Wood. She needed his guidance during a difficult emotional period due in no small part to her on-again, off-again relationship with Ladi Blatnik, who had accompanied her to Mississippi. Pollack broke some of his rules by allowing Wood to have a couple of glasses of wine in preparation for a drunk scene.

When interviewed by Lawrence Quirk on the set of *This Property Is Condemned*, Natalie Wood obviously had deep feelings—she couldn't quite hide them—for her costar, Redford. She was never to realize another project that was dear to her heart: costarring with Redford on Broadway in the play, *Anastasia*. Years later she began rehearsals for the play in Los Angeles, sans Redford, who had decidedly moved on from the theater. She never finished the project because of her death by drowning.

The original one-act play, *This Property Is Condemned*, was simply an encounter between two grubby urchins. As mentioned, in altered shape the play forms the prologue of the film version. The movie, set in the 1930s, tells the story of a doomed love affair between Alva Starr (Natalie Wood), who lives with her mother and sister in the cheap boardinghouse her mother owns, and Owen Legate (Redford), who shows up in town on a mysterious mission. It turns out that he's there to let most of the railroad workers go because of the Depression. The layoffs will probably spell finis for the boardinghouse as well. Alva's mother, Hazel (Kate Reid), wants her daughter to marry a middle-aged man with money, but Owen wants her to leave town with him. Separated from the man she loves by her mother's manipulations, Alva impulsively marries another man, but then runs off to New Orleans to find Owen. Hazel follows and tells Owen of Alva's marriage. The film ends on a flat note with Alva running away from the apartment she shared with Owen, presumably back to her aimless and wasted life, making everything that came before seem pointless—a script without an ending. *This Property Is Condemned* has the bare bones of a sad story, but a combination of twelve screenwriters only served to strip it of its potential power, making each version more superficial than the one before. Each day Pollack would take a scene from one script, add it to a scene from another script, and somehow hope it would all turn out okay. Then producer Ray Stark would add his two cents, which irked Redford even more than it did Pollack. Adding to the anxiety level was Charles Bronson, who had a small role as the man who eventually marries Alva and wanted his part to be beefed up. This mishmash is, of course, no way to make a movie; but far more movies are made like this than the public ever realizes. As if things weren't bad enough, the residents of one Mississippi town where many scenes were filmed were not at all thrilled to have a film crew in their midst, especially because they were afraid the picture was going to be some Tennessee Williams production full of perversion and bad depictions of Southerners. Their mayor was unsuccessful in his attempt to get the production to leave.

Pollack and Redford would have many arguments on the set. Pollack was already insecure—for one thing, it was strange giving orders to Redford, with whom he'd previously only acted. He was initially mortified when Redford would question his decisions and act like the director, and he responded by snapping at him to concentrate on his part and let *him*, Pollack, direct the picture. Eventually Pollack came to feel that Redford needed to share his ideas, which were often good ones, and he was not necessarily trying to take over. (Although an associate of Redford's now says that "Bob *always* had an eye on directing. He *always* thought he could direct a picture as well if not better than the actual director could. It was *no* surprise to anyone who had worked with him that he would eventually turn to directing his own pictures.") Early on, however, Pollack was concerned that Redford would strip him of his power and authority, undermining not only his image as a director but his ability to direct the other actors. He was especially nervous about handling Wood, who was a big star. In any case, Pollack and Redford eventually worked out any differences they might have had, and they worked together many, many times after completing *This Property Is Condemned*.

Playing yet another under-written character, Redford is actually quite good in the film, maintaining an interesting, restrained insolence throughout. There is a nice moment when he sees Wood's face lighted by the candles of a cake, and a good scene when they tell each other off and wind up making love. The obvious affection that Redford and Wood shared in real life is up there on the screen and informs their performances. Wood gives an excellent performance, although the movie is nearly stolen by Mary Badham as Alva's adoring younger sister, Willie, and by Kate Reid as their mother, Hazel. Robert Blake, who decades later was acquitted of murdering his wife, had a small role in the film; he would work with Redford again in a larger capacity.

This Property Is Condemned, like *The Chase*, got mostly negative notices; but most critics also noticed that Redford had star quality and made an impressive leading man. *Variety*, still smitten with the man, praised Redford to the skies, making him sound like some kind of young Olivier committed to total acting. *The New Yorker* observed that in one scene Redford "flats his lines in the awful, self-doubting way of an actor falling out of his part." It may not have been a great performance, but it was by no means bad. Redford did all that the part required of him with competence, and, at times, with a little extra.

By the time *This Property Is Condemned* had opened in theaters, Natalie Wood had replaced Ladi Blatnik with British agent Richard Gregson, who worked out of the Los Angeles office of his talent agency, London International Artists. She talked Redford into becoming one of Gregson's clients, and soon the two men were fast friends. Natalie and Richard would fly out to Robert and Lola's Utah ranch and spend happy weekends together. Gregson tried to come up with joint projects for Redford and his girlfriend—an idea to team up the two in a play went nowhere—and was interested in getting more involved in the motion picture business. To that end he sold his agency, making a huge profit, and formed a production company called Wildwood with Redford. "He was a pretty ambitious guy," remembered Redford.

Whatever the critics thought of the film, *This Property Is Condemned* got Redford a lot of attention and plenty of offers, not all related to the movies. Fan male from women and sometimes men came into the studio with proposals of marriage and everything else imaginable for a man who was rapidly becoming a matinee idol. This kind of thing would intensify after his breakout role in *Butch Cassidy*. Most actors would have pored over the scripts, anxiously deciding which would be the best bet for major stardom. They would talk earnestly with their agents and advisors and prepare for a comparatively grueling schedule of movie assignments, interviews, publicity tours, and so on. Never one to do the obvious, Redford decided just to . . . drop out.

Redford had reached that certain point of recognition where more and more people knew his face on sight, if not his name. He described this period, as many actors did, as "unreal," but it was also overwhelming. Redford knew that he was on the brink of stardom: once he passed a certain point, there would be no going back; every bit of privacy for himself and his family would be gone. As badly as he wanted to succeed, he wasn't certain he was willing to pay the price. He wasn't even certain if he wanted to continue with acting.

Ironically, Redford was also just at the point where casting directors and producers knew who he was. They had seen his work, and many specifically requested him for a specific role, but he was not yet a superstar who could land any part he wanted. Some actors would have reveled in this situation, but to Redford it was only worrisome. Would he really make it in the stratosphere of superstardom, joining the ranks of hallowed actors like Jimmy Stewart and Cary Grant, or would he have to spend the rest of his days deciding which of the mostly mediocre scripts he would spend months of his life working on? If he did have a shot at major stardom, would he ever really be ready for it?

If Redford at that point thought most plays were pabulum, just imagine what he thought of the average Hollywood script. He never thought much of soap opera stuff like *Inside Daisy Clover* and *This Property Is Condemned*, but he knew that producers would want him for such swill because his good looks made him catnip to the largely female audience who enjoyed these pictures. Fancying himself as a kind of intellectual—though he had never graduated from college or had any real, long-lasting love affair with books—Redford worried that he would spend his days walking through unchallenging, mindless assignments and be seen only as a pretty boy that no real person could take seriously. He was embarrassed by the prospect of taking such roles, yet the idea of sticking to and starving on Broadway with its own mediocrity didn't appeal to him either.

Redford needed time away from Hollywood and New York to really *think* about what he wanted to do, and he desperately wanted time alone with his wife and children. He decided to take all of them to Spain, where they would stay in a village well off the beaten track and no one would have the vaguest idea who Robert Redford was. On the family's first day some adventurous tourists showed up, and someone did recognize Redford from TV or the movies. He decided to pack up the gang and travel to Greece. They resided on Crete for the rest of their European stay. Redford had wanted to share with his family the excitement he'd felt when seeing Europe for the first time. To that end he tried to find places that weren't all touristy and Americanized, that still conveyed the Old European feeling, but the quest was difficult.

Some feel Redford had other reasons to get away from Hollywood. Says one insider, "Lola was afraid that Bob was getting too close to Natalie Wood. Everyone knew how *she* felt about Bob, but whether Bob fooled around with her or not—I suspect not—Natalie was a beautiful woman and Bob was only human. It was Lola's idea to get Bob away from Hollywood for awhile. She was hoping that if there was anything going on between Bob and Natalie it would cool off after six months of separation." Redford was not really the type to have affairs with his leading ladies, at least while he was married, but no one could help noticing the chemistry between Wood and Redford both on- and offscreen.

It was lucky, in retrospect, that Redford had his six months of quietude and anonymity; it would turn out to be his very last chance. When Redford's self-imposed exile from Hollywood finally ended, he would return to the States and the movie business and soon find himself possessing one of the most recognizable faces in the country, and indeed the world.

Because of what had happened with *Sunday in New York*, Redford was certain that he would be passed over for the movie version of *Barefoot in the Park*. (In truth, the studio originally wanted to put then-current heartthrob Troy Donahue into the movie; but he wound up on *Surfside Six* on TV instead, clearing the field for Redford.) Redford had affected a blasé attitude toward this development, saying that he was not certain he even wanted to repeat his Broadway performance by doing the film if it were offered. He was surprised when the offer came, but he'd never seriously intended to turn it down. He thought the story might well be as big a hit on the screen as it had been on Broadway. He returned from Europe specifically to make the film.

Redford had gotten this deal before leaving with his family for Europe, so his "dropping out" wasn't quite as insane as it may have seemed to many. He knew he'd have a firm assignment waiting for him when he returned. But he did entertain notions of not honoring his commitment, of staying in Europe with his little family and taking up painting again, of having a much, much simpler life than the one he wound up with. Once he decided to return and make *Barefoot in the Park*, there was no turning back.

Elizabeth Ashley never really had a chance of getting the film assignment for *Barefoot in the Park*. At one point Natalie Wood was considered, but she may have been too expensive. According to producer Hal Wallis, "Jane [Fonda] was developing into a big box office name, and I needed her to carry Redford, whom I also wanted, but who was not that well known at that time." Ironically, Redford would eventually emerge as the bigger and longer-lasting star. Although Fonda had hardly gotten to know Redford when they were filming *The Chase*—she had scenes with many other actors in that movie and was mesmerized by the star Marlon Brando—she finally noticed him when they did *Barefoot in the Park*. "That's because we have mutually liberal ideas, which we discovered when we worked together again," she says. Of course, at that time neither Fonda nor Redford were as involved with the environmental and social issues about which they later become obsessive. Later Redford would say of Fonda, "She's like a phoenix who keeps rising from the ashes."

For the film, the setting was moved from New York's East Side to 10th Street in Greenwich Village. Although *Barefoot in the Park* has its admirers and is often seen as the picture that "launched" Redford, the movie has not aged well. Redford, because of his characterization, displays little charm in the film—so little that you wonder what Jane Fonda's free spirit even sees in him. Consider the scene—once viewed as quite daring—in which Fonda, who at first seems too sophisticated for the blushing-bride routine, rushes out to the elevator bank at the Plaza in a towel and pretends to be a hooker to embarrass hubby Redford. Actually, for today's audience, the film's biggest laugh comes when Fonda mentions that they're paying thirty dollars a day for a room at the Plaza! It is equally funny when we learn the newlyweds are renting a Manhattan apartment (which today might cost thousands) for $125 a month. Neil Simon, who scripted from his play, was probably trying to be hip and not homophobic with the line about neighbors who are "a lovely young couple who just happen to be of the same sex, only nobody knows what that is." The picture briefly perks up a bit when upstairs neighbor Velasco (Charles Boyer) takes the newlyweds and Fonda's mother, Ethel (Mildred Natwick), over to Staten Island for an unusual supper. Fonda and her mother gamely soak it all up, while Redford, a bore, only sulks. This situation leads the couple into a contrived and pointless argument that is improbably resolved when Redford gets drunk and acts crazy, trying to show that he, too, can be a free spirit. But anybody can act all "free" and uninhibited when they're plastered. It's hard to foresee a happy future for this couple. All in all, Redford's performance is a bit dull and not that funny, although he's fine when he does the drunk scene in the park. Natwick, and especially Boyer, easily steal the picture from the leads.

While making the film, Redford was anxious to make sure that no one would confuse him with the tight-assed character he played, the guy who needed to get bombed to let his hair down. When he wasn't in front of the cameras, he wore cowboy hats and boots that were as far removed as possible from the "Paul Bratter" outfit of suit and tie with buttoned-down collar. He took the director Gene Saks for a ride in his car one night and had Saks nearly pissing in his pants. Saks made up his mind that he would never let Redford drive him anywhere again. Many years later, Redford would say he'd based that portrayal on his father. "I was playing my dad. He was a good man, but he was pretty locked up by unfortunate circumstance. . . . He was dogged all of his life by being told 'don't try this, don't try that, you're going to fail.' That was one of the reasons I was so impatient and rebellious. I didn't want that legacy."

Saks remembered: "Bob was trying to impress everyone that he hadn't gone Hollywood, so to speak, now that I look back on it. He had played Paul Bratter for so many performances on Broadway and, I think, come to hate the character, who had none of his sense of whimsy and humor. He might have tried to impress upon people a bit too hard that he was this wild, crazy guy, when he really wasn't. Fun, yes, but not as zany as all that."

The apartment set was quite realistic, but the sound stage was not lit to compliment Redford's features. Never have the bumps on his right cheek been so pronounced as under the harsh lighting of *Barefoot in the Park*. Although some women were undoubtedly turned off by his facial irregularities, it couldn't have been too many of them, given the superstardom that was in his future. No critics or writers ever mentioned it—in those days, such personal references would have been considered in bad taste—although the bumps are glaringly evident, as if the makeup meant to disguise them only made them bigger.

Reactions to the film and Redford's performance were mixed. The clueless Murf. in *Variety* called Redford an "outstanding actor" and predicted that he would have "a successful film career for decades," but went on, incredibly, to call him "the logical follow-up to Cary Grant" despite there being no similarity whatsoever between the two actors. Redford did go on to have a long career; but he did not follow in the footsteps of Cary Grant, a wise move on his part.

Jane Fonda once said, "There's something about Bob that's impossible not to fall in love with. We've made three films together, and each time I was smitten, utterly twitter-pated, couldn't wait to get to work, wouldn't even get mad when he was his habitual one to two hours late. He never knew it, of course. Nothing ever happened between us except that we always had a good time working together. I remember the first day he and I showed up in the Paramount administration building. As we walked down the corridors, secretaries stuck their heads out their office doors to watch him go by. 'Ah,' I thought, 'he's going to be a star.' But one of the things I love about him is that instead of puffing up his ego, this made him uncomfortable. I have never seen women react to a man the way they do to Bob: In Las Vegas once, when we were filming *The Electric Horseman*, a woman threw herself on the ground at his feet. He seems to want to disappear at times like this."

While making *Barefoot*, Fonda and Redford talked about their mutual love of horses, about studying painting, and about traveling and living in Europe. Fonda remembered that most of all, Redford talked about a certain piece of property he had bought in Provo, Utah. "I find a Hepburnesque quality about Bob: You feel that he is somehow better than most other mortals. You *want* Bob to like you, so you are loathe to do or say anything that might make him think less of you. This is not someone you would want to gossip about. Maybe this is why, in a town known for gossip, no one tries to get into his business."

Although Redford was happy that *Barefoot in the Park* was so successful, the euphoria began to fade when months went by without his getting another major role. His frustration had eased up a bit when he was getting a lot of publicity in the wake of the film's release, but there had been too much time between contracts. Redford wasn't kidding himself. He was wise enough to know that the movie was perceived primarily as a vehicle for Jane Fonda. Now he was concerned that the screen role was a fluke, one of the rare times a Broadway actor actually got to play his stage role in the film adaptation. There was absolutely no guarantee that it would lead to anything else.

According to Hollywood folklore, Redford was offered the lead in

The Graduate; but he turned it down, supposedly because no one would believe he had trouble attracting women. While Redford might have been considered for the part that put Dustin Hoffman on the map, he was never the front-runner. What is true is that Mike Nichols *did* approach Redford for *The Graduate*, and he went so far as to have Redford make a test. But both Nichols and Redford agreed that Redford simply did not look right for the part. "Bob was not too happy with this," Nichols recalled. "He loved the script and I think in a way really wanted to do the movie, but I never actually offered it to him and he never actually said he would do it. He was afraid he would be stuck playing nothing but pretty boys for the rest of his career."

Redford had appeared in a hit movie, but he still didn't quite feel like a movie star. He began to wonder if it had been such a wise idea to bring himself and his family back to Hollywood, to leave himself wide open to the savaging of his dreams and to ultimate disillusionment. He read for a variety of roles—including some outlandish thing about outlaws in the Old West who eventually came afoul of South American soldiers. He even tested for a few things, but nothing materialized. Redford was unaware that a mighty struggle for his services was going on behind the scenes.

In the meantime, he was contacted by director-writer Abraham Polonsky, who wanted him to play the title role in a new movie for Universal. Called *Tell Them Willie Boy Is Here*, the picture was based on a novel, *Willie Boy*, that had in turn been inspired by historical events. In it, a posse hunts down a Native American who has killed his girlfriend's father, supposedly in self-defense. Polonsky was blacklisted during the McCarthy era but had continued to write screenplays under pseudonyms; thus he was attracted to what he perceived as a story of social injustice, which also appealed to Redford's instincts. But Redford absolutely vetoed the idea of his playing the title character. He felt Native Americans should be portrayed by Native Americans. Redford told Polonsky that he was much more interested in playing the part of the sheriff, that it was more interesting and ambiguous. He wanted to explore that "gray area" in which the sheriff functioned. He saw the sheriff as someone who was conflicted in that he had to maintain white law and order over Indians, yet didn't share the hatred of them that infected his white peers.

The studio, with a much less finely honed social sense, nixed the idea of casting an unknown Indian in the title role, or in any speaking parts for that matter. Universal felt this would be a good time to put to good use some of its contract players, who were drawing salaries but doing little to earn them. Redford later claimed that he was the one who suggested Robert Blake for the part of Willie; he'd even taken on the studio bigwigs who wanted to pass on Blake. It might be said that it was selfless of Redford to recommend and fight for the actor, who'd been in films since he was a young boy (Blake was not only in the Little Rascals shorts but also played John Garfield as a youngster in *Humoresque*); but Redford may well have realized Blake would be no real threat to him. In any case, Redford would later file his gesture of recommending Blake in the "no good deed goes unpunished" category. The irony is that Blake is all wrong as Willie, being much too contemporary in his deportment. In one anachronistic moment, he even calls someone "meathead."

In the film, Willie is a bitter fellow with a white girlfriend named Lola—played by Katherine Ross, who later wound up in *Butch Cassidy* with Redford (although *Tell Them Willie Boy Is Here* was released after *Butch*.) As Willie and Lola make love in the woods, her father sneaks up on them with a gun. Willie sees the man, knocks him to the ground, picks up the fallen rifle, and shoots him, even though the man is now unarmed and helpless. Lawyers could have a good time arguing over whether Willie's act truly constitutes self-defense—"he would have killed *me*," Willie tells Lola—but an even more questionable moment occurs when Lola, with whom Willie flees, is later found dead. In real life Willie murdered the woman, and this seems to be indicated in the film as well, although the movie tries to gloss over it by feigning ambiguity. The fuzziness of this key point rang the death knell for the picture as far as some critics were concerned.

Redford played the part of Sheriff Christopher Cooper, who must track down and bring in Willie even though he feels ambivalent about the whole thing. He portrays this ambivalence mostly by looking perplexed throughout the movie. The film's liveliest scene is when Cooper's equally ambivalent lover, Elizabeth (Susan Clark), a dignified woman in thrall to the more brutish (as "brutish" as Redford can ever be) Cooper, tells him off when they're in bed. Muddled and meandering, *Tell Them Willie Boy Is Here* emerges as a self-consciously "relevant" chase film with pretty western vistas courtesy of cinematographer Conrad Hall. In the end Polonsky's film was no more relevant or entertaining than the overblown *The Chase*, but mercifully shorter.

Redford always felt that *Willie Boy* was not the picture it could have been, and it was not a particularly good experience for him. Polonsky, after so many years of being blacklisted, had not directed a film for some time. Redford observed that Polonsky had an almost desperate need to appear in control at all times, lest anyone think he was past it. Even when he had not quite made up his mind about a certain scene or approach, he had to pretend he had made a decision—to appear *decisive*, when he was not—and it caused numerous problems. Polonsky butted heads with Conrad Hall, who was about to direct his own movie and had definite ideas about how to proceed with *Willie Boy*. Redford also had issues with Polonsky's script, which he felt portrayed Indians unrealistically. "Polonsky had Indians talking like characters out of some of his thirties films," he complained. "Some of it really made me cringe when I read it."

The real drama of the film erupted after it was released to mixed reviews and poor box office, even though it was held over until after the release and tremendous success of *Butch Cassidy*. Polonsky felt his movie was much more serious and worthy than *Butch*. He was furious that Universal, in his opinion, didn't do enough to promote it. Robert Blake did the talk-show circuit, bitterly complaining that the film was promoted as if it were Redford's movie (which in essence it *was*) and that he was shunted to the side despite having the "lead role." Blake could not have been thrilled when the *Christian Science Monitor* opined that "Redford's strength and dramatic magnetism dominate any film he's in; his performance overpowers that of Robert Blake . . . and tips the film away from its focus." Blake had been hoping *Willie Boy* might be the role that would bring him major stardom, the way *Butch Cassidy* had for Redford. When advertisements for the film played up Redford's part to the detriment of Blake's, for obvious reasons, it left Blake disillusioned and rather manic. Redford had no control over how the film was advertised; he could only shrug and rejoin that bitterness seemed to be Blake's stock in trade. Then Polonsky got in the act and attacked Redford in the press, saying that it was his big ego that made him run around taking swipes at the movie. "Redford was a big supporter of my movie until everyone started saying how wonderful Robert Blake was," said Polonsky. "He was jealous of the Indian, so now he *hates* the movie."

Some critics noted that the only thing that made *Willie Boy* different from a formula Western was that an Indian was the (nominal) hero, and that his character was hardly developed sufficiently for anyone to care about his fate.

William Goldman, who had written a novel entitled *No Way to Treat a Lady* as well as the script for *Harper*, had put together a new screenplay based on the real-life exploits of outlaws Butch Cassidy and the Sundance Kid. These two gentlemen had been vicious robbers and murderers—it was all in the official Pinkerton files that Goldman consulted while writing the screenplay—but for some reason, the writer conceived of his story as a comedy. Although it is chicken feed by today's standards, the folks at Twentieth Century Fox paid Goldman what was then a record amount of $300,000 for his screenplay.

Goldman let the powers that be at Fox know that he had always envisioned Paul Newman in the role of Sundance and Jack Lemmon as Butch Cassidy. Fox approved of Newman, and vice versa, but nixed Lemmon as Cassidy. The director they hired, George Roy Hill, was adamant that if Newman should play anyone, it was Butch and not Sundance. Once the studio approved of this casting change— since it was the bigger part as originally written, Newman didn't object—there remained the task of finding a suitable Sundance.

The first suggestion was Steve McQueen; but he and Newman had carried on a fairly friendly rivalry (both on the racetrack and as actors) for many years, and Steve had no intention of playing second fiddle to him. Newman refused to relinquish top billing, infuriating the competitive McQueen, who walked. (McQueen's private nickname for Newman was "Fuckwit.") Hill then brought up Redford's name—after testing him for his film *Period of Adjustment* with Jane Fonda, Hill liked and remembered him (although the part went to Jim Hutton). But the studio execs dismissed his choice. Redford had only had one hit film; he wasn't a superstar along the lines of Mc-Queen and Newman—or even Lemmon, for that matter.

For each actor the studio mentioned, Hill countered with Redford. They wanted Marlon Brando, but Marlon was not at all interested in the project. He'd already done a Western with bandits and Mexicans and deserts, *The Appaloosa* (1966), and had no desire to do another just yet. Again Hill brought up Redford, and again the suggestion was vetoed. Next Warren Beatty's name was bandied about, and Hill even offered him the part with a $3.5 million salary. Beatty took so long making up his mind, and made so many different demands, that Hill finally told him to go fuck himself.

In the meantime, Newman grew tired of the casting roundelay and added his considerable opinion to the mix. He agreed with Hill that Redford would add the suitable dash required by the part and offer the right chemistry. Sundance was the more "romantic" of the two men, and Redford had the right look for the role. Besides, Hill wanted Redford, and Newman knew it would make for a more pleasant experience all around if the director was happy. Shrewdly, Newman also knew that with Redford instead of McQueen or Brando opposite him, he, Newman, would be the picture's main star. He told the studio to cast Redford, and that was that.

Although Redford had reservations, he was excited and relieved. Director Hill was a cipher, but Bob knew that with Newman's participation *Butch Cassidy and the Sundance Kid* was going to be an important picture. No one had any idea, however, how incredibly successful the film was going to be. For his part, Hill felt that Redford could bring out the humor in the character, that he had an underlying warmth under his surface remoteness that would make him at once believable as a robber and yet likeable. Hill felt it would have been disastrous if a cold man played "a potential killer." Redford liked that the screenplay often depicted the old-time Western desperadoes as "just kids doing what they did—robbing banks, holding up trains—as much for the sheer fun of it as anything else."

Redford knew how much was at stake, and he wasn't about to take any chances. He hired a special makeup man to do what he could to disguise the bumps on his right cheek; a couple of day's growth of whiskers, which were appropriate for the part, didn't hurt either. By then there was no way he could not know that his good looks were going to be his ticket to major stardom.

Redford knew he still didn't have a lot of Hollywood clout at this time, so he stayed out of the way when the inevitable on-set battles between star Newman and director Hill exploded. From his first picture way back in 1954 (*The Silver Chalice*), Newman always had a lot to say about the way a picture was made. Things had only gotten worse as he became a bigger and bigger star. (He had also directed his first film, *Rachel, Rachel,* the previous year.) Big-time directors developed their own methods for dealing with Newman: Robert Wise let him try it his way, hoping he would realize that his approach wasn't working; Otto Preminger told Newman to just act and let him direct the picture; Alfred Hitchcock just glared and cut around him.

George Roy Hill was a comparative neophyte next to those gentlemen, so Newman felt confident he could force his viewpoint through with no problem. Hill surprised him; he was not about to buckle under so easily. Redford was inclined to let Hill direct the picture as he was inclined to do, but he wasn't about to say as much to Newman. Paul was already angry with him for occasionally showing up late for filming. Eventually Newman became quite irritated by Redford's lack of punctuality, although he tried to deal with it with a sense of humor, sensing that Redford could be prickly if pushed.

Redford often found Newman's practical jokes a little tiresome. Newman was getting bored with acting—by that time, Paul was addicted to car racing—and he drank a lot of beer on the set. The result was that Hill once returned from lunch to find that his desk had been sawed in half; or there'd be so many pebbles in his hubcaps that it sounded as if his car was falling apart when he drove it. Later, when they worked on *The Sting* together, Newman had one of Redford's automobiles compacted and then deposited in front of his house like some kind of modern sculpture. Redford sent it back with instructions that the whole two-ton, squashed metal mess be dropped right in Newman's front foyer.

Practical jokes—whether they dissipated some of the tension or only increased it—were one thing, but as filming progressed, Hill and Newman were coming to figurative blows more and more often. Redford had a bad feeling that things were going to get worse before they got better. Then one day an assistant director tipped him off that there was talk of shutting down production—at least until a new director could be hired, one who was more to Newman's liking.

One of the biggest bones of contention between Hill and Newman was known as the Bledsoe scene. Butch and Sundance are being chased by a huge posse when they stop to talk to an old sheriff named Bledsoe. Newman felt that it made much more sense for this scene to occur at the end of the chase sequence and not in the middle of it, that what Bledsoe tells the two men would further convince them that fleeing to South America was the right thing to do. Hill did not agree. Newman persisted in arguing about the scene on a daily basis, and each day the argument took more and more time. Finally a fed-up Redford said, "Why don't we just call the fucking movie *The Bledsoe Scene?*"

As Redford braced himself for the worst, he thought that one way to avoid the helpless feeling of dependence on Newman and the studio was to make sure he himself was in charge of future projects. In his youth, Redford had noted the vacuous glory of certain egotistical athletes—one of the reasons he had never pursued a career in sports—and he wanted to do a study of one such individual, a competitive skier. A script then making the rounds was one that he wanted to not only star in, but produce as well. The picture would be called *Downhill Racer*.

But Redford's attention was diverted when he learned that production of *Butch Cassidy and the Sundance Kid* was not going to be suspended; Hill and Newman had settled their differences by agreeing to compromise. Still, whenever Hill gave the two men their directions, the tension was palpable. Hill and Newman would work together in several more films (not the least of which was *The Sting*, which also starred Redford), but they'd never really like one another. Redford and Hill would have a more amiable relationship on such future films as *The Great Waldo Pepper* (1975). Redford and Newman eventually became fairly good—if not terribly close—friends.

Filming wrapped without further incident. *Butch Cassidy and the Sundance Kid* was a smash at the box office and with most critics, although some had serious reservations. In retrospect neither Newman nor Redford, with their brilliant white teeth, were especially convincing as Old West desperadoes; but they both perform with charm and charisma, and the chemistry was on. Redford is a bit better than his costar, in fact. Newman's oft-quoted comment that the film is a "love story between two men" seems apropos since nominal love interest Katherine Ross has very little to do in the picture. Newman was referring to platonic love, of course; Cassidy and Sundance are buddies through thick and thin. But the picture incited cocktail-party gossip about a possible homosexual relationship between Butch and Sundance—not to mention Redford and Newman! *Butch Cassidy and the Sundance Kid* made Redford a male sex symbol on the order of Newman, if not greater. (He was the younger of the two.) Although Redford never really got into the overcompensatory race-car driving practiced by Newman and Steve McQueen, he did take part in a celebrity race at California's Ontario Motor Speedway in 1969. Newman was on the board of directors and talked him into it, as he later did with Tom Cruise.

Butch Cassidy and the Sundance Kid was successful not because it was especially wonderful, but because it was the perfect date movie. The film doesn't so much glorify as glamorize two decidedly unworthy individuals. When they're shot dead by Bolivian soldiers after robbing payrolls, it's unlikely that even scriptwriter Goldman or director Hill expected anyone to shed a tear. The characters are one-dimensional, some scenes play like a parody on *Saturday Night Live*, and the musical score (by Burt Bacharach) is nauseatingly insipid. Goldman, however, saw the men as romantic figures trying to recapture the past by fleeing to Mexico to continue their lives, escaping the posse that had been put together in the States to take them down. Suzie Mackenzie of *The Guardian* explains the film's appeal as well as anyone: "[Goldman] took all the iconography of the genre—running horses, an almost religious feeling for landscape, a sense of the astonishing speed with which things change, the pioneer stubbornness of characters battling on against hopeless odds—and he gave it a spin. He invented the buddy movie."

The public's reaction was tremendous, however, and Robert Redford became a major star and a household name. Whatever his aspirations to being regarded as a serious *artiste*, there was no doubt it was sex appeal that got him across. Although plenty of men admired his dash and panache (as they had Newman's) and saw themselves, too, as romantic, misunderstood outlaws, the large majority of his fans at that time were female. One fan mag that put him on its cover underlined this fact by superimposing several lipstick kisses on his photograph. Part of Redford would always be embarrassed by this harping on his physical appeal to women.

He would always be tactful when discussing the film. "There were problems," he said with consummate understatement. "But we worked through them and the picture was better all around." One big problem was that Newman liked to rehearse the scenes a lot, and Redford felt it was better to be spontaneous. "Newman was calling the shots so I rehearsed," Redford said later. This difference in approach to film acting would also become a problem with at least one megastar leading lady in the future. Many years later, Redford claimed never to have seen *Butch Cassidy* all the way through. "When George Roy Hill showed me a rough cut he didn't tell me there was a song in it called *Raindrops Keep Falling on My Head*," Redford told *People*. "I said, 'what the hell is that? First of all, it's not raining. Boy, you killed this project.' Talk about being wrong."

"I had known [Redford] a little socially," recalled William Goldman. "He was attractive and a wonderful storyteller and a good athlete and nobody ever said he was dumb—but rooms did not hush when he entered them. Suddenly everything was different . . . he was an international cover boy." And an international sex symbol who appealed to legions of hungry women. "That's bound to be just the least bit unsettling, You've spent three decades walking along being one thing, and you're still that thing—part of you is—but no one's seeing that. You don't know for sure what the public is reacting to, but you do know it's not *you*. And you don't know how long the reaction will last, but you do know that chances are, it won't be forever. Stars have to live with that madness." Redford was no exception.

William Goldman recalled that Redford appeared on the cover of *Life* magazine not long after *Butch Cassidy* opened in theaters. Underneath his photo, the caption read, "Robert Redford, Actor." Redford told Goldman that he kept thinking it read, "Robert Redford, Asshole." Goldman said: "Well, he wasn't an asshole anymore. Now he was a phenomenon." Throughout the seventies Redford would be a top box office attraction, along with Paul Newman, Steve McQueen, Burt Reynolds, and Clint Eastwood—the big five. "But if

Marlon Brando, Steve McQueen or Warren Beatty had said yes to the part of the Sundance Kid," Goldman recalled, "Redford might well have remained what one studio executive told me he was when talk of hiring him first came up: 'He's just another California blond—throw a stick at Malibu, you'll hit six of him.'"

A bizarre by-product of Redford's newfound fame was that an old project came out of the woodwork to haunt and nearly embarrass him. Paramount chose this moment to finally release the "unreleasable" *Situation Hopeless . . . But Not Serious* as the latter half of a double bill with another weird comedy, *Oh Dad, Poor Dad, Mama's Hung You in the Closet and I'm Feeling So Sad.* An official at Paramount insisted that the film had merely been held up due to unavoidable and unnamed difficulties over the years, but the movie was not shown to the press this time out. Redford was not surprised by Paramount's actions, which he knew centered on the money to be made off his name. For his part, Robert Shaw lobbied to have his name removed from the credits. *Situation Hopeless* got very little attention in any case.

In the mid-seventies producer John Foreman thought it would be a good idea to bring Redford and Paul Newman back together in a new movie that would reintroduce their Butch and Sundance characters, but in a contemporary milieu. They would be New York City detectives in a film directed by Sam Peckinpah. Foreman got in touch with husband-and-wife screenwriters John Gregory Dunne and Joan Didion (who later wrote Redford's film, *Up Close and Personal*), but they realized that all Foreman had was a concept and no real story and turned the project down. The film never materialized. As of this writing, Redford claims to be "depressed" by recent reports that *Butch Cassidy and the Sundance Kid* will be remade with Matt Damon and Ben Affleck in the leads.

While waiting for *Butch Cassidy* to be released, Redford mulled over the possibility of starring in a film adaptation of William Goldman's novella *The Thing of It Is*, which Natalie Wood had given him. At first this project had really interested Redford, and he initiated the whole thing. Redford asked Goldman to write a script on spec, and told him he would be interested in starring if he liked the screenplay. Redford would play Amos McCracken, a suddenly successful songwriter married to a beautiful Wasp who doesn't know that he is secretly half Jewish. Ulu Grosbard, helmsman of the film adaptation of *The Subject Was Roses* and a director of whom Redford approved, was brought on board.

Then *Butch Cassidy* opened, and everything changed. Redford had many more options. And, as always, like an old-time movie star, he had his image to consider. He told Goldman that he could no longer commit to *The Thing of It Is*, because the character Amos McCracken was kind of weak and his fans would never accept him in the role. The film was never made. Redford also may have felt that, with his newfound clout as a Major Movie Star in a Big Hit Movie, he wanted to work on a production in which he would have more control. He might have found himself butting heads with Goldman, who had written the original story, the way Newman continuously clashed with George Roy Hill.

Since acquiring his plot of land in Utah in the early sixties and building his house, Redford had been buying more lots surrounding his land whenever he had some extra cash. This land was mostly semi-wilderness in a gorge in the Wasatch Mountains. After the success of *Butch Cassidy*, Redford and some partners bought the Timp Haven ski lodge and all of the property attached to it; Redford hoped it would be a backup for possible hard times, or at the very least a source of extra income. In this he was disappointed, because the lower elevation ensured that Timp Haven's skiing season would be shorter than that for other places in the area. Not enough people came to the lodge to make it profitable; but then Redford thought he would turn it into a resort and arts colony similar to Aspen. Even this idea proved disappointing; the Sundance Resort, as it was eventually christened, did not exactly attract droves of people, despite Redford's connection. But that would all change many years later, when "Sundance" came to mean much more than a resort.

Redford's choice for his next film, *Downhill Racer* (1969), was ironic in that he meant it to present him to the public as a serious artist, and yet the role—of a skier-playboy—traded primarily, as expected, on his looks. This was the first production of Wildwood, the company

Redford had formed with Natalie Wood's boyfriend, the former agent Richard Gregson. Gregson had, for a time, been Redford's agent as well as Natalie's. As Redford remembered it, "It was really Natalie who came to me and said 'You oughta go with this guy. . . . He's a hotshot guy from England. She suggested it because I wasn't happy with my agency situation. I met him, I thought he was suave, I said yes, he became my agent." For a time, at least. "He had bigger fish to fry," said Redford. When Gregson married Wood in May of 1969, Redford was his best man, but the two did not stay partners or close friends for very long.

"[*Downhill Racer*] wasn't supposed to be a film about skiing," Redford recalled. "Although the studio never got that through their heads. . . . I wanted this movie to be the portrait of an athlete, of a certain kind of person in American society. It annoyed me the way athletes were portrayed in films. They were always clean-cut, middle American types who came off the farms and had great wives behind them and great moms and dads. It was a Norman Rockwell depiction of America and that's not the way I saw it. I said, 'What about the athlete who's a creep?' We do tend to tolerate creeps who win. Who remembers who came in second? I wanted to see that in a film and it only happened to be skiing because I was into it at that time and thought it was something very beautiful and visual that hadn't been dealt with in film before."

Downhill Racer was originally slated to be a project for Paramount Studios, who would back the film once Redford finished making a Western for Paramount entitled *Blue*. Roman Polanski was assigned to direct *Downhill Racer*. Understandably, Paramount wanted to take advantage of the publicity over *Butch Cassidy* and immediately put Redford into another Western. In *Blue*, Redford was to play an American-born loner who is raised in Mexico and has trouble trusting people until he falls in love with a woman for the first time. Silvio Narrizano was to helm the film. It was an important break for the Italian director, although some feared that he was not the best choice to direct a Western, and his lack of interest in such details as locations and cast were worrisome. Redford agreed to do the film, but had second thoughts—mostly it was the mediocre script that was the problem—and backed out at the last minute. The studio rushed British actor Terence Stamp (*The Collector*) into the role—an odd choice to replace Redford—and promptly filed a lawsuit against Redford. Redford countersued, and shortly thereafter learned that Paramount had lost all interest in *Downhill Racer*. Things between Redford and the studio were settled amicably, however, and Paramount remained involved in the skiing film. *Downhill Racer* was eventually released under the Paramount banner—but not before being canceled yet again, until the budget was severely downsized from $3 million to $1.8 million. As for *Blue*, it did not do much business without Redford's participation, but it may have become a forgotten film—like, say, the later *Little Fauss and Big Halsy*—even if Redford had been involved.

Redford lost out on one good role in an important film because of his litigation with Paramount. Roman Polanski wanted him for the part of Mia Farrow's husband in *Rosemary's Baby*. Polanski had been turned down flat by Warren Beatty, who felt the material beneath him. Paramount, with a nod from its lawyers, said, "No way!" The part went to John Cassavetes, who did not become a superstar although the film became a big and highly influential hit. Redford wouldn't work with Farrow until filming *The Great Gatsby*. This was neither the first nor the last time that Redford and Beatty were offered the same role. Jack Nicholson, although not cut from the same pretty-boy cloth, was also offered many of the same roles. According to Peter Bart of *Variety*, Redford and Beatty had other things in common: "When they wanted to talk about something, they were in your face. When problems arose, you couldn't get them on the phone."

Michael Ritchie, who had previously directed only for television, seemed an odd choice to helm *Downhill Racer*. But Redford admired his work and had no intention of turning his film over to some martinet or powerful director who would completely take over. Redford wanted someone he could deal with and, if necessary, overpower. The two men had long meetings in which they jointly decided upon the picture's look and feel. They both believed that the picture would benefit—have an added veracity—from the use of mostly unprofessional actors, and they both agreed that the role of the ski-team coach would have to be assayed by a fully professional actor. "Somebody like Gene Hackman," Redford suggested. Redford had known Hackman—and future costar Dustin Hoffman—since his New York theater days; the other two always had thought that pretty-boy Redford would make it, but they didn't hold out the same hopes for themselves. Ritchie thought it would make sense to actually get Hackman, so they set up a meeting on the set of Hackman's latest film. Hackman agreed to do the picture. Ritchie noted of Hackman that "he brought such strength and authority to the part that the only problems we had were over those scenes where Redford was supposed to leave Hackman bewildered and plowed under." Redford would occasionally ask the director for a comment on his approach to a particular scene, generally a minor touch of some sort, but otherwise he felt he had conceived and nailed down the part and simply directed himself.

Downhill Racer was filmed in Colorado and in the Alps over a period of seventy days, with an extra twenty-five days for second-unit shooting. Most of the extras, who numbered over seven hundred, couldn't speak English. Each day's footage was sent to London for processing, making it impossible for Ritchie to determine if it were even usable. Upon learning that an early thaw was predicted, the company decided to have a seven-day workweek so that all the footage could be shot before there was no more snow on the ground. Fortunately, the Bond film *On Her Majesty's Secret Service* was also being shot at the same time in the general area. With a budget much, much larger than that of *Downhill Racer*, the British company was able to fly in a lot of artificial snow. As soon as the crew for the Bond film packed up and left, the *Downhill Racer* crew moved in and used their fake snow.

In *Downhill Racer* Redford plays David Chappellet, who comes from a small town in Colorado and hopes to find fame and fortune as a member of an Olympic ski team. The trouble is, he's not a team player, he's completely self-absorbed and tactless, and he won't take advice from anyone, not even his coach (very well-played by Gene Hackman). Despite all this, he manages to win a gold medal before the picture ends.

Notwithstanding its very sixties ambiance and cinema verité approach, *Downhill Racer* is a very old-fashioned movie. Stories about men who come from humble backgrounds with parents who fail to encourage or even understand their dreams (Chappellet's father is a disinterested farmer), have been told again and again in the movies, although in the old days stars such as John Garfield or Paul Muni would have been cast as the antihero. *Downhill Racer* not only fails to break new ground, it doesn't even present its story or protagonist in especially dramatic terms. James Salter's screenplay is full of minor incident but contains no plot.

Redford is miscast as Dave Chappellet; he's not nearly scruffy or hungry enough to suggest an uneducated small-towner who lives on dreams. He does have his moments, however, such as when he visits a teammate who's broken his leg (and lost all chance of competing) and convincingly evokes the awkwardness he or anyone would feel in such a situation. He also maintains the properly arrogant and blasé demeanor that his character would exude.

The picture makes the most of the skiing background, having been filmed at the Olympics and other European competitions, with much location filming in Austria. Since the Olympic committee wouldn't let anyone film the competition in Grenoble, Redford and his crew set up their base in a room in a crummy hotel and then used disguises to get past the guards with their hidden cameras. The photographer, Brian Probyn, was outfitted with a fake wig and putty nose so that no one would recognize him. In this way, they managed to get 20,000 feet of film.

Despite the near-documentary style chosen by director Michael Ritchie, the cinematography is always slick and handsome. Director of photography Brian Probyn had an eight-man team covering the action from every conceivable angle. One astonishing bit—a shot from the subjective viewpoint of a skier as he slices over the ice on the final stretch of a race, speeding aggressively toward the finish line (Joe Jay Jalbert took these shots)—almost makes you feel as if you're on skis yourself. These subjective shots were not used when the skiers slid down a mountain, however, because the constant, jerking body movements would have damaged or detached the cameras.

Right before filming was to begin, Redford almost broke his kneecap in a skimobile accident. While accidentally hurtling over a small cliff, he decided he might suffer less injury if he stayed with the vehicle instead of jumping clear. Ritchie noticed that Redford was limping in the early shots and tried to save the ski scenes until the very end of the shoot as his star mended. Then the studio insisted that Redford use only a stand-in for his skiing scenes, but Redford pretended that he hadn't gotten their communications way up in the mountains. Redford loved skiing, was fairly good at it, and he was damned if somebody else was going to ski for him in his own movie.

Dramatically, the picture has few highlights, but one memorable scene occurs when Redford goes back home to visit his father. The two sit at opposite sides of the room, sharing space but hardly speaking. It's a very realistic moment that perfectly captures the lack of communication between them. It also partially explains why Chappellet has so little interest in the private lives of other people. He tunes out when his hometown girlfriend starts asking his advice on her future plans after they make love in his car; in another car scene, when his new girlfriend goes on and on about her Christmas vacation and her relatives, he angrily honks the horn to shut her up.

Another notable moment occurs when a sportscaster talks about Chappellet while the TV cameraman inadvertently focuses on another skier who happens to look like him. The extra chosen for this scene has an uncanny resemblance to Redford. Redford took a perverse pleasure in this; he incorporated the scene only because everyone kept remarking on how much the young day player looked like him.

Although he took no screen credit for it, Redford was executive producer and called all the shots. All of the actors understood this situation, said their lines, and stayed out of his way. Hackman as the coach, and Camilla Sparv as the classy European lady he becomes involved with, had more scenes than the other cast members did, although even their screen time was limited. Of Chappellet's teammates, Dabney Coleman gets hardly a line of dialogue, while Jim McMullan (as the skier who breaks his leg) fares only a little better. Some feathers were ruffled when scenes were dropped or hastily rewritten—or left on the cutting-room floor—but no major fights broke out. Filming the assorted hotel and lunchroom scenes proved no problem, and only inclement weather was a drawback to some of the outdoor location work. Most of the film consisted of footage of various skiing competitions, and Probyn and his crew had that well in hand.

Downhill Racer is very atmospheric and full of flavorful details, but it never shows all the hard work that goes into becoming an Olympic champion. Chappellet is meant to be shallow; but he has enough intestinal fortitude, skill, and stick-to-itiveness to accomplish his goal, which may or may not have been the point of the film. For *Downhill Racer* says whatever it means to say in the most languid and undramatic way possible. "I don't think the picture was quite what I hoped it would be," Redford admitted years later. "It took two years of my life, but it wasn't very successful commercially. The films I've wanted to make and have really been behind haven't made much money. That's the way it is. But you end up with the satisfaction of doing something on film that you have a kind of passion for."

During the filming, Redford's partner Gregson and gal-pal Natalie Wood showed up to observe. "[Natalie] helped out and loved doing it," Redford remembered. "She went around and carried things. It was just fun. She was just a lot of fun." Though Natalie may have been dating Gregson, many feel her heart still belonged to a disinterested Redford. Accepting that her feelings for Redford would never be returned, Wood married Gregson in an elaborate Russian Orthodox ceremony not long after she returned from Austria.

Downhill Racer was previewed that summer in Santa Barbara. It was shown on a double bill with the vastly superior *Midnight Cowboy*, with no intermission between films. When Redford noticed droves of people getting out of their seats, Natalie Wood, who had accompanied him with her new husband, assured Bob that they were only going to the bathroom. "Remember, Bob," she told him, "there was no intermission." But the droves of people weren't coming back. "Finally *whole rows* were getting up and leaving!" Redford recalled, until "there were about eight people left in the audience." Natalie told him that when she attended a preview of her film *All the Fine Young Cannibals*, the audience had "thrown stuff at the screen!" As usual, Redford was utterly "charmed" by Natalie and her efforts to cheer him. *Downhill Racer* was not a big success. "I put my heart and soul into it," Redford said.

Redford did everything he could to make the movie a success, including taking his cause to the universities, arranging special screenings, and giving interviews to pimply college reporters. He hoped that students en masse would support the film and through word of mouth make it a hit, or at least help it to have more visibility. "He was soft-spoken and humble," remembered one student, Hal Rubinstein, who was granted an interview after praising *Downhill Racer* in his university's paper, "and he asked for help for his movie without a trace of arrogance because he believed in its message. By the time he'd left, I wanted to rent a theater to show *Downhill Racer* to all my friends." Yet Redford also felt he had the eyes of Hollywood upon him; and being only human, he did not like the idea of falling on his face in front of people who'd figured that he'd never pull it off.

Natalie was already pregnant by Gregson by the time of the screening. She and Redford would remain friends and see each other from time to time, but she had moved on. Eventually her husband would do the same. *Downhill Racer* would be the first and last production the two men did together, although the Wildwood company would continue under Redford's direction.

Francis Ford Coppola was in preproduction for *The Godfather* when Redford's name came up as a contender for the part of Michael Corleone, the title character's youngest son. It was not Coppola who wanted Redford, however, but producer Al Ruddy. Coppola wanted a relatively unknown actor named Al Pacino—a "homely runt" compared to Redford—to play Michael. The studio, its eye ever on the bottom line, wanted a major star. If not Redford, then one of the usual suspects: Warren Beatty, Jack Nicholson. Mario Puzo, who'd written the novel, stepped in and insisted on Pacino or no one. Redford and Beatty were out. Frankly, it's hard to imagine either of them doing as good a job as Pacino, who is the superior, and more passionate, actor.

Redford did *Little Fauss and Big Halsy* for Paramount in 1970. Another buddy-road movie so popular during that period, this film was set among the small-time racing milieu. It focused on the one-sided friendship between the handsome user Halsy Knox (Redford) and a mechanic–wannabe racer named Little Fauss (Michael J. Pollard). Both men, despite their marked differences, are essentially losers; but Little has a kind heart, and Halsy bothers with people only if he thinks he needs them. The duo briefly becomes a trio when the two men hook up with Rita Nebraska, played quite well and against type by a gap-toothed Lauren Hutton. Little Fauss falls for Rita, but of course Rita only has eyes for Halsy.

Redford plays his role in *Little Fauss* a bit "sexier" than usual, but he's not and never really has been what's known as a "crotch" actor or a "bad boy"; he doesn't have that kind of dark, dangerous, highly erotic appeal. He is more the high school athlete, the jock grown up. He can certainly love up a woman but may lack imagination in the bedroom, and he would never, ever resort to anything kinky or slightly brutal. Yet he almost hits the mark in this film as a sort of good-looking loser—he admits that the only girls he can get are "stupid" or "pigs"—except swaggering simply isn't his forte. His essential good breeding always comes through. Still, many women in the audience surely swooned anyway when he flashed his wicked grin of pearly whites.

Redford was attracted to the role because he liked the idea of playing someone so raunchy and low-life and obvious for a change. "I was a bike nut when I was a kid," he told one on-set reporter. "I grew up with motorbikes and hot rods and loved that whole scene, thought it was wild, fun." To another interviewer he said, "You could say my love of motorcycles has something to do with the sexual drive, but if you try to analyze why you like things you take the sense of fun out of them." Some of his coworkers theorized that Redford saw Halsy as what he feared he might have become had he had less luck and talent. The film's director, Sidney J. Furie, like many others, was impressed by Redford's directness and practical nature. "He got right into his work, talked about his role, didn't get off the subject or talk about anything else; he was very focused. More like a business executive than an actor, and I've worked with many."

In the picture, Redford also can't seem to disguise his fondness for Michael Pollard; but this may simply have been good acting, because the two did not exactly bond while making the movie. There were no real arguments between the two actors, but not even a temporary on-set friendship developed between them. Reportedly Pollard, who'd found fame in *Bonnie and Clyde* at about the same time Redford hit it big in *Butch*, was jealous of Redford's major stardom and disdained him as a pretty boy. Furie reported that Pollard was so stoned throughout shooting that he had difficulty relating to anyone.

Pollard always looked mentally deficient, no matter what role he played. Despite all this, Pollard easily outacts Redford in the movie.

Everyone had a different opinion about how to proceed. The film's writer, Charles Eastman, wanted to direct the film and didn't like director Furie's interference and script changes. He walked off the picture and refused to do any more work on it. "They should have let him direct it," Furie said some years later. "It was not a happy experience for me." Furie was bothered because he thought the ending just didn't work. He wanted to write a new one, or to have Eastman come up with one that came naturally out of the characters and story. Furie saw himself as an auteur who should have input into the storytelling process and was annoyed that he was perceived only as the hired help.

In the late 1970s, Redford declared that "[*Little Fauss*] was the best screenplay of any film I've ever done, in my opinion. It was without doubt the most interesting, the funniest, the saddest, the most real— and original." Anyone who has actually seen the picture may wonder what on earth Redford is talking about, but the picture may well have worked on paper. A major bone of contention was the ending, which Redford felt should be left alone. He argued that Furie didn't think the ending worked because he didn't understand it, and he didn't understand it because the entire movie eluded him. He ranted years later that Furie's tremendous ego prevented him from listening to suggestions—his suggestions, of course—and that a sensitive script had been turned into a cartoon. "There was a terrific ear that went into writing that script and it was a bad ear that went into making it. The author was done a disservice. Furie really can't blame anyone but himself for the way the picture turned out—it was his interpretation."

The movie was filmed in a lot of small towns as the cast and crew traveled about in much the same way that the racers and their groupies did. Some of the racing scenes were shot at Sears Point during the national championship road races, while others were filmed in speedways in Phoenix and outside Los Angeles. Before long, tempers flared on the set, especially between Redford and Furie. Furie told the actor that they were having a problem with lining up a shot because of his movements and they needed to talk. Redford snapped "Too bad!" Embarrassed in front of the crew, Furie called Redford over and told him off, telling him that they could talk about their differences of opinion but that merely saying "too bad" was not an option. Redford was more cooperative after that, and he later explained that all during the shoot of *Little Fauss and Big Halsy* he was preoccupied with thoughts of *Downhill Racer*. In truth, neither Furie nor Redford would remember that much about making the movie. A gracious Furie contended that Redford gave one of his best performances in the film, insisting that far from being the type of actor who always played himself, he did indeed become the character he was portraying.

Whatever opportunities might have been missed with *Little Fauss and Big Halsy*, the film is not memorable. Redford's disgust with the way it turned out may have had to do with his hope that it would cast him in a new light, that the critics who didn't think much of him might see him as a serious actor in a serious, artful film and not a superficial pretty boy in a mere Hollywood product. Although the picture tries for a kind of naturalistic or cinema verité approach and has some interesting details along the way—a sad Little Fauss watching Rita and Halsy dance—it mostly meanders along in an uninteresting manner with characters who hardly deserve or hold our attention. Nobody seems to be having a good time, least of all the audience. Far from the level of, say, *Midnight Cowboy*, *Little Fauss and Big Halsy* emerges as a real bit of nothing much. One critic suggested that at least the picture would have made some sense, had some poignancy, or been about *something* if the Pollard character were in love with Halsy!

Redford had always inspired a sharp division of opinion among film critics, but at that time they seemed more polarized than ever. *Newsweek*, clearly impressed by Redford's performance, wrote that the actor "realizes Halsy through small gestures; his eyes never still, always searching out some advantage; his smile the counterfeit amiability of the used-car salesman; his speech the quick, slick cadences of the pitchman who wants to be heard but not understood." On the other hand, *Newsday* noted that "Redford's performance demonstrates that he is an actor of limited dimension and range . . . the ex-ingenue of *Barefoot in the Park* is the new antihero athlete of *Downhill Racer* and *Big Halsy*, but it's just repacking the same product in different plastic." Pauline Kael played close attention to how Redford as Halsy was always "fiddling with his zipper and juggling his genitals (on one occasion, in what is possibly a movie first, in a close shot). . . . Was it only a few months ago he seemed a promising actor? He's already an overripe star."

Molly Haskell of the *Village Voice* admired the actor but noted that "from film to film, he carries this aura of betrayed promise, something sad and inaccessible which should be drawn on as the stuff of characterization instead of hovering like a mist around the edges . . . you keep thinking he could do anything, yet somehow he never does." Some critics were mesmerized by his looks and screen appeal, his obvious ability and ease in front of the camera, and they may have taken them as signs of a budding genius. Redford had charmed many of the critics, but with others he clearly had his work cut out for him.

Although Lola Redford had for many years seemed content to be a stay-at-home mom, her own brand of social activism encouraged her to step outside the household in 1970. She and Ilene Goldman, wife of screenwriter William Goldman, had become good friends. The women were much closer, in fact, than their husbands were. Concerned about the deteriorating environment, they decided to form C.A.N., or Consumer Action Now. "It actually began with the first Earth Day," recalled Lola Redford. "I think the event inspired many of us in the city to talk about our environmental feelings and concern. Ilene and I, especially, found that we felt women were helpless to exert meaningful pressure in the marketplace because information was being withheld." She added: "Just being for trees, fresh air and pure water isn't enough. We're all for ecology but few of us know how to begin living our lives in ecologically sound ways. We need information that will help us distinguish between environmentally 'good' and 'bad' products so that we can vote for (buy and/or recycle) the good and vote against (not buy or use at all) the bad every day of our lives." With fifteen other women in tow, Lola and Ilene decided to start a new organization that would gather pertinent information and alert the public via newsletters, a speaker's bureau, tours of universities, and lobbying in Washington. One of their first actions was to march through midtown Manhattan supermarkets putting up charts that listed which detergents and cleaners were safe for the environment and which weren't.

But this newfound political activism did not keep Lola away from home all *that* much. On October 22, 1970, Lola Redford gave birth to their third child, a girl they named Amy Hart Redford.

In 1971, Redford may not have been aware that over in France, all hell was breaking loose on the production of the race-car picture *Le Mans*. Star Steve McQueen, having marital and career troubles galore, was acting like a prima donna. The original director, the estimable John Sturges, quit in a huff over the antics of his protégé, McQueen. "I'm too old and too rich for this shit," he was reported as saying. Then McQueen nearly punched out the replacement director, merely because the man had the audacity to call him "Steve." Studio execs flew over to France to decide whether to shut the production down if they couldn't reign in their star. They very seriously considered firing McQueen and replacing him with Redford. After several hours of negotiations, McQueen and the studio came to an agreement; Redford's services were never enlisted.

McQueen would come to see Redford as an even bigger threat to his security as a movie star and cocksman than Paul Newman was. This was especially true when McQueen's wife, Ali MacGraw, came home from a Redford film and talked about him as if he were a "serious" actor and McQueen was not.

Redford did *The Hot Rock* (1972) because he claimed to be "flat broke" at the time. While this was surely an overstatement, and the term *broke* applies differently to movie stars than to ordinary people, in truth Redford was feeling a pinch. Like most actors who hit it big, they spend, pay off debts, buy big houses, and make such huge financial commitments of different kinds that they often find they've overextended themselves despite the money they make. They have to keep getting those big salaries to maintain their now much more extravagant lifestyle. Redford, although by many accounts more practical than other actors, was no different. He later claimed that

The Hot Rock was one of the few films he did primarily for the paycheck.

Redford also liked the cast. Originally, George Segal was to play Redford's role, with George C. Scott as his long-suffering brother-in-law—the role Segal actually played. Redford was much more bankable at that time than Segal was, so Segal was pushed into the supporting role and Scott was out entirely. Zero Mostel was signed as another devious crook who tries to outwit Redford and company, and Paul Sand, Ron Liebman, and Moses Gunn were cast in smaller roles. The movie was filmed over a three-month period on location in New York City, adding a certain energy and veracity.

The plot of *The Hot Rock*, like most caper films, is constructed to make you wind up rooting for the crooks. William Goldman adapted Donald Westlake's novel about a team of inept thieves trying to snatch a diamond known as the Sahara Stone. Although Peter (*Bullitt*) Yates's direction was fairly routine, *The Hot Rock* managed to emerge as one of Redford's more entertaining pictures of the period. The highlight of the film is a great copter ride over Manhattan that leads into a break-in at a New York Police precinct. This is necessitated because one of the gang, Paul Sand, tells everyone that he hid the gem in his jail cell. Although Faye Dunaway later felt Redford could not be convincingly menacing in *Three Days of the Condor*, Redford manages to be pretty intense as he threatens Sand's father, Zero Mostel, late in the picture. He even orders Mostel's son to be thrown down the elevator shaft (which turns out to be a trick). Redford, or at least his character, seems a little wimpy, however—by movie standards—when he meekly hands over his expensive watch to a weirdo with a knife. The terrible jazzy score by Quincy Jones does its best to ruin the movie, but fortunately it doesn't succeed.

By and large, *The Hot Rock* got mildly positive reviews when it opened, although its reputation has improved in recent years. Redford felt that the British Peter Yates didn't have the right feel for a film with American humor. "His speciality was action," Redford observed, "and this was more of a comedy. The trouble was he didn't understand our humor." Despite its shortcomings, *The Hot Rock* is clever and often quite amusing. As usual, Redford's own notices were very mixed; *Newsday* noted that "Redford's supercool pose of *Butch Cassidy and the Sundance Kid* and *Downhill Racer* has sunk to the inexpressiveness of catatonia." *New York* Magazine felt that "Redford is just a little too all-American handsome, a bit too sophisticated and 'star quality' for the company he keeps in this film. He is actor enough to carry off the role—but in context it seems more role than realism."

William Goldman was watching them shoot *The Hot Rock* at a prison in upstate New York. Redford simply had to walk out of the prison wearing clothes that did not fit him. Then he walked over to director Peter Yates and conferred with him for a while. One of the guards began chatting with Goldman during this lull and said, "[My wife] said to me today that she would get down on her hands and knees and crawl just for the chance to fuck him one time. *One time.*" Goldman noted that "here was this goddamn guard using every word in his vocabulary to try to convey to me the extent of his wife's sexual passion for a guy who was basically a fine actor from California who had made some disastrous movies."

Zero Mostel, coming off his high of starring on Broadway in the megahit musical *Fiddler on the Roof*, was disappointed to be only a supporting player in *The Hot Rock*. He hoped that being signed to the lead in the film version of *Fiddler on the Roof* would bring him back on top, and he was eventually mortified when the role instead went to Israeli actor Topol, who had starred in *Fiddler* in London. Wondering whether he would get the role he'd created on Broadway preoccupied him during *The Hot Rock* shoot, although he performed with his usual professionalism. When asked about the film, he also seemed preoccupied; he said, "It was fun to make, fun, but there were other things I would rather have done. I liked Bob, a serious actor, a real professional. But it was fun. A good picture."

A good picture it may have been, but some of Redford's most important and famous movies lay just ahead.

The *Candidate* (1972) came about because of an evening when Redford sat in front of his television set watching 1968 presidential candidates Richard Nixon and Hubert Humphrey holding telethons. Redford was negatively impressed with the utter phoniness and blatant staginess of the events. He hated the way people applauded like automatons at simplistic slogans and seemingly ate up everything their candidates said. He wanted to do a movie that would expose the whole process, lay bare the facts of politics and campaigning. Redford had always deemed himself as apolitical; the phoniness of the process was one reason why. Although Redford was determined to make what he felt would be an important film, it did not turn out to be an entirely pleasant experience for him. *The Candidate* was Redford's second stab at producing.

Redford went to director Michael Ritchie, who'd helmed *Downhill Racer*, and told him what kind of movie he wanted to make. Ritchie was surprised to learn that Redford had neither screenplay nor source material but found the idea interesting nevertheless. Redford suggested they get together, talk about what they'd like the movie to say and be. Then they could hire the appropriate screenwriter, ideally someone with a political background and some knowledge of the campaign trail and its tribulations. It was determined early on that the film would not be based on any particular political figure, although after the film came out, there was a lot of speculation. Many saw Redford's character, Bill McKay, as Bobby Kennedy. Although both Bill and Bobby came from political families, Bobby was a professional politician—ready, willing, and able to run—while Bill had to be carefully talked into running for office. Redford thought it would be best to film the picture in New York, but Ritchie told him that someone like Bill McKay would be taken more seriously in California, so the locale was changed without a hitch.

Despite his success in *Butch Cassidy*, Redford discovered that studio heads had seen the disappointing grosses for *Downhill Racer*. Redford found himself in the humiliating position of having to shop the manuscript almost door to door, standing in the offices of disinterested movie executives who told him that political movies were dead—or too dangerous. Using all of his charm and acting chops, Redford tried to convince these wooden-faced business types that he could make a timely, entertaining, and—best of all—profitable movie. He failed to convince most of them, but he would later laugh that Paramount President Stanley Jaffe almost fell asleep in the middle of what he thought was a highly energetic presentation. Finally, Dick Zanuck, who had come from Twentieth Century Fox to Warner Brothers, gave Redford carte blanche.

Once a script was cobbled together—most critics agreed that the film was badly under-written—Redford discovered that he did not at all enjoy playing Bill McKay. He had to film many scenes where McKay was giving speeches, attending rallies, greeting his constituents, all of which the somewhat shy—or disdainful—Redford hated. To make matters worse, for added veracity it was decided that at certain small towns or whistle stops the crowd would be told that Redford himself was actually running for office. (Apparently the big "Vote for Bill McKay" signs weren't employed during these sequences.) Redford found that he was continually being besieged by his fans. For a ticker-tape parade in San Francisco, secretaries in buildings along the street where filming would take place were importuned to throw pages of their calendars out the window at noon. Most of the women, swooning at the thought of *Robert Redford*, were only too happy to comply.

Redford recalled that before filming the sequence, he was in a sour mood because he had hoped to take some time off to go skiing in Utah. He'd gotten only four days away from the set at that point, and he was mighty sore that he had to return early to do the parade sequence. But it was such a heady feeling to see all the people outside the car reaching for him, screaming, most of them thinking he was actually running for office, and to see all the calendar pages raining down, that he came out of his funk in a hurry. It also cemented in his mind the dangerous unreality and phoniness of politics. He later likened the experience to finding a piece of Kryptonite, the metal that can take down Superman.

Redford was also disquieted when he gave speeches in which by his own admission he said nothing whatsoever of consequence, but inspired the people to cheer at every pause. He was convinced that he would have gotten many votes. Of course, some people in the crowd may have figured out the gag and gone along with the joke, and others were simply reacting to his celebrity rather than his words. Redford made it clear that he had no desire to run for office, although he has given it some serious thought. "You can't be your own man no matter how hard you try," he said. "I think a politician has to sell a little piece of himself, and I don't want to."

It was planned to include a sequence in which a sixteen-year-old groupie jumps naked into a pool just so she can get close to Bill McKay, who's working out his frustrations as he swims. In that certain hopeful teenage way, she would ingenuously ask if he knew a friend of hers from Van Nuys, Pinky King—a line that was supposed to get a big laugh. The scene was filmed; but when nobody laughed at a preview, it was cut from the film. The young actress was so nervous about appearing naked on camera, however briefly, that Ritchie had to give her several glasses of Manischewitz before he could start filming. Just as he started, some of the other actors in the film, both men and women, rushed out in the altogether and dived in the pool, only to jump out and rush like hell out of camera range and offset. They were trying to put the girl at ease, but their efforts apparently had the opposite effect. Said one crew member, "It was just meant as some gentle joshing, but she thought she was being made fun of. Too bad, 'cause it was very funny."

Redford was delighted when Natalie Wood agreed to do a cameo as herself in *The Candidate*. She flew into Oakland and arrived at the set wearing blue jeans and wrapped in a mink. Wood looks gorgeous in the movie as she and "Bill McKay"—who does not know who she is—talk about, of all things, yogurt. "She just came and did it," Redford recalled. "There was no calling the agent, no deals. She said, 'I'm just gonna do it.' That kind of stuff. I'm a pretty old-fashioned guy about that kind of loyalty and commitment. That meant a lot. And we had great fun, doing it." It was the last time Redford would ever see his old friend, a woman who had once loved him with all her heart. (There was some talk that Wood might play Daisy in *The Great Gatsby* with Redford, but apparently her reconciliation with Bob Wagner took precedence and she did a telefilm with him instead of really going after the part, as she had done on many previous films.)

Redford wanted the great veteran actor Melvyn Douglas to play his father in the film and sent him a copy of the script. "It puzzled me," Douglas recalled. "It read more like an extended TV documentary than a feature film. The major character was reputed to be based on Ted Kennedy, though in the early scenes he reminded me more of Jerry Voorhees, the idealistic California congressman Nixon rampaged over to get into the House of Representatives." Douglas was afraid that the "staccato cutting between scenes" would prove too confusing to the audience. Jeremy Larner, the screenwriter, had been an advisor to Eugene McCarthy. His book *Nobody Knows* documented his disillusionment with the campaign. Larner later claimed that he had to fight tooth and nail with Redford over virtually every point of the script. "In the end he's a star who wants his way," said Larner. "Bob is very tough in lots of ways that relate to getting along in show business."

Redford flew to New York to meet with Douglas, where he told the older man that he wanted him for the role because of his political work as well as for the political roles he had played. Redford told Douglas he "needed a character with a touch of arrogance, a shrewdness, the suggestion of political skill" and explained that while the script was rough, Douglas would only have to commit to a little over a week of shooting, with Redford there for him every step of the way. Douglas agreed—because of Redford. "He struck me as an artist with integrity and guts."

After shooting wrapped, Redford sent Douglas a note: "I know your feelings going into the project were somewhat ambivalent, and that is not a state I would be comfortable in. I know that I . . . [wasn't] articulate in explaining it all; that we had a script that was very lean in spots and vague in others, that your role in the effort no doubt seemed slim and sketchy, that the film had to be shot a certain way. What I'm sure was clear was that it was a labor of love, and that you responded to this is very moving to me."

In the reception room scene when Douglas grins and gives Redford the double-handed compliment, "Son, you're a politician!" viewers can see that some spinach is caught in his teeth. Douglas was always amused by the speculation over whether that happened by accident or was his comment on his character. "That is an argument I couldn't settle for anything in this world," he said.

Melvyn Douglas told Lawrence Quirk not long after *The Candidate* was released that he was impressed with Redford's acting skills and his professionalism. "A pleasure to work with," was his opinion. Douglas had met with Franklin Delano Roosevelt in the White House and used his memory of FDR's "astonishing smile" in portraying John McKay.

The Candidate got mostly good and respectful reviews, with several critics noting that it worked despite the lack of a strong script. Redford and Ritchie were tinkering with bits and pieces, creating and throwing out scenes, all during the filming. Some real politicians, such as Bella Abzug, felt the movie was entirely too negative and predictable. In fact, its basic story had been told on celluloid many times; it showed the tried-and-true: an honest guy first compromising and then becoming corrupted by the process and selling out. Abzug felt the movie was superficial and ignored the fact that there was still room in politics for men and women "with passion and principles." After the real-life events of Watergate and the filming of *All the President's Men*, the comparatively tame *Candidate* would be virtually forgotten.

Bill McKay is a role perfectly tailored for Robert Redford, who is at his most handsome in the film. But while the movie has interesting moments and performances, it is not new in any way, and it is hardly riveting. Redford is good in the movie, but he's no match for the marvelous Melvyn Douglas as his father. Don Porter, as his opponent Jarmon, also gives a scene-stealing performance. The biggest problem is Jeremy Larner's screenplay, which inexplicably won an Academy Award. The relationship between McKay and his wife, Nancy (Karen Carlson), is barely delineated, and it appears to undergo dramatic developments that occur only offscreen. It's possible, of course, that many scenes, especially if they did not showcase producer-star Redford, were left on the cutting-room floor. The ending, after which a clueless McKay actually wins the election, has him sighing and asking, "What do we do now?" This comment is kind of stupid, considering the important issues he is facing.

While publicizing the movie in Florida Redford learned—as did the rest of the country—that five men had been arrested for breaking into the Democratic National Committee headquarters at the Watergate Hotel in Washington, D.C. Overhearing some reporters who had come along on the publicity junket for *The Candidate*, Bob was dismayed that they seemed to think there was nothing especially unusual about what had happened. In this he may have been naive, but he was hardly the only one. At the time he couldn't have dreamed that the Watergate break-in would have surprising repercussions on his own life and career. But that was in the future.

Years later, when asked why he never ran for office, Redford replied: "I like my freedom too much. I like to have a good time. I don't want to be held to such compromises." *The Candidate* is the one film that Redford wants and plans to do a sequel to, although he took many years to make the decision. According to Redford, "[the script] is moving into final draft form [as of mid-2004]. I had never really wanted to do it, but the thing that inspired me was imagining myself watching myself on ads run by my opponent, drawn from the first film. Showing ads from me as a young guy running for office. Whatever happened to this guy? I thought, that'd be a hell of a thing, to play a guy thirty years later looking back, where you could actually use your own film turned around as negative ads against you."

Redford and his friend Sydney Pollack wanted to work together again, but they were having trouble agreeing on the right project. Pollack had wisely passed on *Downhill Racer*. In turn, Redford refused to do Pollack's *Castle Keep*, which Burt Lancaster did.

Jeremiah Johnson began life as a script by Edward Anhalt and John Milius about an old mountain man called "Liver Eatin' Johnson." Redford enjoyed the script until Johnson actually did start eating livers—"yuck!" was his reaction. Still, Pollack felt there was potential in the basic material of a mountain man facing the elements and triumphing, a study of the indomitable human spirit. He talked Redford into seeing the possibilities, and Bob agreed to do the film, provided they had a good script.

The story that emerged concerned a young man who takes to the mountains, intending to be a hermit and eke out his living. He discovers a frozen corpse in the snow, but that doesn't deter him; he eventually meets up with a grizzled old-timer named Bear Claw (Will Geer), who becomes a mentor. After spending some time with Bear Claw, Johnson comes upon a woman (Allyn Ann McLerie) whose husband has been murdered by Indians. Recognizing that the woman has been driven insane by grief, Johnson takes her little boy, Caleb (Josh Albee), along with him. From a tribe of friendly Indians, Johnson receives a surrogate wife, Swan (Delle Bolton), to go with his surrogate son. After some initial awkwardness, Johnson seems happy with his little family until he encounters a cavalry troop whose officers ask him to lead them to some snowbound settlers. Against his advice, the troops take a shortcut through a sacred Crow Indian burial ground. In retaliation for this, the Indians murder Swan and Caleb before Johnson can arrive home. Johnson becomes the legendary Indian hunter known as the Killer of Crows.

Redford was still financially haunted by the lawsuits filed against him by Paramount. "He wasn't making a lot of money off his pictures because part of them were being done as court settlements," explained Pollack. He had not expected these financial problems when he bought and began to develop his property at Sundance, and the property was taking up most of his income. He was determined not to lose it, so he badly needed the $200,000 that Warner Brothers would pay him for his participation in *Jeremiah Johnson*.

A fresh problem arose when the bean counters at Warner Brothers sat down and figured out their total expenses for the picture. Whatever it was, it was too much for the studio. They decided that *Jeremiah Johnson* would have to be shot entirely on studio sound stages and preexisting sets on the back lot. This announcement struck horror in the hearts of both Redford and Pollack; they knew the picture just wouldn't work in the current day and age if it was studio-bound and played against phony sets. Stark realism was the creed of the day, and some of the conditions of the script simply could not be re-created convincingly on a set. They needed the mountains; they needed the snow, the scenery, the whole look and smell and atmosphere of the great outdoors. The public might accept classic Westerns shot on the back lot *because* they were classics, but a modern-day Western had to have veracity.

Because Warner Brothers had a contract with Pollack, they told him he had another option if he couldn't see shooting on the back lot. They would pay him a certain amount, effectively dissolving the contract, if he agreed to drop the project altogether. Redford, however, was appalled when Pollack told him they should forget about *Jeremiah Johnson*; he told Pollack that he'd have to either lose or pay back the $200,000. (It is not certain whether Redford had received the money at that point. Certainly Redford had a contract, and the studio would have had to work out some kind of deal or buyout with him, as they did with Pollack. Undoubtedly Redford had, at least on paper, already spent or committed the $200,000 and did not consider pulling out of the film and accepting less cash as an option.) When Redford told Pollack that he *had* to do the film no matter what, Pollack rejoined that that was not the case with him. Redford was furious. He felt that they had started this project together and it would be unfair, indeed despicable, of Pollack to pull out just to save his own skin. Pollack argued that the film would be a disaster and do neither of them any good if it was shot on the back lot. His agent was on his back, telling him Redford had no right to force him to commit possible career suicide just because he had to have a big house in Utah.

Redford exploded at Pollack, calling him traitor and worse. Pollack, whose career had been greatly aided by Redford's intervention, felt ashamed. He backed down, admitting later that Redford was right. He rejected the offer from the studio and decided they would just have to figure out a way to make *Jeremiah Johnson* without spending a lot of money. They absolutely could not do it on the back lot—but what was a cheaper solution? Pollack scouted locations after promising Warner Brothers executives that he would stay within the prescribed budget without shooting on sound stages. The sweeping vistas of Utah, where Redford had his estate, seemed made to order.

Pollack rarely started filming with a finished script in hand, and *Jeremiah Johnson* was no exception. "I'd like once in my life to start a picture with 'THE END' written," he recalled. "In *Jeremiah Johnson* I was writing sections of the farewell scene six weeks into the shooting. I was in a motel on a Sunday fiddling with that scene and trying to find the end of the picture." Some feel he never quite succeeded. A major problem was figuring out a solid reason for the Indians to kill Redford's surrogate family, leading him to become the almost mythical Indian fighter at the end of the story. All things, all scenes pointed in the direction of the ending they had finally decided upon, but they couldn't simply have the Indians attack without cause just to create an ending. "We hadn't stopped to work out the details," Pollack recalled. "Indians sometimes massacred white men; we figured we'd work out the details later." As the shooting progressed, this major point began to gnaw at and obsess both Pollack and Redford. It was all they could think about, preoccupying their thoughts even at mealtimes and causing sleepless nights. Finally, Pollack solved the problem with the help of Edward Anhalt.

The production was decidedly no-frills, because there was no money for expensive script doctoring or dressing-room vans or fancy flown-in catering. A costume designer couldn't be fitted into the budget, so the cast improvised by taking clothing they already owned and mixing and matching, tearing things here and there for the proper weathered look. "We thought the picture was going to be the bomb of all time," Pollack later recalled in an interview. "We were flying by the seat of our pants. I didn't know what I was doing half the time. In spite of all that it turned out much better than we expected."

The snowfall in Utah caused considerable problems. Because the horses were unable to walk in the heavy snow without sinking into it, hundreds of yards of chain-link fencing from Sears had to be put on the ground. Everyone quickly became horrified at the thought of having to do retakes, because then all the foot- and hoofprints had to be covered up before they could proceed. Makeshift toilets served the seventy-man crew, and the temperature was often frigid. Before shooting was completed, many of the crew members quit. On the final day no one remained except Redford, Pollack, and a helicopter pilot who was instructed to take a long shot of Redford walking across the snow far below and disappearing into the distance. Redford walked and walked and walked, until he felt it was okay to stop and turn around, and then discovered that the helicopter had disappeared. At first he thought a disgruntled Pollack had decided just to leave him there; then he realized they had probably run out of film and had to fly for some more. *Jeremiah Johnson* became Redford's favorite of all his films up until that time and for a few years afterward.

While not a masterpiece, *Jeremiah Johnson* is a credible seriocomic adventure film that is almost campy at times. The tragic moments are kind of dropped in unsentimentally, which strips these scenes of needed emotion—a sure sign of filmmakers who think an audience should shed tears only when watching a soap opera. Redford looks good in a full beard, and he is not bad—albeit miscast—in a role that would probably have better suited the stoic and older Robert Mitchum. Redford is not quite up to the scene in which he finds his "family" dead. Will Geer is superb as Bear Claw, and there are other flavorful performances by character actors who fit the basic tone and style of the piece far better than Redford does.

Jeremiah Johnson premiered at the Cannes film festival—the first Western to do so—and it was on the Ten Best Pictures lists of the *Los Angeles Times, Reader's Digest,* and *The New Republic. Parents* magazine gave it a "Special Medal of Merit" award. Much of this acclaim had less to do with the film's quality than with its de-emphasis on graphic sex and violence, both of which seemed to dominate movie screens during the seventies. *Jeremiah Johnson* was a certified hit, grossing more than $22 million in North America alone. It was presented in theaters as a "prestige" item, promoted as a special event; although it was less than two hours long, it was played in theaters with a musical introduction and intermission. The musical score by John Rubinstein and Tim McIntire is decidedly Coplandesque.

Jeremiah Johnson got many respectful and positive notices, with Judith Crist opining in *New York* that the film was a "poetic legend, a ballad-like epic of man and nature." The *New Jersey Press* felt that it was "the movie that *Tell Them Willie Boy Is Here* hoped to be." Redford got high marks for his performance from many reviewers, although some saw him as just being on an historical "I'm not just a pretty boy" kick. But at least two prominent critics—who had never been carried away with Redford's acting, or at least had been disillusioned by him—went on the attack.

Joseph Gelmis of *Newsday,* who liked the film, devoted much of his review to Redford's acting style, or lack of it. He complained that "Redford is Redford" and mocked how his style of speaking was allegedly inconsistent from scene to scene and asserted that he was "one of those lightweight talents who go a long way on looks, on knowing when to turn up the thermostat on his clean-cut boyish California-surfer sex." In his opinion, Redford was "saved by supporting actors and by spectacular views." He even felt that Redford didn't have much charisma. "Blue eyes aren't enough, Bob, because to us you'll always be the aging ingenue." There were many who agreed with some of Gelmis's assessments, but Redford's fans would have argued vociferously about his alleged lack of charisma.

Pauline Kael of *The New Yorker* entered the fray and attacked Redford's habit of underplaying, which she wrote seemed "lazy and cautious and self-protective." She suggested that he needed to open up, to stop playing old-style star games when the rules had changed. "Probably young audiences can no longer relate to what the Westerner stood for, but are they supposed to like Redford because he's so sheepish and silent and straight? Hell, so was Lassie . . . there are no depths in Redford that he's willing to reveal; his cool is just modern, existential chic."

What particularly irked Redford about Kael's review was not the attack on his acting—or so he said—so much as her misreading of the final scene, when he confronts an Indian warrior across the distance and the two look at and signal to each other with a certain respect despite their mutual hatred. Kael wrote that Redford simply gave the Indian the finger. "This criticism really bothered the hell out of me," Redford recalled, "because of my respect and feelings for the American Indian. I thought this was a case of a critic being completely irresponsible, simply disregarding what was actually up there on the screen just to embellish a personal attack. Disgraceful."

Ray Stark, who'd produced *The Owl and the Pussycat* starring Barbra Streisand, wanted her in another movie for his production company, Rastar, because *Pussycat* had performed well at the box office. He hoped to interest her in a script about the bittersweet love affair between a campus radical and the more conservative boy next door. Barbra Streisand agreed to play the female lead in what became *The Way We Were* long before Redford was signed as her costar. The screenplay, and the novel it was based on, was by Arthur Laurents.

Years before, Laurents had directed a Broadway musical, *I Can Get It for You Wholesale*, in which a very young Streisand had one knockout number.

After Barbra agreed to do the film, Sydney Pollack was quickly signed as director. With Pollack on board, it seems hard to imagine that any other leading man besides his good friend Redford was ever considered; but such blond and blue-eyed actors as Dennis Cole and Ken Howard were considered and rejected by Streisand. Pollack nixed Ryan O'Neal, Streisand's costar in *What's Up, Doc?* because he didn't think O'Neal's presence was strong enough to keep Streisand from swallowing up the picture. Pollack didn't immediately approach Redford because Bob had already read the script—producer Ray Stark had sent him one—and rejected it. In fact, Redford hated the screenplay for *The Way We Were*.

Streisand then set her sights on Hollywood's premier lover boy, Warren Beatty. Beatty, of whom it was said that he would sleep with virtually any woman as long as she was breathing, took Babs to bed practically as she wagged the screenplay in his face. It seems that Beatty had no real interest in *The Way We Were* or in Streisand, but did want Barbra to sing at a rally for George McGovern. Therefore he refused to make any commitment to the film while still dangling hope before Barbra's nose like a half-eaten carrot. Barbra tried to get out of the fund-raiser; but Warren only had to remind her of how he was still thinking of doing the picture with her, and she suddenly renewed her commitment to McGovern. The night of the concert, Warren's date was Julie Christie, not Barbra. Streisand still couldn't see the handwriting on the nostril. Finally she demanded a yes or no from Beatty, and he complained that the part was simply too small. "I'll have it beefed up!" she rejoined. When Warren still refused to commit, she decided she'd go with the possibly prettier Robert Redford and show Warren that she and the movie could live without him. So Beatty lost out on yet another hit movie; *The Way We Were* grossed fifty-six million.

Pollack had an ally of sorts in signing up Redford. Coproducer Julia Phillips pitched the idea of Redford teaming with Barbra Streisand for *The Way We Were* at lunch, for which Redford was late as usual. "I just can't see her and me in the same move . . . we're, like from different generations," he told Phillips. Phillips suggested that he see *The Owl and the Pussycat*. After seeing the film, Redford told Phillips: "I don't see me and Barbra Strident in a movie together." Phillips, however, still saw the two as a good team, thinking it would work to contrast "the rawness [of Streisand] against Redford's gentile pseudo-intellectuality."

At these lunches, Phillips was amused by Redford's habit of dressing himself up in "scarves and mufflers and hats and shades, which only make him look more Redford-ish." Not so amusing was his other habit of always meeting at out-of-the-way restaurants that had no customers, simply because the food and service were abysmal. Worst of all was how he would blow Phillips off, call to say he couldn't make a meeting, and then expect *her* to call him back "even though he's being the rude one."

Still Redford resisted, feeling that the part of Hubbell Gardiner was vapid and uninteresting. He wanted to play parts that were challenging, that had—to his way of thinking—some emotional or intellectual rigor to them. He had no great interest in being the male lead in a Barbra Streisand movie. He may have appeared in some romantic soap-opera-style pictures—such as the ones he did with Natalie Wood—early in his career, but that was before he was a major movie star in his own right. *The Way We Were* did not appeal to him on any level.

Although Redford did not really want to do *The Way We Were*, he didn't want to disappoint his friend Pollack, who told him that once he was signed he could use his considerable clout to insist upon script changes. His part would not only be expanded, but given much more depth. Pollack told Redford that he wouldn't and couldn't make the movie without him. Pollack was so sure he had Redford sewed up that Ray Stark issued a press release to the *Hollywood Reporter* stating that Redford had signed to do the picture. Oops—the next day they had to retract the report because it turned out that Redford had not quite made up his mind. An exasperated Stark told Pollack that if Redford did not sign by midnight of that day, he would go ahead and hire Ryan O'Neal, who at least had a certain box-office appeal and had worked well with Streisand in other films. Pollack pointed out to Redford that they could delay filming until the fall, so that they could shoot in New York, where Redford's children would be starting a new year of school. Pushed to the wall—and prodded by

Pollack (as well as the promise of a higher salary than Streisand's and a percentage of the profits)—Redford finally agreed to do the movie. The *Hollywood Reporter* took back its retraction; Redford was now officially Streisand's costar.

Next the problem of the rewrites had to be dealt with. Arthur Laurents did not care for the way things were developing now that Redford had jumped on board. As far as Laurents was concerned, *The Way We Were* was essentially the story of Katie Morosky (Streisand). The character of Hubbell Gardiner (Redford) and her romance with him was just one element of her story. Pollack was afraid that Streisand's forcefulness would unbalance the movie, but now Laurents was afraid the opposite would occur. His protests falling on deaf ears, Laurents was summarily dismissed from the project altogether. A series of writers—everyone from Francis Ford Coppola to Dalton Trumbo—were brought in to cobble together a script that gave Streisand and Redford equal time and equal opportunities for emoting. Eventually Arthur Laurents was brought back, at Streisand's insistence. "He's such a weasel," Laurents later said of Redford. "He's impossible, egocentric." Redford insisted on a confrontation scene between Katie and Hubbell, so that Hubbell would be more than just a passive love object for Katie. He felt the primary difference between the two characters was that Katie was for causes and Hubbell was for people.

A bigger battle than the one between Pollack and Laurents was the one between Pollack and producer Ray Stark. Pollack felt that the two lead characters should not just be observers of and commentators on the 1950s McCarthy witch hunts, but actual participants. Pollack thought it was important to include a scene in which Gardiner would testify before the House Un-American Activities Committee and name names, causing the biggest crisis of all in his relationship with Katie, who refuses to inform and hates him for doing so. In this way, Pollack hoped to make a much bigger statement about this controversial period in American history and how it divided and shattered families and destroyed lives.

Stark, however, would have none of it. He saw *The Way We Were* as primarily a simple love story and thought box office opportunities would be destroyed if Redford were seen as a villain. The characters might not stay together at the end of the movie, but they would still

CHAPTER SEVEN   101

respect one another. Katie could not respect Hubbell if he turned in his friends as communists. Pollack wanted the film to open with Gardiner testifying at the hearings while Katie flashes back to their life together; instead, she simply sees him dressed in his Navy uniform at the bar at El Morocco in Manhattan, practically asleep. The flashback then consists only of their college days when they were bare acquaintances; their actual romance and relationship begins at El Morocco. In Pollack's version, the flashback would have encompassed most of the story.

Once the script was ironed out, there were more problems. For one thing, Redford seemed to have no great desire to meet with his costar before filming began. Redford agreed several times to see her, but he kept putting off the actual date. Streisand certainly knew that Redford had the right chemistry, but she also needed to get some sense of him as a person before they worked together. As weeks went by and Redford kept putting her off, Streisand became angrier and angrier.

Afraid that some new nightmare might ensue, Pollack went to Redford and asked him as a personal favor to meet La Streisand face to face. Redford said that he would go, but Pollack had to go with him. The two men made a date to have dinner at Streisand's house—they talked mostly about the property both men owned in Sundance, Utah—where Redford worked his charm and Streisand became a little smitten. This did not, however, thaw the ice between the two stars; the ice had not entirely melted even when the picture began filming. Redford was still not thrilled with the script or his character and wanted further changes. Streisand and Laurents were sure that the film was being heavily swayed in Redford's direction, that "Katie's story"—and Barbra's big moments—were being lost. After a while, both stars simply went through the motions, convinced that the movie was hers—or his. They rarely spoke except during their scenes together, although observers noted that they were always outwardly cordial.

Another problem was that their acting styles were poles apart. Streisand fancied herself an "intellectual" actor who liked to discuss scenes with director and costar before they shot, while Redford—like Frank Sinatra—wanted to shoot while the energy was high and he was at his best. Too much dissection and rehearsal blunted the edge and bored him. Pollack had a hell of a time trying to reach that certain point, a happy medium, where Streisand was ready and Redford hadn't passed his peak. Too soon, and Barbra would feel rushed; too late and Redford would go stale.

Cast members later observed that Redford and Streisand not only did not bond, but hardly talked to one another. Costar Bradford Dillman, among others, noted that both of them tended to stay to themselves during filming. Redford was much more accessible to cast and crew—although he was frequently off on the phone or tending to something or another—while "Barbra finds it very, very difficult to socialize," according to Dillman. "I think I saw her laugh twice during the months we were together." Of the two, Redford was definitely the more pleasant, although Barbra was seen more as shy than as unlikable. She got into the habit of calling up Pollack late at night to discuss the following day's scenes, and she tried to do the same with Redford. But her leading man made it quite clear that he would discuss the picture only on the set and in the daytime. "I won't say Barbra was exactly panting for him over the phone," said a production assistant, "but I think she made Bob nervous."

To everyone it seemed apparent that Streisand—the strong, sturdy, in-your-face, unflappable Streisand—had developed quite a yen for Redford, and she knew it was hopelessly unrequited. Cast member Viveca Lindfors recalled, "I could tell from the way she looked at him when he wasn't watching. Not during scenes, although her feelings for him empowered her acting in those scenes."

According to another cast member, "Streisand had a definite crush on Redford, but that didn't mean she wasn't 'on' to him. Like most movie stars, like Redford himself, Barbra was extremely protective of her territory. She appreciated the fact that Redford was doing a good job in the movie, but she was afraid he would wind up dominating it, casting her aside, which was ridiculous, as she had the better part. Still, you could tell she was developing a real love-hate or like-dislike for the guy. Part of her was just as crazy about him as Katie was about Hubbell in those early scenes—a schoolgirl infatuation with a good-looking guy—but she also didn't trust him. Whether it was because he didn't respond to her obvious interest, or because she was afraid he and Pollack were conspiring to steal the picture away from her, or both, she became too wary of him to ever become friends with him." Redford admitted in later interviews that he was aware that Barbra was generally "untrusting," because she had been used and hustled by too many people, sycophants, and hangers-on; he could identify with this, as he often felt the same.

At one point during filming Barbra became nearly hysterical when, the story goes, producer Ray Stark, whom Redford reportedly detested, called her and told her that the camera man was lighting her all wrong. "It looks like you've got a beard in every shot," Stark told her. Horrified, Streisand complained and got the camera man fired. Later on it was simply seen as a control stratagem of Stark's.

When all was said and done, Streisand was convinced that the final result would have been much better—and perhaps it would have been—had she had complete control over the movie. She had several arguments with Pollack over her character and different scenes—especially her crying scenes (she thought they made her weak; Pollack thought they made her human)—but Pollack refused to make changes. Seeing the final cut, Streisand was furious with the director. While she no longer necessarily felt that he had favored his friend, Redford—something that had worried her all throughout filming—she resented the fact that Pollack didn't listen to or understand the points she was making. Redford stayed out of it. He had never wanted to make *The Way We Were* in the first place. Redford has often been quoted as saying that doing the movie was like "doing overtime at Dachau," a thoughtlessly tasteless remark. Redford had developed a sincere dislike of Ray Stark by the end of filming; he was convinced that if Stark had gotten his way, he would have been cut out of the movie entirely. Redford thought he had given a lousy performance until his wife Lola went to see it on opening day and told him he was marvelous.

The "Cornell University" scenes were actually filmed on the campus of Union College in Schenectady. Because this was the early seventies, most of the college students—male as well as female—sported long hair, which was unacceptable for the time period of the movie. Trying to round up male students for extras, the studio offered them a few dollars and a hot meal if they agreed to get their hair cut. There weren't that many takers, so actual actors had to be bused in for the scenes.

Many observers of the film noted that it reversed the usual formula. The guy doesn't move heaven and earth to get the gal; it's the other way around. Katie picks up Hubbell in a bar, brings him home, and takes advantage of his inebriated, confused state to climb in bed with him and make love to him. The man is the object of lust and the woman is the ardent pursuer.

Viveca Lindfors played the part of Salke Viertel, whom she had known during her days in New York. Exiled from Germany, Viertel had hosted a salon of Hollywood thinkers and liberals. Laurents's original novel had been based on the lives of Viertel's son Peter and a woman named Jiggy Schulberg (Redford does not play Lindfors's son in the movie, however). "The viciousness of the McCarthy period was easier to handle in retrospect," she remembered. A few years after making the film, she told William Schoell: "Yes, I guess I would have to say *The Way We Were* was 'Hollywood schlock' all right, although it did do a service in re-introducing a difficult period of American history to the public at large. Robert Redford and Barbra Streisand were very interesting characters, she more than he, probably because powerful women are always more interesting. But I thought both of them were nice, if a little distracted, which is understandable." The final scene of *The Way We Were* was to have depicted Katie watching her grown daughter leading a campus protest against the Vietnam War, but it was never filmed.

Redford gives a very good performance in *The Way We Were*, although both he and Streisand are woefully unconvincing as college students in the early flashback sequences. However, what is very convincing is Hubbell's look of embarrassment and self-consciousness as the teacher picks out his story among many to read to the class. This scene mirrored Redford's embarrassment over all the fuss being made over him in real life. In a voice-over, Katie thinks, "It was too easy for him, but at least he knew it," a comment that could also be made about Redford. Redford also seems good because his costar completely fails to create a *real* person. Nasal and too "cute" by far—even when she gets into bed with Hubbell for the first time—Streisand comes off as a caricature. A self-absorbed artist in real life, Streisand has no understanding of real activists and no real identification with Katie. Redford's suggesting that one character is a "dyke" seems counterproductive in a film supposedly condemning prejudice and name-calling. The picture-postcard shots of New York do little to capture or illuminate the real city. *The Way We Were* may resonate for people who have discovered that, like Katie and Hubbell, they just can't live with the one they love; but its superficiality, which most critics noted, keeps it out of the league of other great Hollywood romances.

With a major ad campaign mounted by Columbia, which promoted the teaming of two beloved stars, *The Way We Were* cleaned up at the box office, garnering over $25 million in the United States alone. Sydney Pollack and Redford estimated that their cut had to amount to over $5 million, which was not forthcoming from Columbia. The two men had to sue the studio and producer Ray Stark for what was owed them.

Redford had already been big, but he was a superstar after the release of *The Way We Were*. He was not especially happy with this development. He felt it typecast him as a romantic figure when he felt he could do so much more, and he thought that people were beginning to see him in an unrealistic, superhuman light. Worse, he would have to fight harder than ever to maintain privacy for himself and his family. Still, even he would have to concede that superstardom had its compensations.

Strictly because of the movie's huge grosses, Streisand, Redford, and Pollack agreed to eventually do a sequel to *The Way We Were*. Pollack came up with the idea of having Katie and Hubbell coming back together for the sake of their daughter, Rachel, who is a sixties radical (which pleases Katie) and a drug abuser (which does not). When the film did not happen, there was talk among the stars and Pollack of doing a kind of reunion movie instead of a sequel, which would have been titled *After Love*. Both projects failed to materialize, because it was understood that it would be hard to get the two stars to agree upon a script and because most studios would balk at their combined salary demands. After *The Way We Were*, Streisand and Redford were two of the biggest—and most expensive—film stars in the world. Redford's next picture, *The Sting*, would only make Redford hotter.

John Huston wanted to make *The Man Who Would Be King* with Redford and Paul Newman, but British actors Michael Caine and

Sean Connery, who did play the leads, were considered more sensible choices even by Newman and Redford. Instead, George Roy Hill—whom producer Julia Phillips described as "a tall, mean-faced goy"—planned a new picture, *The Sting,* with Redford. As originally conceived, the movie was to have a single star, Redford. But everyone connected to the film was hoping lightning would strike twice, and *The Sting* (1973) would be a box-office smash as big as *Butch Cassidy*; when approached, Paul Newman was only too happy to sign up.

Redford was frankly thunderstruck when he found out that Hill had offered the part to Newman and even more stupefied that Newman had accepted. The part Newman played was originally conceived as a supporting role for a grizzled old character actor, but it was heavily beefed up to make *The Sting* a natural follow-up to *Butch Cassidy.* Both actors received $500,000—not a lot by today's standards, but a hefty sum in the seventies—to make the film, plus a percentage of the profits. The film took in $69 million at the box office. Redford almost turned the picture down when it appeared that the screenwriter, David Ward, would also direct. He did not want to work with a neophyte and felt Ward was unlikely to revise his own script, which in Redford's opinion needed work.

The movie focuses on two 1930s con artists, a veteran (Newman) and an ambitious neophyte (Redford). The two men team up to pull a classic "sting" on the man responsible for the death of a friend and fellow grifter. Along the way there are assorted twists and turns and double crosses, all sheathed in a handsome and reasonably atmospheric production gloss. Again Redford is somewhat better at this material than Newman is, and he received an Oscar nomination for Best Actor. *The Sting* was also nominated for Best Picture, and Hill got the nod for Best Director. *The Sting* was perfectly entertaining if minor fluff that traded on the undeniable chemistry between the two stars. According to George Roy Hill, "What puts Newman and Redford over so well together is as much chemistry as acting. When they're in the same frame something exciting happens even when they're not talking or even moving."

Redford liked working with Hill this time, and would work with him again. He liked the fact that Hill ran a tight ship, knew what he wanted and when he wanted it. He admired Hill's thoroughness and professionalism. He likened being on a George Roy Hill set to "being in a bomber squadron." Redford would probably not have wanted to spend much time socializing with the man, but he respected him. For his part, the only problem Hill had with Redford was when Bob squirmed in his seat while watching the finished movie—which he did during a screening of *Butch Cassidy*. One observer put it bluntly: "Let's face it, Redford, like all actors, especially the good-looking ones, is vain. He doesn't like seeing himself projected on the movie screen because those bumps on his face are as big as manhole covers. The joke is that it didn't stop him from being a sex symbol and having millions of women panting after him like crazy." As one woman fan put it, "I'd kiss each bump if I could!"

Redford was not necessarily being humble, but perceptive and honest, in admitting that he didn't think he deserved to win the Oscar. He knew it was hardly a performance that stretched his talent or showed genius. He also felt that if he was nominated, then Newman certainly should have been as well. He had never been all that impressed with the whole award system in the first place, noting that "best performance" Oscars were often given to people who had done much better work in the past or wouldn't do their best work until several years in the future. Redford felt that it was one thing for a fellow in a footrace to win because he reaches the finish line first and is clearly faster than his competitors are, but the "Oscar Race" had too many variables; it simply couldn't be as clear-cut.

"[Warren Beatty] systematically let it be known that he had read and rejected every script to which Robert Redford had committed," said Peter Bart of *Daily Variety*. It has been said that one of these scripts was *The Sting*, which Beatty found rather tedious. A studio exec or agent may have sent Beatty the script. It is doubtful, however, that George Roy Hill would have wanted to work with him, and even more doubtful that anyone would have found the combo of Newman and Beatty as appealing—or as box office—as Newman and Redford, considering the grosses for *Butch Cassidy*.

During the making of *The Sting*, Newman played more of his practical jokes on Redford and Hill, which they took with as much grace as they could muster. Newman had apparently been annoyed by Redford's late arrivals on the set of *Butch Cassidy*, so he had his wife, Joanne Woodward, make a needlepoint for Redford with a message about the virtue of being on time. This was a good-natured but serious admonishment.

Redford and Newman eventually became fairly good professional friends, although it could not be said that they were terribly close. For one thing, their temperaments were very different. Although Newman could be quite political in his own way—Joanne was the catalyst in this—he was not quite as committed as Redford, who occasionally found Newman to be rather frivolous.

Paul Newman said that he admires Redford: "He's not been sucked in by fashionable things and he keeps his life to himself, and he's very comfortable in his own skin, I think." But he admits that when the two try to have a conversation, there are always long pauses because they are both very private people. "We both look at the floor," said Newman. On another occasion Newman said, "I have known the man for over forty years and I don't know him, not really." For his part, Redford said of Newman that he admires the way acting came naturally for Newman when it didn't for him.

Redford undoubtedly noticed that the characters of *The Sting* have absolutely no depth to them; but after a few attempts to improve the screenplay, he probably figured it wouldn't matter too much if the audience felt the story was compelling and the film fun. Redford was not crazy about the fact that most of his lines were exposition, telling the audience what was going on or the other characters what they would have to do; he also spent half the movie *running* from one place to another. Although early in the film, Redford seems to have a sexy girlfriend—played winningly by Sally Kirkland—the only woman he beds is Dimitra Arliss as Loretta. An excellent actress, Arliss, with her plain looks, gave hope to average-looking women in the audience that they, too, might actually have a shot at Redford. Newman sleeps with a character played by Eileen Brennan. *The Sting* may be the only movie in history where the female love interests, if they can even be called that in a buddy film, were less attractive than the male leads (although the women may have been better actors).

Robert Shaw, who played the victim of the scam in *The Sting,* had written the novel on which *Situation Hopeless . . . But Not Serious* had been based. The chances are good that Redford and Shaw did not swap stories about the disastrous film version. Shaw had injured his leg before filming began and remarked that he was grateful for how solicitous Newman always was toward him, but of Redford he had little to say.

As with *Butch Cassidy*, Redford did not actually see *The Sting* until many, many years later, when he finally watched a DVD of it with his eleven-year-old grandson. "He was looking for a film to see this summer." he recalled. "We're going through the videos under 'classics' and I saw *The Sting* there. So we watched it. We had a hell of a time. He loved it."

As mentioned previously, when two good-looking actors appear in "buddy films" together, the rumor mills begin churning with generally apocryphal stories of backstage homosexual affairs. One critic referred to Newman and Redford half jokingly as "the screen's leading romantic couple." Although there *are* plenty of hidden homosexual encounters and full-fledged gay relationships between famous Hollywood movie stars, the rumors of an affair between Newman and Redford have never been even remotely substantiated. When Newman toyed with the idea of filming the gay novel *The Front Runner*, which delineated the affair between a coach and a younger athlete (an idea he dropped in order to do *Slap Shot*), some people believed the stories that Redford would play Newman's younger lover. It is unlikely Newman approached Redford about the film— although not impossible—primarily because there was a much greater age difference between the characters in *The Front Runner* than there is between Newman and Redford; the coach is middle-aged and the athlete he falls in love with is in his twenties. In any case, it is doubtful that Redford, who fretted so over his gay/bisexual role in *Inside Daisy Clover*, would have had the courage to even consider playing a part in *The Front Runner*. Newman certainly lost his courage when he opted for the less controversial *Slap Shot*. While Newman and Joanne Woodward seem to be supporters of gay rights, Redford has never stood up for gays in any strong public manner, although he has allowed many gay-themed films to be shown at his Sundance Festival and openly supported them.

One critic suggested that the Newman-Redford pairing was not a "perversion" of the old romantic movie pairings such as William Powell and Myrna Loy, but more along the lines of the Lew Ayres– Lionel Barrymore relationship from the old Dr. Kildare films (years before the TV series with Richard Chamberlain) in which Ayres was young Dr. Kildare and Barrymore was his mentor, Dr. Gillespie. Of course, the age difference between Newman and Redford was not quite as marked (this was a problem in *The Sting*, because Newman was supposed to be a mentor to Redford). Finally, Newman and Redford's dalliances with members of the opposite sex in *The Sting* almost seem dragged in to prove their characters' heterosexuality, although one such scene does set up an exciting twist.

Warren Beatty—wouldn't you know it?—was first offered the role of Jay Gatsby in the third film version (after 1926 and 1949) of F. Scott Fitzgerald's novel, *The Great Gatsby*. Beatty took too long mulling it over and let it be known that the contract would have to be renegotiated before he would sign. It was decided to look elsewhere. Redford took the title role in *The Great Gatsby* after Jack Nicholson, wisely, turned it down. Redford should probably have done the same. While neither Nicholson nor Beatty might have been right for Jay Gatsby, they might have offered more flavorful performances. Redford was seen by almost everyone as being just a little too bland.

The film came into being because film star Ali MacGraw of *Love Story* fame wanted to play Daisy Buchanan. Her husband at the time was Robert Evans, a former actor who was then the production chief at Paramount. Completely smitten with Ali, Evans was determined to make the dream a reality for his wife. He contacted producer David Merrick, who normally worked on Broadway, and asked him to produce the film, flattering him that he would give it the right panache and class. Nicholson did not want to work with MacGraw (it was said that Beatty had similar concerns), so Evans sought out Marlon Brando, who was much too old for the part. Evans might have signed him anyway, except that Brando demanded too high a salary. Redford got the role by default. Ironically, when word originally got out that Evans wanted to do the movie, a bidding war for the rights began, and Redford was a major bidder. Evans bought the rights from Fitzgerald's daughter for nearly half a million.

Once they had their stars, the problem became finding a director who thought the distinctly limited MacGraw would be convincing as Daisy. Several major directors flatly refused to make the picture with MacGraw as the leading lady. Jack Clayton had no objections, but it became a moot point when MacGraw began a highly publicized affair with Steve McQueen, her leading man in *The Getaway*. Evans headed for divorce court, and his once-beloved Ali was unofficially out on her keister. Evans decided to let David Merrick run the whole show as sole producer, although he remained involved to a lesser extent as one of the front office men at Paramount.

Ali MacGraw had not given up, however. She and lover boy McQueen decided that they would make the perfect Daisy-Gatsby duo and to hell with Bob Evans. Through agents, they approached David Merrick, who told them in no uncertain terms that Redford had been signed and that was that. Now MacGraw was officially off the film; without McQueen by her side, she refused to do the picture and asked for a release (some claim she still wanted to do the picture, but McQueen forbade her to do it without him). Merrick was happy to release her. Then Evans got a cable from a quick-thinking Mia Farrow, who asked if she could play Daisy. A few other actresses had already been tested—Candice Bergen, Katharine Ross, Natalie Wood, Tuesday Weld, Faye Dunaway, Cathy Lee Crosby, and Lois Chiles, who was awarded a lesser role in the movie—but everyone agreed that Farrow had the right aristocratic, almost ethereal quality for the part.

Faye Dunaway had badly wanted the part of Daisy; she had especially wanted to work with Redford. "I flew down to Los Angeles to do a screen test for the role," she recalled. Some of the Paramount executives wanted Clayton to consider Dunaway and test her, but he had already made up his mind that Farrow was to be his Daisy. "I would never have agreed to the test if I had known that the director had his mind made up otherwise going in," Dunaway recalled. She would later work with Redford in *Three Days of the Condor*. The year of *Gatsby*'s release, 1974, both Dunaway and Redford were named America's favorite film stars.

Mia Farrow was pregnant with her third son, Fletcher, while making *The Great Gatsby*, which was filmed at the Pinewood Studios in England. "What I remember best about *Gatsby*," she recalled, "are my earnest and mostly successful efforts not to throw up on Theoni Aldredge's gossamer costumes. I also remember the Watergate hearings, which riveted Bob Redford and me to the television set in his dressing room, and provided us all with an endlessly fascinating topic for discussion. Nor will I forget Bob's good heart, and the pleasure of his company." Farrow objected to the "cotton candy" wig that she had to wear in the film because her own hair was so short. Wearing a wig bleached absolutely snow-white by the hairdresser, Farrow felt that her performance was severely undermined; but no one else seemed to notice.

Producer David Merrick showed up on the set of *Gatsby* far too often to suit the director, Jack Clayton. Redford, preoccupied by Watergate, seemed somewhere in outer space to most of his colleagues; "certainly his mind wasn't on the film," one of them reported. Most of Clayton's previous films had been "sensitive small films," as Mia Farrow put it, and *The Great Gatsby* had not been conceived by him as a "big" picture. But the studio hyped it "as if it were *Gone With the Wind*," according to Farrow, with all sorts of tie-in promotions. "The delicately balanced script was blown up into something it never was meant to be," she recalled.

In one scene, Farrow as Daisy has to pick up and sob into about a dozen hand-tailored silk shirts that Gatsby throws at her feet. After each take, everyone—actors included—would pick up the shirts and carefully refold them and return them to Gatsby's wardrobe. Then Redford would throw them again, Farrow would weep, and the refolding would again take place. Again and again. This simple sequence took an entire day to shoot. On another occasion, Clayton and actor Scott Wilson—who played the garage owner, also named Wilson—argued about Clayton's instructions for the man to bang his head against a post after he learns his wife has been run over and killed. Wilson was afraid it might be too much, but the next day he was ready to shoot it that way and felt that it worked.

The studio was determined to turn *Gatsby* into a blockbuster. Nowadays merchandising of a movie is fairly common, but in 1974 it was basically a new approach. People connected with the movie thought the film's reviews were particularly savage because the critics were offended by the tie-ins with everything from hair salons to sportswear (to create "the Gatsby look"), Scotch whisky, and even Teflon cookware, which had F. Scott Fitzgerald's daughter joking that "daddy would have loved being a Teflon pan more than anything else."

Part of the hype was to schedule even more interviews with entertainment reporters than usual. Redford hated being chased around the set when he hoped to get some rest or privacy, answering the same pat, dull questions asked by one reporter after another. Still, all of this publicity worked to get the film an unheard-of $18 million in advance bookings, which meant that the film had already earned back its costs times three. Although *The Great Gatsby* has always been considered a Redford turkey because of the bad press—few people who went to see it enjoyed it very much—it actually made a lot of money.

The Great Gatsby is not an awful movie, just a very disappointing one. It is handsomely produced and well directed, if a bit on the slow side. Redford looks great with his dyed-brown hair, but he and Mia Farrow are not a good pairing. With their differing acting styles they don't even seem to be in the same movie, and Farrow overdoes the wide-eyed fluttery posturing that she affects. Redford is too controlled, too drawn in, for a man who is supposed to be passionately in love. But he has his moments, for instance, a wonderful sequence when he wears a perfect, frightened-hopeful expression on his face when Daisy catches sight of him in a mirror. Redford isn't necessarily any less convincing than Alan Ladd was in the earlier sound version; maybe only Zachary Scott would have made an effective Gatsby.

The film has good supporting actors, including Sam Waterston as Nick Carraway and Bruce Dern as Tom. Every star vehicle seems to have one or more actors whose raw and obvious ability reminds the audience of what really good acting is all about, and in *The Great Gatsby*, that actor is Scott Wilson. As the husband of the woman who's run over and killed by Daisy, he gives a consummate and impassioned performance. He steals the picture from the superficial, lightweight Redford and even from an excellent Dern and Waterston, who admittedly have less showy roles.

"Robert Redford chose to play [*Gatsby*] recessively rather than assertively," said John Harbison, who composed an operatic version of Fitzgerald's novel that premiered at the Met. Harbison had his own struggles in bringing Gatsby to life in musical terms, but he was determined to avoid Redford's approach. "I mean, once he's there, it would seem to me entirely necessary for him to take responsibility for being there. He seemed to interpret the part in terms of 'This is a mysterious person; I will behave mysteriously and noncommit-

tally.'" In his opera Harbison created a Gatsby who was more assert-
ive, "spellbinding and impressive."

There were those who admired Redford in the part, however.
Writer Leonard Leff found his portrayal "subtly detailed. Waiting
for Daisy in Nick's cottage, for instance, Redford's Gatsby glances
through a magazine. Before he turns a page, he licks his finger in a
gesture that betrays the humble origins beneath the character's high-
priced clothes. Later, when Daisy reached out to him, he extends his
hand but will not let their fingers touch. He cannot consummate the
dream."

Years later, though, Redford talked back to his critics, saying that
if they had actually *read the book* they would have realized that he
was only trying to give an honest interpretation of the character based
on what (little) Fitzgerald says about him. Fitzgerald described Gatsby as being a fine figure of a man, so there was no reason he couldn't
be good-looking. He also said that he was awkward and rough, and
some critics did pick up that Redford tried to get this across, that he
was "surprisingly good at conveying Gatsby's uneasiness, [that] the
social graces are not natural to him." But Redford could never be
called "an elegant young roughneck." In the end he was a victim of
blatant miscasting. Mia Farrow was not spared the critical barbs either, with the *New York Daily News* stating that "she has all the romantic allure of Little Bo Peep."

Jack Clayton and David Merrick had a final contretemps some
months after the release of the movie. Clayton felt that his use of
such period songs as *What'll I Do* and *When You and I Were Seventeen*
were crucial to setting up the mood of the film, and he was nearly
apoplectic when he found out that Merrick had failed to secure video
rights for these tunes. Therefore they had to be cut from the sound-
track of the videocassettes.

Twenty-one years after the release of *The Great Gatsby*, Patsy Ken-
sit, who played Farrow's daughter in the film, played Farrow herself—and could not have been more like her—in the television film
Love and Betrayal: The Mia Farrow Story, which detailed her marriage
to Woody Allen and his affair with their adopted daughter. Howard
Da Silva, who played Wilson in the 1949 version of *The Great Gatsby*
with Alan Ladd in the title role, played Meyer Wolfsheim in the Redford version.

The Great Waldo Pepper (1975) looked at the barnstorming pilots of post–World War I. These men found that the only way they could keep flying and make a living in the air they loved was to become stunt pilots at air shows across the country. Waldo Pepper (Redford), one of these pilots, tells everyone a fairy tale about how he had a dogfight with the infamous German ace, Ernst Kessler. Waldo has a not-so-friendly rivalry with Axel Olsson (Bo Svenson), but the two are talked into teaming up for a flying circus in Nebraska. After a young woman is killed during a wing-walking act the pilots cook up, and other tragedies occur, Waldo is grounded and finds work in Hollywood under an assumed name. There he finally meets the German ace Kessler, who is technical advisor for a movie about his life (the film completely glosses over the fact that he presumably shot down many American boys). During filming of an aerial sequence, Pepper and Kessler engage in a dogfight for real; Pepper wins, and salutes his adversary.

The Great Waldo Pepper (1975) had its origins in talks between William Goldman and George Roy Hill during the making of *Butch Cassidy*. "Hill had been a marine pilot in both World War Two and Korea," Goldman recalled, "but his heart was then and forever with the Jennys and the other flimsy machines surrounding the period of the First World War." From the start, Redford was seen as the star—the only star—for *Waldo*. Yet according to Goldman, who wrote the screenplay: "It is my firm belief that because of his presence in the film, giving a superb performance in a role tailored solely for his talents, that the movie was a commercial disappointment."

Goldman believed the problem was in the scene when Redford transfers from plane to plane (the feat was actually performed by a sixty-eight-year-old stuntman) in an attempt to save the life of Susan Sarandon's wing-walking character, who is frozen to the wing in sheer terror. "Now we're on Redford," said Goldman, "stunned, alone on the wing. She's fallen. We hold on Redford's face a moment, distraught, stricken; he's come so far, risked his life, tried so hard. But she's gone. . . . So was the audience."

During their very first preview of the film in Boston, Goldman and Hill sensed this might happen. They had tried to prepare viewers for the fact that the story, initially lighthearted, would turn grim. They showed photos of wrecked planes and dead pilots during the opening credits; but this was too abrupt and chilling, almost grue-some and grotesque, a change in mood (the fears of falling and of flying, combined in *falling off or out of a plane*, create a kind of psy-chic, gibbering terror in most people). "For the first hour of the movie," Goldman commented, "[the audience was] in love with us, and in that instant when the girl went off the wing, the affair ended."

Goldman felt that the scene, and movie, might have worked with a leading man who as of 1975 was seen as being more flawed and less heroic than Robert Redford—maybe Jack Nicholson or Robert De Niro. In his opinion the audience felt cheated, if not downright out-raged, when Redford failed to save the girl. In any case, the film did not do that well at the box office. Some critics felt the real problem was that the movie mixed slapstick with drama and wasn't satisfac-tory in either capacity.

Hill took Redford up in his plane and showed him his aerial moves, which he claimed that Redford loved. Later, however, Hill said that Redford began to develop an uncomfortable feeling while in the air. He told stories of how Redford would seem to do every-thing he could to stall and delay the time he would have to actually get inside the airplane, trying on different gloves, talking to the crew, having to make a last-minute phone call. The trouble was that Red-ford had not learned to fly, and he felt completely out of control up in the air.

During the flying sequences, licensed pilots were situated behind machine guns while the camera made it appear as though Redford, who was seated in the rear cockpit, was doing the flying. Because the real pilot would be flying blind, if anything happened, Redford would not have been able to take over the controls and land the plane. Two planes crashed during filming, seriously injuring the pi-lots.

The publicity department let it be known that Redford had done his own stunts, including the scene when he walks out on the wing after Sarandon—which of course was not entirely true. According to Hill, Redford did walk out to the first bay on the wing while they were three thousand feet in the air—"what the hell am I *doing* here?" Redford wondered—but after that the stuntman took over. For the scene when he looks as if he's about to transfer from the wing of one plane to another plane above, Hill simply instructed Redford to stand up in the rear cockpit and angled the shot so that it looked as if he were standing in space.

One of the young actors in the supporting cast was Scott Newman, Paul's handsome actor son, whose experience as a parachute jumper came in handy. Redford and Hill were happy to have Paul's son in the film. Although he may have been hired as a favor to Newman, or gotten the job due to his obvious contacts, Scott was still a promising actor.

The Great Waldo Pepper opened to lukewarm reviews. The film is full of striking aerial footage, but it contains nothing new. It's as superficial as any Grade C poverty-row pic on stunt pilots, such as *I'm Still Alive*, with Kent Taylor. The picture does nothing to help us understand these men or what drives them. Redford never seems like a real person, only a feathery Hollywood conception of mock heroism. Sarandon's death is sanitized; no close-ups show the poor woman's terror, no screams are heard as she falls. Her death is forgotten about almost immediately, making the whole scene almost meaningless; it should resonate for the rest of the movie, but it doesn't. The audience may have been more turned off by the nonreaction to Sarandon's demise than by the death itself. But then, women are pretty disposable in the world of Waldo Pepper, if not of Hill, Goldman, and company. Margot Kidder, another potential love interest for Redford, is on-screen for what seems like thirty seconds. The only effective scene in the movie occurs when the camera shows us the blank stares of the townsfolk as they watch a downed pilot burn to death with utter dispassion.

Redford was not only busy appearing in several films in 1975; he was also being burned in effigy, and more than once. This came about because he had become aware of plans to build a power plant in southern Utah. Always a committed environmentalist concerned about everything from land-use legislation and global warming policies to radioactive waste disposal and mining reform, Redford went on the attack. He was famous enough to get lots of media attention, including an interview on CBS's *60 Minutes*. Redford received a great flood of hate mail and threats, and pronuclear protesters burned effigies. Plans to build the plant were halted, however, and many people who encountered Redford offered him their thanks and appreciation for his efforts.

Redford's first experience as an activist had occurred a few years previously in 1970, when he learned of plans to build an eight-lane freeway through a canyon not far from his property. Redford contacted other interested parties and formed a group that successfully prevented the freeway construction. He learned not only that numbers of concerned citizens acting together can bring about change, but that the importance and influence of celebrity cannot be underestimated.

Three Days of the Condor (1975) was a "paranoia" chase-thriller influenced by the events of Watergate. Sydney Pollack directed the film, and Faye Dunaway was tapped to costar with Redford. "Though I was well-established by then," Dunaway remembered, "I was still a bit intimidated at the idea of being in a film with [Redford], particularly since he and Sydney had worked together on three earlier films. They would be old pals and I would be the newcomer." Still, Dunaway was an admirer of Redford and his "extraordinary presence on-screen," so she agreed to do the film. Dunaway, who worked with Warren Beatty in *Bonnie and Clyde* and with Redford, had this to say of them: "They are brilliant men, passionate about what they produce, and boy are they not dumb."

Redford plays Joseph Turner, an intelligence analyzer for the CIA. One afternoon he comes back from lunch to find all of his coworkers murdered. It seems they had discovered something that might lead to the uncovering of an unauthorized operation within the CIA. This renegade agent makes it look as if Turner is a murderer, and he has to go on the run, kidnapping a young woman along the way for cover. CIA operatives try to bring in Turner while the renegade agent's hit man does his best to kill him. The hit man, however, winds up killing the renegade, and the CIA wants Turner back. Turner, however, refuses to play ball and turns in the whole story to the *New York Times*.

The movie was filmed on location in New York City in November of 1974. Production meetings were held at Pollack's townhouse, where the principals decided that Lorenzo Semple Jr.'s screenplay needed some punching up; David Rayfield was brought in to do the revisions. Redford would constantly joke that Dunaway was getting all the funny lines, and he wanted some for himself. The rewrite, according to Dunaway, made her character of Kathy much more dimensional, and a love scene for her and Redford was also incorporated. Due to the different and often contradictory demands of Pollack, Redford, and Dunaway, Rayfield was constantly revising pages of the script throughout the filming; sometimes the actors got the revised script for a particular scene only a short while before shooting it.

Redford and Dunaway worked well together on camera, but they did not exactly bond. "We just never hung out," Dunaway recalled. "Redford was intellectual, I think, very preoccupied with the business and with other projects and with the world . . . when he wasn't in front of the camera, he was on the phone. I liked working with Redford, though he was at times difficult to connect with." No wonder—although Redford claimed to like Dunaway personally, he admitted finding her—and acting with her—"difficult." She always seemed to be off somewhere in her own troubled world, a world that Redford had no need or desire to enter, so he excused himself when the scene was over and went about his own business. Many have found Dunaway, while likable, to be a somewhat overbearing presence—larger-than-life, somewhat fussy and affected like a "grand dame"—and while Redford may have appreciated her strengths, he would have found such a woman off-putting. Even Redford's detractors have never described him as being "affected" like many movie stars, both male and female.

Dunaway had a terrible time acting the scene in which Redford first kidnaps and threatens her; she has to play it as if she's terrified of him possibly raping or beating the hell out of her. "Now I'm sorry," Dunaway recalled, "but the idea of being kidnapped and ravaged by Robert Redford was anything but frightening. And Turner's character was very much like Redford's—serious, kind, down-to-earth, and very good-looking." Picking up on one reason that Redford is never very convincing in "evil" roles, she added, "Redford has such gentle eyes, it's just very, very hard for him to look menacing. And the wire-rimmed glasses they had him wear to fit the character, who was a CIA bookworm, made him look more sensitive and vulnerable than ever."

Dunaway nearly burst into laughter every time Redford acted menacing and made a grab for her. After a few aborted takes, Pollack told Redford to take a break in his trailer while he spoke to Dunaway about how to handle the scene. Instead of talking to the actress, he kept the cameras rolling, and being an actor himself, played Redford's part as the camera remained fixed on Dunaway. Wearing a very realistic and frightening sneer, he advanced on the woman and told her the terrible things he was going to do to her. In this way he was able to get the proper reaction from the actress.

While working on *Three Days of the Condor*, Redford had acquired the rights to the book *All the President's Men*, had committed to producing and costarring in it, and was extremely involved with preproduction concerns. This was one reason that Dunaway found him so remote; but worse, Sidney Pollack also thought that his star was less reachable than usual. Pollack was entirely sympathetic with the fact that Redford had many chestnuts in the fire—"everybody wanted a piece of him," he recalled—but he was frustrated with trying to keep his star's mind on the project at hand. *Condor* was not an easy shoot, because Pollack was constantly having to wait until Redford was through with one phone call or meeting or another. There were constant delays, Redford was always late, and sometimes he didn't show up at all after a hasty, apologetic phone call.

Originally, Redford had not liked the idea of working too often with the same director. He thought it would be better to work with and learn from a variety of directors, some of whom might bring out different things in the actor. Then Redford realized that he and Pollack had come to know each other so well, and worked together so instinctively, that they hardly had to communicate; Pollack concurred, describing their on-set communications as a kind of shorthand. Each man understood what the other wanted and needed from him.

Although it received some good reviews, and was bolstered by contemporary reports of real-life CIA covert operations, *Three Days of the Condor* failed to rise above a prosaic level. A fight scene when a "mailman" tries to murder Redford is very well executed, but otherwise Pollack reveals no great touch for Hitchcock-like material; Hitchcock would never have touched this convoluted, prosaic script in the first place. Both Dunaway and Redford tried to deglamorize themselves—the latter with a pair of wire-rimmed glasses—but only the former was successful at it. Dunaway easily outacts Redford in their scenes together, but the whole business with Redford kidnapping her and keeping her prisoner in her apartment is contrived from start to finish; the obligatory love scene between them is particularly unconvincing. When Redford returns from lunch to find all the dead bodies of his colleagues, some of whom he appeared to be close to, his acting is on the college drama club level. *Three Days of the Condor* is the kind of movie in which people with no medical training can tell for certain that someone is dead and, therefore, never call an ambulance. Redford is much better when he's confronting CIA bigwig Cliff Robertson late in the picture. At the end Redford simply allows the hired killer—Max Von Sydow in a role that wastes his talents—to get away. The picture was "presented" by Dino De Laurentiis, prompting one critic to call it "De Laurentiis dumb." *Three Days of the Condor* made some money, but it hardly made a ripple in film history.

Redford's next film, however, would focus on some real-life political skullduggery. And it would be a very different story.

Redford wanted to star as Bob Woodward in the film version of Woodward and Bernstein's book, *All the President's Men*. He also wanted to produce it, and to that end he secured the rights to the best seller before it was even completed—for nearly half a million dollars of his own cash. Redford's suggestions to the two authors even influenced the direction they took in the manuscript. They had intended to tell the story from the burglars' point of view, but Redford convinced them instead to tell the story of their own investigation. Redford the producer hired William Goldman, the writer of *Butch Cassidy* and *The Great Waldo Pepper*, to do the script for *All the President's Men*.

Woodward, Bernstein, and even the *Washington Post* had to approve their depictions in the film, and hence the script. There was some concern that top directors would be skittish about working on the project, because they didn't like the star to be their boss—and the producer as well. And what if they couldn't get a costar as big as Redford to appear in the film? The only two who seemed right to play Carl Bernstein were Al Pacino and Dustin Hoffman; however, Hoffman agreed to do the film after reading Goldman's first draft.

In truth, Hoffman had tried to secure the book rights at the same time as Redford and was planning to offer $450,000. Redford was just a bit quicker and nailed the deal first. It was reported that Redford offered Hoffman the part of Bernstein as a way of apologizing, to mend fences, but he may simply have seen it as a smart move. Redford may have intuited that he would be blown off the screen by the more charismatic and dynamic (than Hoffman) Al Pacino. Redford did allow Hoffman to get top billing in the picture. Redford told reporters, "[Hoffman]'s a fantastic actor. Working with him is like working with a stream of pure electricity. He's so intense and fluid, you can't help but react." As previously noted, Hoffman and Redford, along with Gene Hackman, had been casual friends during their early New York City theater days; and the connection continued, more perhaps for Redford and Hackman than for Redford and Hoffman. "Redford I hardly see," Hoffman said, "because he spends all his time up in Utah, I suppose."

Redford initially had mixed emotions about playing Woodward; he felt the character was a bit plodding, and the role did not interest him as much as the part of the spirited madman in *One Flew Over the Cuckoo's Nest*, which he was offered. Having committed so much of his time, money, and energy to *All the President's Men*, he decided to stick with the Woodward role, with regrets. Jack Nicholson was given the part in *Cuckoo* and, a quirkier performer, proved to be a much better choice than Redford would have been. Redford had no real reason to regret his participation on-screen in *All the President's Men*, as it would prove a triumph for him in many ways.

Part of the problem, however, was that he wasn't certain how to play Bob Woodward, who told him "I'm a very, very boring person." Redford told him, "That's very nice, but you know I can't play a very boring man. And then I thought, why not?" He found his key to the role when he recognized that "Bob Woodward uses that bland polite exterior to hide the fact that he is really a killer. He'll charm and charm, he'll let Bernstein do all the dancing and flag-waving, and then he'll go for the throat to get a story. I liked that."

On July 2, 1975, a press conference was held at the Burbank Studios replica of the *Washington Post*'s newsroom, with Redford and Hoffman presiding. The set, which cost nearly half a million to build, took up two full sound stages. Over one hundred journalists crushed into the set, along with quite a few fans who were hoping to see or meet the stars. When one fan got too persistently close to Hoffman, he took that as his cue to lead the reporters on a tour of the duplicate news room while Redford kibitzed.

There was some worry about how the two stars, both of whom could be perfectionists in their own way, would get along while making the film. It was remembered by all that Hoffman had hoped to buy the rights and make the film himself, and he undoubtedly had his own ideas about how to proceed. (In his next film, *Marathon Man*,

Hoffman would force a frail and ill Laurence Olivier to rehearse a particular scene over and over and over again, despite the older actor's obvious discomfort.) However, things went smoothly for the most part, even though Redford and Hoffman did not see eye to eye on everything. Hoffman had some problems with the picture's cinema verité approach.

"I told Bob that he was drying the picture out," Hoffman recalled. "I said he should add a scene where Woodward and Bernstein were really having it out. But he didn't. I would have fought more, but by the time I saw the film, it was too late to make the radical changes I wanted. In my opinion, the film is a little too smooth. I would have left a few hairs on the lens." Still, in his public statements a gracious Hoffman was full of praise for his costar. "The film is really a landmark inasmuch as it's the first movie that really said anything even half-assedly true about the press. Bob deserves this success. Not to take anything away from Alan Pakula, who directed it, but this was Redford's project all the way. He may be the hardest working actor I've ever known."

More problems began when Goldman innocently referred to the true story of *All the President's Men* as "comic opera." Carl Bernstein took offense at this, as if it demeaned the seriousness of their effort, which was not Goldman's intention. After that Bernstein seemed not to involve himself much in the movie, although that turned out not to be the case. A big-name director agreed to do the film; but then it turned out that he was mad at Warner Studios, in the middle of suing them in fact, and had only said he'd do the picture to cause delays and hassles. He had no intention of being at the helm. The editors at the *Washington Post* took forever to approve the script because they objected to the jokes Goldman had inserted into sequences of their editorial meetings. Goldman found their response bizarre; he had heard the lines being spoken by these same editors when he sat in on their editorial conferences. The editors were afraid the gags made them look foolish.

Alan J. Pakula was tapped to direct the Woodward-Bernstein Watergate opus. He'd produced *Inside Daisy Clover* long ago and had since directed such films as the chilling political thriller *The Parallax View* (1974) with Warren Beatty, and Redford had admired his film *Klute* (1971). Redford had wanted to take on this challenge himself, but wisely realized he would be taking on too much if he did; he was sleeping only four hours each night as it was. Pakula couldn't make up his mind what he wanted and asked Goldman to write multiple versions of virtually every scene. Redford was sick of being in buddy movies—insecure about the homoerotic talk they engendered, perhaps—and insisted that Goldman insert several sequences involving Bernstein with a love interest. Redford's rationale was that the scenes would show how the budding affair was affected by Woodward's obsession with his investigations, but the sequences simply did not belong in the movie and were eventually scrapped. "I think he always knew a romance didn't belong in the picture and this picture always had a length problem," Goldman recalled. "It wanted to center on the two reporters and there was more than too much for them to do." Another problem for Redford was that both costar Hoffman and director Pakula were the type who liked to discuss scenes endlessly and do many different takes. Redford, who with every additional take was afraid that he was losing his edge, indulged them.

One afternoon Redford summoned Goldman to a meeting at the Redfords' New York apartment. When Goldman arrived, he saw Carl Bernstein and his future wife, Nora Ephron, sitting with Redford in the living room. Redford explained that the two had been quietly working on their own script of the book behind his back and asked Goldman to take a look at it. He explained that they were all on the same side; they all just wanted the best possible script, so maybe he could take a look and find something of use. Only one scene from this script made its way into the movie, and Goldman later claimed it was entirely fictional; he also noted that in Bernstein's version he had turned himself into something of a lover boy and Woodward into a kind of hero-worshipping sycophant of his. Goldman later recalled that he was appalled and hurt that Redford didn't defend his work—he had written three movies that starred Redford—and told Bernstein and Ephron what they could do with their script. Reportedly Redford did wryly tell Bernstein that "Errol Flynn is dead."

Goldman later conceded that Redford as producer was in a bit of a bind. A long, drawn-out battle with Bernstein might have only delayed and damaged the picture. "But I still think it was a gutless betrayal," he said. Woodward later apologized to Goldman for ever allowing Bernstein to write his own script. When news of this second script leaked out, it got around that Goldman had muffed the assignment, which was not true. One afternoon at CBS, a mutual acquaintance introduced Goldman to Walter Cronkite. All the famous newscaster said to Goldman was, "I hear you've got script trouble."

Goldman was not the only one to note that Redford had developed a bit of a "star attitude." Even though they and their respective wives and children had now known each other for years, even though Goldman was working for Redford as screenwriter, Redford would not give him his phone number. "In order for me to contact him, I would have to call his secretary, and she would then call him and he would then call me," Goldman remembered.

Jane Alexander remembers that she played, as she puts it, "the 'slush fund' bookkeeper who blew the whistle on John Mitchell. . . . It was a great film to be a part of, coming as it did on the heels of Nixon's 1974 resignation. Those of us of a liberal persuasion could feel self-righteous about our beliefs at last. Yes, we *were* right about the Vietnam War, and yes, Nixon *was* a dirty dog. But the film was more than just a historical triumph; filmically it was outstanding because the brilliant Alan Pakula directed it." Alexander received a supporting actress nomination for "my four minutes on screen." As for Redford, Alexander noted that "celebrities are the most generous people I know. Not only is Robert Redford extremely active with environmental organizations such as the National Resources Defense Council, but he founded the Sundance Institute in Utah to nurture independent film, making it the leading organization of its kind in America today. This could not have been accomplished without Redford's personal contribution of time and money."

Although time has stripped *All the President's Men* of some of its luster, it remains an excellent and absorbing film, and one of the best movies that Redford ever did. He was in at its conception—and even before, for that matter—and obviously cared very deeply about the film's quality and success. While Redford always exudes too much "success" and sheer confidence to come across as "hungry" as Bob Woodward was when the events took place, his performance is still quite good. Hoffman is as effective as always, if a little mushmouthed. The cinema verité approach works very well, and the film is superbly cast down to the smallest roles.

Redford had a reunion with Jason Robards, with whom he had acted so long ago in *The Iceman Cometh*. Robards recalled that "Redford was a committed actor, he cared about what he was doing, he gave it all he had, two hundred per cent." He observed that Redford had of course changed over the years, now that he had gone from newcomer to one of the most famous movie stars in the world, but he also noted that "even back then he was kind of cocky and confident underneath."

Many years before his involvement in *All the President's Men*, Redford had met Richard Nixon. It happened in Los Angeles at an event called Boys' Week, for which the thirteen-year-old Redford had won a special achievement award from school (this was clearly before the "rebellious" period that began a couple of years later). The trophies were presented by Governor Earl Warren and Nixon, who was then a senator. "I didn't have a clue who Nixon was," Redford recalled. "He handed me the award, shook my hand, spoke to me, and I absolutely got a chill. I thought, 'This man is as cold as ice—there's not a real bone in his body.'"

All the President's Men was eventually viewed—even by Redford—as having some unforeseen negative repercussions. "When did the press start snapping at its own tail?" wrote Michael Gross in his first media column for *GQ* in 1996. "It probably began with the film *All the President's Men* when Robert Redford and Dustin Hoffman played Watergate reporters Bob Woodward and Carl Bernstein and the public got the idea that reporting was glamorous work. Worse, reporters decided the same. Suddenly we didn't just write news and gossip; we *were* news and gossip." Then Liz Smith reported that during an interview on *Extra*, Redford said that after the film's success he saw reporters "drawn to journalism for the wrong reasons—less of truth-getting and more about getting exposure . . . at some point the news media was taken over by a profit-share mentality and there was less emphasis on news. Entertainment is an issue here, and you can feel it." Redford has also commented that whereas the reporters of *All the President's Men* had more than one source and double-checked everything, nowadays "rumors are printed as fact."

In June 2005, when W. Mark Felt of the FBI revealed that he had been "Deep Throat" and it was all over the news, DVD sales of *All the President's Men* began to soar. Redford told Chris Matthews of

MSNBC's *Hardball* that he was never told who Deep Throat was back when they were making the movie. "Obviously, that was a huge attraction for me," he said, "because of the cinematic, theatrical value. I queried it in the very beginning. And Bob and Carl—it was mostly Bob, because Bob had the contact not to reveal. And I chose to honor that. I didn't feel it was my position to be aggressive about it and I didn't." Redford said that he had not suspected Mark Felt but had always thought it must be someone in the FBI.

Neither Redford nor Hoffman received Academy Award nominations, although Jason Robards won Best Supporting Oscar and William Goldman was awarded the Best Screenplay statuette. The movie was also nominated for Best Picture and Best Director. Redford took some badly needed time off after making *All the President's Men*. He wanted to spend time with his family and work on a new solar home he was building on his property in Utah. He said at the time that he wanted to take at least a year off from the movie business, regardless of any momentum that might be lost. He needed his personal time, and that was that. But he still wound up spending a few days in front of a camera when he signed up for the monster production of *A Bridge Too Far*.

But in 1976 another project on Redford's mind was interesting him a lot more than *A Bridge Too Far*. Redford had always been interested in land preservation and the restoration of national parks, and he signed a contract to do a book that would reflect these concerns. *The Outlaw Trail* documented the actual route taken by many Old West desperadoes, including Butch Cassidy and the Sundance Kid, when escaping from their pursuers in a way that was considered foolproof. "[The trail] is in danger of total obliteration because so few people know about it," Redford told *Publishers Weekly*. "There's no hope unless someone tries to identify it, and some kind of heritage trust is arranged."

The book was expanded from an article in *National Geographic*. Redford and eight other men, including photographers, rode on the trail on horseback for three weeks. Traveling from Hole-in-the-Wall, Utah, to Circleville, Arizona, they gathered stories and took pictures that were generally described as "breathtaking." Redford and the others interviewed people living on or near the trail, including some descendants of the outlaws who'd used the trail to escape the minions of the law. One book critic opined that the book was "history told with flair" by Redford. Reportedly, Redford's prose was fixed up quite a bit by editors.

Joseph Levine was considered a real Hollywood character, a major independent producer who had come up from poverty and was not afraid to take risks and gamble on huge profits. He was the man who in 1957 had bought American rights to the Italian production of *Hercules,* starring Steve Reeves—which every studio had passed on. Levine then spent a fortune re-dubbing the film and promoting it heavily on television. Everyone thought he was crazy, but *Hercules* made over $20 million. After coming out with more prestigious films such as *The Graduate,* Levine, very rich, retired; then, nearing his seventies and bored, he decided to make a comeback. He bought the rights to Cornelius Ryan's book, *A Bridge Too Far,* and decided to make himself a blockbuster.

The $25 million production of *A Bridge Too Far* (1977) was Levine's attempt to make a movie from the real-life events of World War Two's "Operation Market Garden"—the subject of Ryan's book—in which General Montgomery hoped to end the war in one great thrust of cooperative efforts. Director Richard Attenborough had originally wanted Steve McQueen for the part Redford was to play, but McQueen made too many demands: an astronomical salary for a little over two weeks' work, and money to house his entire entourage on location during shooting. Attenborough might have met those terms; but the topper was that McQueen, who did not like to deal with realtors, demanded that Attenborough get the studio to buy his house for half a million. Although McQueen and Redford were not exactly interchangeable, Attenborough figured Redford would be much, much easier to work with. In any case, Redford received the highest salary—two million dollars.

A minor contretemps erupted when Sean Connery, who'd been hired for $250,000 to play Major General Roy Urquhart, commander of the First Airborne Division, read in the newspaper that Redford was being paid two million. "At first I thought it was a mistake," he remembered, "then I learned it wasn't. Now, considering the size of my part in the picture, the salary I'd agreed on seemed fair. But when I found out how much others were getting—for the same amount of work and with no more acting ability—it became unfair." Connery renegotiated with Levine, who gave him another $125,000 to keep him from walking. Connery might have walked had he known that American actors (besides Redford) such as Gene Hackman were receiving a cool million apiece for their participation.

Much of the film was shot in Deventer, near Arnhem, in the Netherlands. The production team numbered three hundred, and there seemed to be at least as many actors. Tanks, artillery, and aircraft of World War Two vintage—or reproductions thereof—were flown in from all over the world. The real-life events behind the sequence wherein boats filled with soldiers row across the river to capture the bridge caused some problems for screenwriter William Goldman. The Allied forces had originally planned to take the bridge at night, but the boats didn't arrive on time. It was then decided to mount the operation during the daytime, but when the boats—flimsy concoctions of canvas and plywood—were examined, they were deemed dangerous and inadequate. There also weren't enough oars. Still, there was no choice but to use the boats. At least, it was reasoned, the first wave of boats—led by Major Julian Cook (Redford's part)— would be camouflaged from what turned out to be armed and waiting Germans by a cover of smoke caused by deliberate Allied tank fire. Cook got into his designated boat with the troops, and everyone began rowing toward the bridge. Unfortunately, the wind came up and blew away all the smoke. The men were left out in the open, easy targets; a great many soldiers were slaughtered by German fire. Still, with the help of a second wave of Allied troops in the makeshift rowboats, the bridge was taken.

In the movie Cook/Redford is seen leading the first wave, which seems brave enough to begin with. But as William Goldman noted, "Sure, the first wave was a tremendous undertaking. But they *didn't* know that the Germans would be waiting for them, and they *thought* they had smoke cover. The second wave, standing there, watching it all, *knew* when their turn came they were going to get slaughtered. But when the boats returned, they got right in and rowed into the bloodbath." The second wave of this operation was referred to by one British general as "the single most heroic action of the war." Yet Goldman was frustrated that he lacked the resources and ability to depict this amazing, inspiring, and heartbreaking moment in the film.

"Even though it was true," he recalled, "I didn't know how to make it believable. The star [Redford] must be the center of the action. What's he supposed to be doing during all this [the second wave]—running up and down the embankment shouting encouragement?" So the true story of the horrible, wonderful sacrifice of all those young soldiers was itself sacrificed so that a movie star who had never seen combat could look heroic. The movie *could* have depicted the heroism and probable terror of the soldiers of the second wave as they rowed to their deaths, but this event was inexcusably excised. This is one of the most meretricious examples of how Hollywood can simply undermine humanity in the name of dollars and no sense.

Speaking of dollars, in addition to his hefty salary Redford nearly earned himself a financial overage of $125,000. A climactic scene involving his character was to be shot at the massive Nijmegen Bridge in Holland, but the actors and crew could film only from 8 a.m. until 9 a.m. and only on several successive Sundays. The rest of the time, the bridge would be in use. Each Sunday Redford, the other actors, and Attenborough and his crew would arrive at the bridge and film for one hour only. Finally, only one Sunday was left to finish the sequence before Redford was contractually free of his obligations to the film; it was also the last Sunday the bridge would be available according to Levine's arrangement. If the weather was bad, they would have to pay Redford overtime—that would account for the $125,000—to stay over until the following Sunday, assuming they would even be allowed to film on the bridge at all that day. The other 275 people in the cast and crew would also have to be paid extra. Although there was a lot of tension in the air that morning, the weather was good, the sequence was completed, and Redford flew back to the States. Redford gained the admiration of many crew members by pitching in and moving roadblocks along with everyone else.

As if Steve McQueen didn't have enough reasons to hate Redford, he was given one more on a March afternoon in 1977. He had just signed a contract to star in a film about the real-life bounty hunter, Tom Horn. That very same day, Redford announced that he was also developing a movie about Horn. "Every time I look in the rear view mirror," McQueen said, "I see ol' Bob." Redford decided there was no point in going ahead with his film, which the McQueen version would probably beat into theaters in any case. David Carradine decided to do a quickie TV version called *Mr. Horn*, while *Tom Horn* became McQueen's penultimate movie. Redford went on to other projects.

When making the film *The Electric Horseman* (1979) with director Sydney Pollack, Redford had a chance to deal with some of his ecological and animal rights concerns. In this movie Redford plays a former rodeo champ, Sonny Steele, who has been reduced—for rather good money, however—to becoming spokesman for a breakfast cereal. But Sonny is dissatisfied and heartsore and has taken to drink; his wife Charlotta (Valerie Perrine) has left him, and he's unhappy with his job. Worse, he's unhappy with the way his employers are treating their racehorse, Rising Star, which he is supposed to ride as part of a huge Vegas spectacular. On the big day Sonny rides out into the crowd on Rising Star, then continues through the casino and onto the Vegas strip and out of town. Turns out he doesn't like the way the horse is being drugged and intends to turn the animal—who he thinks has "more soul than most people"—loose in a canyon in Utah. Coming along for the ride is a television reporter, Ally Martin, who develops a brief romantic relationship with Sonny after a wary and combative beginning.

Redford's costar for *The Electric Horseman* (1979) was Jane Fonda, who got her asking price of one million bucks to play the role. As if that weren't enough, she looked forward to working with Redford (as both an actor and an activist) as well as director Sidney Pollack, who'd helmed *They Shoot Horses, Don't They?* in which Fonda had starred. Then there was the fact that the movie dealt with such matters as animal rights and the excesses of big business, both of which inflamed Fonda's passion and ire. Fonda also enjoyed being in St. George, Utah, where the movie was filmed; this was close to Redford's Sundance resort. Redford and Fonda were now the number-

Redford as a young actor in New York. (QR Photos)

Appearing on the TV show Moment of Fear *in the early 1960s. (QR Photos)*

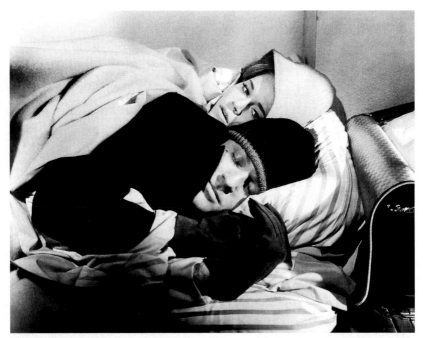

Redford and Jane Fonda as Paul and Corrie Bratter in the 1967 film Barefoot in the Park. *(© John Springer Collection/CORBIS)*

With Paul Newman in Redford's breakout film Butch Cassidy and the Sundance Kid. *(© John Springer Collection/CORBIS)*

Redford as the Great Waldo Pepper. (QR Photos)

Redford and journalist Bob Woodward, whom he portrayed in the 1976 film All the President's Men. *(QR Photos)*

Directing Mary Tyler Moore in the 1980 film Ordinary People.
(© Bettman/CORBIS)

Directing The Milagro Beanfield War *in 1986. (© Doug Menuez/CORBIS)*

Redford with granddaughter Lena at a gala dinner at the State Department in Washington as a 2005 Kennedy Center honoree.
(© Mike Theiler/Reuters/CORBIS)

one male and female box-office attractions in America, and the film was bound to make money—which it did. Fonda earned herself extra income and practically found herself with a new career by teaching exercises at night in the basement of a spa in St. George. This would lead into the Jane Fonda workout tapes that proved so successful.

One afternoon, a sequence of Fonda and Redford kissing kept being interrupted by thunderstorms that would blow up a squall and just as suddenly vanish. Fonda and Redford would wait for the thunder to recede, pucker up, start to kiss—and bam, back came the thunder. The 20-second sequence required 48 takes to satisfy the director; it cost $280,000 to shoot from different angles. "It would have been cheaper if I had kissed the horse," Redford said, "like in the old Gene Autry westerns."

"My playing Hunt Sears [Sonny's employer] in *The Electric Horseman*," says John Saxon, "must've come from Sydney Pollack's and Redford's memory of me in *War Hunt*. Though my agents thought it wasn't much of a part, I thought otherwise and jumped to do it; though it wasn't easy since Redford's and Pollack's careers and mine were now inverse to when we did *War Hunt* fifteen years before. At the 'looping session' of *Electric Horseman*, Redford complimented me for a 'textured performance.'" Saxon is very effective in the film.

The Electric Horseman has phony-baloney "star vehicle" written all over it, and it never ascends above that level no matter what the intentions. Although Redford looks great with a dark mustache against his lighter, loosely coiffed hair, he is completely miscast as an aw-shucks kind of guy. Sonny would have been a funny role had it been played by a performer with a lighter touch—Burt Reynolds, for instance—or by a genuinely grizzled character actor à la Broderick Crawford. Played by Redford, Sonny is never real; he's simply a romantic Hollywood symbol of ersatz activism.

Redford isn't even funny as a drunk. The movie's title comes from the way Sonny in his role as spokesman wears a white outfit with little electric lightbulbs on it as he rides around the stadium in a near stupor. (Some people joked that Redford's primary reason for taking the part wasn't its subtexts, but because he thought he looked great in the outfit!) Before one imagines that the actor had suddenly stopped worrying about his on-screen image—Sonny is more than a little dissipated, for instance—it must be remembered that the cowboy isn't an ugly drunk or alcoholic. Redford probably wouldn't have consented to play such a character, nor had the range to portray him convincingly.

It's hard to tell what everyone intended with *The Electric Horseman*, which has almost no entertainment value. According to Ray Stark, "the damn thing wasn't funny and it wasn't a drama and it didn't add up to much of anything if you ask me, but it made money and the stars looked good. What else is new?" Although *The Electric Horseman* is constructed like a comedy with serious overtones, it's amusing only in fits and starts. Redford and Fonda are not exactly Hepburn and Tracy, but even that famous couple couldn't make something out of nothing. Scenes that might have looked funny on paper barely get a giggle due to the miscasting and the heavy, overproduced quality of the picture. Everyone and everything lacks the light touch. The characters—such as they are—are lost in widescreen vistas. All the viewer takes away from the film is that Jane Fonda is arguably more attractive in this movie than she was during her Roger Vadim/*Barbarella*/sex-kitten phase.

The movie also doesn't come to terms with the fact that Sonny could have brought attention to the animal's plight *without* running off with a twelve-million-dollar racehorse and risking arrest. The idea that he felt it was the only way he could get attention is invalid for the simple reason that throughout the first half of the film, Fonda is *constantly* trying to get an interview with Sonny—with instant access to the media, why didn't he just tell her what was bothering him? Of course then there would have been no movie. Although there are a few well-staged sequences—such as the cops chasing after Sonny—*The Electric Horseman* is a good example of how Redford allowed his private and public concerns to dictate his often extremely poor movie choices.

Redford did not just see himself as a movie star. He saw himself as a man who was committed to quality, a serious Man of Film who believed in the medium's power to enlighten, educate, and transform. He made the occasional mindless movie for the money—he and his family lived well and lived alone, sheltered by the isolation that only money could buy—but he really wanted to make films that *said*

something, that had real characters doing real things; he wanted to be part of the cinema of substance. But he figured the studios with their big budgets were never going to be behind projects such as these, movies that would undeniably be deemed risky—if not utter losers—at the box office. Redford would eventually prove, along with other filmmakers, that a project could be serious, meaningful, full of three-dimensional characters, and still make money; but he would think of such ventures as being independent *spirited* even if they originated with a studio. He saw independent films—films that were not made under the auspices of any major or minor studio—as being the saviors of cinema. "Indies" were the movies made by the driven and passionate filmmakers who had something personal and important to say. How ironic that Redford would inadvertently help bring about a climate in which independent films increasingly resembled the types of studio movies for which they were supposed to be the antidote.

There was a time when the phrase "independent films" made people think of movies produced on a very low budget, featuring amateur actors and grainy film stock, filmed in the director's garage in black and white and in 16mm, and financed with mommy and daddy's credit cards or by a trust fund. Many of these films were worthless, but now and then something came along that indicated genuine promise and artistry, that struck a chord; the story and characters or the sheer originality triumphed over poor and even inept production values. There were even a few genre gems that offered something different and less formulaic than the standard studio item. In 1962 Herk Harvey of Lawrence, Kansas, put together a cheap but imaginative horror film called *Carnival of Souls*. Filmed entirely on location, it boasted interesting and professional acting and some eerie and outstanding sequences. It eventually became a cult item. Independent films were an exhilarating, often exasperating alternative to the more polished but often less fertile Hollywood product. Redford would always remember his struggles to get *Downhill Racer* financed, made, and distributed—it was not an independent, but an "independent spirited" production—and the disappointments that followed. Because of it, he wanted to make things easier for those who wanted to follow the independent route.

Redford was getting a big idea. And he could not have imagined what a mighty oak would grow from this acorn, or the far-reaching consequences it would have on the film industry in the not-so-distant future. But that would have to wait, because Redford was also very much a family man. And his family needed him.

Since age fifteen, Redford's son Jamie had suffered from poor health. Although Redford did his best to shield his children from the spotlight, some theorized that Jamie's conditions were psychosomatic, caused by having an intense, driven father, a mother who repressed her own ambitions, and the unspoken tensions between the two. Others simply thought the boy's various health concerns were a reaction to an overprotective, almost smothering maternal presence and an almost inevitable paternal absence due to the long weeks when his father was away from home making movies. In truth, Redford tried to be with his family as much as possible, but it may not have been enough. In any case, the Redfords took their son to doctor after doctor; but no one could seem to diagnose what was causing Jamie's frequent bouts of flu-like symptoms, during which he endured attacks of chills and cramps. Sometimes he had an alarmingly high fever, and at other times he was too exhausted even to get out of bed. The parents, as parents do, wondered if he was sneaking liquor or drugs.

But it turned out that Jamie's problems had an organic cause; in 1980, he was finally diagnosed with ulcerative colitis. Colitis is a serious, painful disease of the large intestine that can ultimately destroy the colon. Jamie was given medications and told to go on with his life as best he could. For their part, his family hoped that no complications of colitis, of which there were many, would make his situation even worse. If it is true that you're only as happy as your unhappiest child, Redford must have carried with him a constant worry over his son, a pain that existed somewhere below the surface of whatever deal or film he was making. Luckily, Jamie—a nice-looking young man with his father's eyes, smile, and hair, if not his "movie star" aura—was said to be a plucky fellow who would take life's challenges as they came.

In the meantime, Redford continued to apply his social conscience in choosing the movies he appeared in, such as *Brubaker* (1980). Brubaker was based on the experiences of Thomas Murton, who in 1968 was briefly employed as a warden at the Cummins Prison Farm in Arkansas. One day an elderly prisoner led Murton to a spot where three "escapees"—who'd allegedly been tortured and beaten to death—were buried in wooden coffins. Murton, who raised a fuss about this and other matters, was fired soon after for having substandard administrative abilities. He further claimed that he was almost accused of grave-robbing as well.

Murton, who became a chicken farmer—a profession for which his opponents felt he was more suited—shopped his story around for years in the hopes that it would be made into a film. Ron Silverman, who produced the movie, took it from studio to studio and did his best to interest a star in the script. The film would never have been made without Redford's name attached. "Although the events of the movie do not follow the specific chronology of my days in Arkansas," said Murton, "the situation of the prison, and the prisoners, is true."

The first director assigned to the film was Bob Rafelson, who'd had hits with *Five Easy Pieces* and other films. Rafelson came to prominence in the seventies, when the director was king and superstar—the actors were almost secondary—and there was no way he was going to take orders or even suggestions from any movie star, even one as big as Robert Redford. Almost from the start, Redford and Rafelson had operatic quarrels that drew the attention of the news media. Rafelson eventually was fired; Redford's participation was seen as far more crucial than the director's. Stuart Rosenberg was chosen as the new director because he had helmed the very successful Paul Newman convict picture *Cool Hand Luke* (1967).

Brubaker is a well-made picture on the subject of prison reform, with Redford giving a solid performance—one of his best, in fact—in the title role of the new warden at the Wakefield prison. The movie's improbable opening scenes have *Brubaker* pretending to be a convict himself, mingling with the inmates and seeing how conditions are firsthand. This dramatic license may have served only to baffle audience members who had already read about the picture, knew Redford played the warden, and wondered what he was doing in jail. Like virtually all movies of the prison reform genre over the years,

Brubaker downplays whatever horrendous crimes the prisoners may have committed to get them locked up. The movie focuses on the more redeemable inmates, although early on Brubaker does say to the men that "most of you belong here."

As Brubaker sets about making his reforms, he discovers that his biggest obstacle is the prison reform board, which advises him to let it go when he discovers that the bodies of murdered men are buried on the prison grounds. How can we lock these men up for murder, he asks, and then turn around and let these murders right here go uninvestigated and unpunished? In another dramatic but suspect sequence, the inmates start clapping for Brubaker as he leaves the prison. Redford had a large and talented supporting cast in *Brubaker*, including Jane Alexander, David Keith, Morgan Freeman, John McMartin, and many others. Redford not only holds his own in the film, but again shows what a good listener he can be as the other actors emote. Of his performance, the *Boston Globe* opined: "[Redford] makes it look easy. He tempers the character's righteous indignation with a smattering of naturalism. He understands the necessity for understatement in a film that is overcrowded with acts of physical and psychological violence."

As the filming began to run overtime, however, Redford started to stress out. He was supposed to be doing preproduction on the first film he would direct, *Ordinary People*, and *Brubaker* was still not completed. He was understandably tense and irritable as the filming went one week over, then two, until finally being completed three whole weeks behind schedule.

Redford then flew off to Chicago to get to work on what he considered his most important film project to date.

Two of the many properties that studios hoped Robert Redford would star in came from best-selling novels: James Clavell's *Shogun* and Colleen McCullough's *The Thorn Birds*. Richard Chamberlain, TV's *Dr. Kildare*, itched to play Blackthorne in *Shogun* and the priest in *Thorn Birds* on television, but his William Morris agent told him they were to be major motion pictures with Redford as star. Australian filmmaker Peter Weir planned to direct Redford as Father Ralph de Bricassart in *Thorn Birds*. Chamberlain, possibly more handsome than Redford, remembered Bob from when he had played a supporting role on a *Dr. Kildare* episode; now Redford was a superstar. Disappointed, Chamberlain bided his time, knowing it would be hard in both cases for a screenwriter to whittle a massive novel down to a mere two hours for theatrical release. This insight proved correct; justice couldn't be done to the books in just a few hours. The rights for *Shogun* were sold to NBC television and *Thorn Birds* to ABC. Starring in both productions, Chamberlain became king of the miniseries. As for Redford, he had other fish to fry.

Redford was the most popular choice to star as the Man of Steel in Warner Brothers' multimillion-dollar adaptation of *Superman*, but he refused to commit until he saw the finished script, which was being endlessly tinkered with by a variety of writers. Redford's salary demands were also off-putting to the studio. His former costar, Gene Hackman (*Downhill Racer, A Bridge Too Far*), was signed, along with Marlon Brando; but negotiations with Redford eventually fell through. Christopher Reeve, a relative unknown who was closer in appearance to the Man from Krypton, was signed. We wonder if Redford would have allowed his hair to be dyed Superman-black if he had agreed to do the film.

The father-and-son producer team of Alexander and Ilya Salkind were behind *Superman: The Movie*. As Ilya remembered, "The main drama was the casting of Superman himself. I was under incredible pressure from my father who said we needed a name. I argued with him about that but he was adamant. So I made an offer to Robert Redford. I knew it wouldn't work out because everyone would say 'That's Robert Redford flying,' and it would have been a joke. He turned it down because he didn't think it was right for him, so I was really pleased."

Redford never regrets turning down certain roles that he simply isn't interested in, no matter how successful the films might eventually become. Along with *Superman*, *The Godfather*, and *Who's Afraid of Virginia Woolf?* he nixed *The French Connection*, *Love Story*, and many others. Like Steve McQueen, Jack Nicholson, and Al Pacino, he passed on spending months in the jungle with Francis Ford Coppola to make *Apocalypse Now*. Producer Dino De Laurentiis fired director Robert Altman, who didn't want to use Redford in *Ragtime*, but Redford passed on the project anyway. Occasionally he was considered for a part he didn't get or wasn't offered, such as the role in *Presumed Innocent* that went to Harrison Ford.

Redford's old friend, supporter, and costar Natalie Wood was desperate to play the part of the mother in *Ordinary People* and probably felt she had the inside track. She was not only a proven talent, a genuine movie star who had handled many a dramatic part with aplomb; she was Redford's friend and had given him his first Hollywood break. Now it was Natalie who needed a break. She had a couple of unremarkable feature films coming up, but otherwise she'd appeared in only one picture in ten years, focusing instead on her marriage and children. "You don't come back easy," Redford noted. By the time he heard that Natalie was interested in the part, he had already pretty much decided on using Mary Tyler Moore. "I would have loved to have made it work [with Natalie]," Redford said, "but I couldn't. Natalie had requested just a conversation about it, and that was kind of painful. I would have loved to have done it, but I just didn't see her for that particular role." Because Mary Tyler Moore was not exactly a box-office draw at the time, Redford couldn't be accused of blowing off Natalie because she was no longer a top-tier star. When Natalie drowned in 1981, Redford was haunted by the fact that their last contact before her death had been awkward and negative. Redford may never have loved Natalie the way she had loved him, but his feelings for the woman were always sincere. "She was a good soul," he said.

Redford told Mary Tyler Moore that he had seen her in the part of the mother, Beth Jarrett, as he read Judith Rossner's novel. Redford and Moore had occasionally crossed paths while walking on Malibu Beach. Redford told Moore that he would spot her and wonder about what might be her "dark side." Moore had heard that Redford wanted everyone to respect his privacy, so whenever she spotted him walking toward her, she looked down at her feet and walked by as quickly as possible. The two had never spoken until she was considered for the role of Beth Jarrett.

Mary Tyler Moore was not coming from a good place. Her long-running and successful sitcom, *The Mary Tyler Moore Show*, had gone off the air. An attempt at a comeback with a new show, *Mary*, had failed. Before doing *Mary Tyler Moore*, she had appeared in Elvis Presley's final film, *Change of Habit* (1969), and in *Don't Just Stand There* (1968) with Robert Wagner; but efforts to reignite her film career after TV stardom didn't pan out. Her marriage to producer Grant Tinker was unraveling painfully, and she was drinking heavily. After arguing with Tinker, she would drive drunk through Brentwood from Sunset Boulevard to Santa Monica Boulevard, running stop signs in a desperate game of Russian roulette.

When Moore heard that Redford wanted to talk to her about the possibility of appearing in *Ordinary People*, she was anxious to meet with him but also nervous. At the studio, Redford immediately put Moore at ease with his casual charm, but he told her that he was concerned that her television image of Mary Richards would impress itself a bit too firmly on Beth Jarrett. Redford told Moore than he felt that Beth's relationship with her surviving son was similar to the relationship he'd had with his own father. Moore empathized, having had a difficult relationship with her own father.

As Moore saw the character, "Everything Beth despised, she was herself. But no matter how far down she pushed it, she recognized herself in her surviving son, Conrad. He was the embodiment of her failure as a woman and as a mother. Conrad had fallen apart; his attempted suicide was the prophecy of her own unworthiness. She couldn't forgive him for betraying her."

Of Redford, Moore recalled that he was "warm and funny, and so charming that within minutes I forgot who he was. Reality, however, would call to me from time to time. I would be immersed in his vision of the story and its characters, even making an intelligent comment or two myself, when I would feel a thunk in my chest as my mind screamed out—THIS IS ROBERT REDFORD! Then I'd have to summon all my discipline to return to the conversation we were having, without revealing my little lapse."

Moore left the studio with no firm commitment from Redford. He later told her that he would stand on a rock—which he later showed her—near a high cliff at Sundance and think about her day after day, "trying to make the decision to put you in the film or not." When *Ordinary People* opened in Utah, Redford invited Moore and the other actors to his home for the weekend.

Although Redford never seriously considered casting another actress, he just couldn't make up his mind about Moore. Moore's agent, John Gaines, made frequent calls to the studio but could never get a commitment. Everyone assumed the main problem was that Redford feared the casting of "Mary Richards" would ruin his movie. Even if Moore's performance was exceptional, her casting might mean people wouldn't take the film seriously.

Gaines hit upon a unique idea. The producer of the Broadway hit *Whose Life Is It Anyway?* needed a replacement for Tom Conti and wanted to hire another of Gaines's clients, Richard Thomas. Thomas was making a movie, however, and Gaines impulsively suggested Moore. Moore agreed to do the play. Gaines felt that it couldn't hurt if Redford and Paramount knew that she was going to appear in a serious theater piece—a far cry from *The Mary Tyler Moore Show*— before *Ordinary People* was released. If all went well, she would prove that she was more than "Mary Richards" long before the picture opened.

While Moore's Broadway assignment may not have done that much to convince Redford to hire her—he had seen her in the part from the first—it may have helped to convince some studio naysayers that she had the stuff for the role. Still, Redford needed more proof before signing her. Three months after their initial meeting, he asked Moore to come in and read with Donald Sutherland. Although Sutherland had originally been cast as the psychiatrist (played by Judd Hirsch in the film), when Sutherland asked Redford if he could play the husband, Redford complied.

The reading with Sutherland went well, and Moore was signed to the role of Beth Jarrett. Moore was impressed with Redford's directorial technique, which she found differed greatly from the TV approach. "Bob touched more responders in the process of character development and integration of that person than I'd ever experienced," she recalled. "By the time filming began, there wasn't a situation in which I couldn't imagine just how Beth would feel and how she might behave." Redford found that he kept having to strip Moore of all of her "Mary-isms," gestures and line readings that had become a part of her after playing Mary Richards for so many years but that would be inappropriate for Beth Jarrett. Redford was seen as a perfectionist by many involved in the film. He kept at the actors for take after take after take, until they were giving him exactly what he wanted. For the last take, the actors had to stick to the blocking (their movements in relation to one another and the camera) that had been worked out for them; but otherwise they had free reign, keeping in mind all that they had learned, all the various approaches, from the preceding takes. Redford hoped they would always go for the unexpected.

One scene that Redford filmed repeatedly was one in which Moore simply had to place a cake in the refrigerator and close the door. Whenever they got done early, they'd go do the cake scene again, but Redford was never satisfied. "Bob was looking for a glimpse of the woman's soul," Moore reflected.

Moore entered into an affair—her first—with a fellow cast member while making *Ordinary People*. "When he touched me that first time with such intense passion and curiosity, I thought I'd die from pleasure," she recalled. The man made her feel young and quelled her restlessness. It was a temporary, on-set affair—the man was also married—that meant a great deal at the time but was never expected to last past the final day of shooting, and didn't. Moore discovered her husband was also having an affair.

During preproduction, Redford contacted Gene Hackman and offered him a part in the film. Afterward, Hackman was uncertain about whether he'd been offered the role of the father, played by Donald Sutherland, or the psychiatrist, played by Judd Hirsch. "We just couldn't make a deal," Hackman said. "I would have loved to have done that film, but I wanted some points, and they were willing to give me points but not enough to make the picture feasible. It was just one of those deals that fell apart." Reportedly, Hackman had some concerns about the script and characterization, but Redford wasn't willing to bend on these areas.

Ordinary People tells the story of the upper-middle-class Jarrett family, whose picture-perfect life has been shattered by the tragic drowning death of the older son, Buck. Feeling survivor's guilt, the younger brother, Conrad (Timothy Hutton)—who was also on the boat at the time of Buck's death—attempts suicide and is institutionalized. His father, Calvin (Donald Sutherland), is a warm, loving presence who does his best to care for a son he doesn't quite understand; but his mother, Beth (Mary Tyler Moore), who loved Buck unconditionally, is embarrassed by Conrad's emotional problems and unable to give him the love and affection he needs. Conrad bonds with a caring, unsentimental therapist (Judd Hirsch) who helps him acknowledge and deal with his guilt and pain, especially after a young woman he met in the hospital commits suicide. Disgusted with what he sees as his wife's coldness and lack of compassion for her own son, Calvin tells Beth that he thinks he no longer loves her. Beth packs up and leaves as father and son try to come to terms with what has happened.

Redford really hit one out of the ballpark with his first directorial effort. *Ordinary People* is a first-class drama full of lovely scenes, a fine attention to detail, superior acting, and a willingness to deal intelligently and unapologetically with matters of *emotion*. The film begins with shots of lonely roads and vacant parks that resonate with the uncertainty, loss, and loneliness of the story that follows. There are quietly powerful moments, such as the scene when Beth refuses to be photographed with Conrad, and the scene when Beth sits in her dead son's room, looks up, is startled by Buck standing in the doorway—until she realizes it is only Conrad. After his friend's suicide, as Conrad washes his hands in the faucet, the water running over the scars on his wrists and into the sink turns into the waves around the boat, in a flashback to the tragedy. (These flashbacks are interspersed throughout the film and always occur at appropriate moments.) There's the quick shot of the disassociated man sitting alone and bored during a party as so-called friends chatter and laugh all around him. The picture is never mawkish or particularly manipulative—it is in no way "soap opera"—which makes it all the more remarkable that it works so well. Hanging over the film, although never stated outright, is the terrible but undeniable notion that Beth simply feels the wrong son died.

Redford drew excellent performances from his cast. Mary Tyler Moore gives a strong, careful interpretation that never descends into superbitch or "Craig's wife" caricature, which it easily could have. Redford managed to reign in Donald Sutherland, who can go way overboard in certain roles, and helped him to give one of his loveliest and most solid performances. Sutherland shows emotion with the kind of subtlety and underplaying that Redford's proponents would say is in the style of Redford. Best of all, Redford—after some give-and-take, arguing, soul searching, and subdued hysteria—allowed Timothy Hutton to give a no-holds-barred emotional performance that at no time can be confused with scenery chewing or overacting. Hutton's portrayal is carefully built and skillfully layered. It is the type of intelligently expressive and volatile performance that Redford himself—at least the Redford of the movies, as opposed to the Redford of the theater—could probably never be capable of, or at the very least would simply be loathe to do. (Hutton should have been awarded the Best Actor Oscar but received an Oscar for Best *Supporting* Actor instead. This is ludicrous. Although fourth-billed after the other three principals, Hutton's name is still above the title and he had the pivotal role and the largest part.) "When Redford asked me to try out for the role as the son in *Ordinary People*, I was flattered," said Hutton. Although he had appeared in some TV dramas, this was his very first theatrical motion picture. "When I got it, I was flabbergasted. I was lucky."

As the therapist, Judd Hirsh pretty much reminds you of his nice-guy cabdriver portrayal on the sitcom *Taxi*, but he is nevertheless effective. Redford wanted someone who didn't come off like the stereotypical shrink, and in this Hirsch certainly succeeded. Dinah Manoff, Lee Grant's daughter and a fine actress in her own right, has a nice bit as Karen, the friend from the hospital who seems so happy and well-adjusted but winds up killing herself. Manoff allows signs of her character's underlying disturbance to come through.

Ordinary People isn't perfect. You don't get a sense from the breakfast scene that opens the film that a tragedy has occurred in this household; but then again, Redford may have wanted to start with a mundane, bucolic portrait and slowly introduce the characters' dysfunction. The ending, with Beth's abrupt departure, seems contrived to create a dramatic coda to the proceedings, and she never quite seems like the monster she is presumed to be. Her true feelings are never really explored—the other characters simply bounce their feelings off of her. She can be warm and loving to her husband, and when she criticizes him for telling people that Conrad is seeing a shrink, she does have a point; it's not anybody else's business. Of course, she's more afraid of scandal and humiliation—what the neighbors will think—then she is of how Conrad will feel. Beth is not a one-note character, but perhaps she isn't allowed a complete rendering, either.

Near the end of a screening for *Ordinary People*, an unpleasant moment occurred when a loud, rude laugh erupted into the air. Julia Phillips had made a remark to a companion which was guaranteed to get him to hoot. Phillips, who by her own admission became a cocaine addict, had deliberately created the distraction. She later explained that Redford had "snubbed" her in the Paramount commissary after asking to see a picture of her child. By the time Phillips extracted the photo from her wallet, according to her, Redford had taken a powder. But many saw her as a rather ditzy, self-absorbed person who easily took umbrage at the slightest infractions and held grudges for a lifetime.

Ordinary People won almost universal praise from the critics, and Redford won the Oscar for Best Director. Alvin Sargent brought home a statue as screenwriter, and the movie won Best Picture. Setting aside all of the assorted considerations and behind-the-scenes maneuverings that go into achieving Oscar nominations, this was no sop to the "pretty boy" and his little movie; *Ordinary People* was a genuine picture of quality. How ironic that an actor so reticent himself to portray strong, genuine emotion on screen should direct—and direct not only capably, but beautifully—a film that was so gloriously awash in it.

Wrote the *Boston Globe*: "Robert Redford, the director of this film, doesn't appear in it. Yet it resonates with a sensitivity and sympathy to nuance that contrasts notably in tone to most of the movies in which he has appeared. It is an astonishing debut for Redford. . . . [*Ordinary People*] is flawed. It's too careful, obviously a debut film by a director who is serious and wants to be taken seriously. But its fierce determination to avoid sentimentality redeems it and makes it linger in the memory."

One afternoon when Redford was in Connecticut looking for houses to use in *Ordinary People*, he dropped by the home of screenwriter Jay Presson Allen. In the living room Redford saw the script for *The Verdict* on a coffee table, and he asked Allen if he could read it. It was then well known to everyone that Redford was as interested in directing as he was in acting. Redford called the film's producers, Richard Zanuck and David Brown of *Jaws* fame, and asked for a meeting. Redford told them that he was interested in doing the movie because of the subject matter but was not a great admirer of Allen's screenplay. He thought they should get writer-director James Bridges, who'd done *The China Syndrome* with Jane Fonda, to do a rewrite. Bridges made two attempts to revise the script, and Redford rejected both of them.

Several months went by; as Bridges worked on yet a third version, Zanuck and Brown seethed with impatience. By then Redford had been announced as the star of the film, but it seemed to be taking forever for somebody to write a script that he would approve. Redford summarily rejected Bridges's third draft. Finally the problem came to light. According to William Goldman, "Redford is still interested in doing a movie about medical malpractice—but the main role, that of the lawyer, Galvin, that's the problem. He's a boozer and a womanizer and Zanuck and Brown hear that Redford thinks the character could be bad for his image." Zanuck and Brown wondered why Redford couldn't have made that clear from the first, although altering the character would have stripped the storyline of much of its power. Redford's concern with "image" was also seen as quaint and old-fashioned and a little exasperating. As one observer put it, "'Image' was something the stars under the old studio system worried about. By the 1980s, if not long before, real actors were more interested in meaty parts than they were in preserving an image that was probably false to begin with."

Zanuck had finally had enough with his star when he found out that Redford was having talks behind his back with his buddy and favorite director, Sydney Pollack. Although Zanuck could not technically fire Redford, because the actor had not yet signed the contract, he did call his agent and tell him they were no longer interested in Redford's participation. Zanuck went public with his fury at what he felt was Redford's off-putting and selfish behavior. Eventually Sidney Lumet was signed to direct *The Verdict.* According to William Goldman, "When Lumet was announced, word seeped down that Redford was available." The part went to Paul Newman anyway.

In November of 1979, before the release of *Ordinary People*, Redford held the first of what would be many three-day filmmakers' conferences at his ski-lodge home in Utah. This would be the beginning of the Sundance Institute—his big idea—which was dedicated to nurturing and preserving the spirit of independent filmmaking. Redford had noticed that the film business had changed a lot since his early days; he saw that many talented people were being shut out of the monolithic system of the massive studios. Minorities and women, in particular, were having a tough time breaking in. He hoped to change that with the institute, which he named after the outlaw he played in *Butch Cassidy* to indicate that Sundance would be helping those who worked outside the system. There was a time when many great filmmakers had started out as "indies" and moved on to the majors, but that no longer seemed to be the case.

A roster of top-name talent attended the conference, which was very informal. Redford and special guests were clad in jeans and boots, and Redford served beer from his in-house bar. Redford told everyone that while the conference had been his idea, he was not "in charge" as such. He was there to listen and share ideas along with everyone else. Eventually this little weekend conference would grow into what seemed to many a giant industry that was far, far from its alleged indie roots. After the release and success of *Ordinary People*, Redford was given the generally affectionate nickname of "Ordinary Bob," a response to his self-effacement, his insistence that everyone should forget that he was Robert Redford, movie star (which, of course, is something that no movie star ever wants *anyone* to forget).

During the conference Redford spoke often of diversity and the need for "unique voices" to be heard. According to one source, "Bob was completely serious about this. Sure he called it the Sundance Institute but he had to name it something, and he knew the use of his name or something along those lines would attract people who could help. This was not a ploy or a stunt. He truly *believed* in independent filmmaking and wanted to do something to help. He wanted to give something back. I suspect he has always been a little bit embarrassed by his success, how easy it came for him with his looks and so on. But he really believed in the notion behind the Sundance Institute."

Redford did not have time to run the Sundance Institute himself, but he kept it in the family and hired Lola's cousin, Sterling Van Wagenen. Some people wondered about this act of nepotism, because Sterling's only real experience had been running the not exactly prestigious U.S. Film Festival. Van Wagenen served as an administrator who reported to a board comprised of a few independent filmmakers, executives from assorted foundations, and a smattering of Hollywood types. Redford was annoyed when in 1986 Van Wagenen took a leave of absence to produce a movie based on Horton Foote's *Trip to Bountiful*, starring Geraldine Page. Redford was even more annoyed when Van Wagenen came back the following year to resume his duties at Sundance.

Relations between Redford and Van Wagenen soured when Bob acquired the rights to a screenplay adaptation of a 1940s novel called *The Giant Joshua*. At first Redford tried to buy the screenplay; but the writers, John and Denise Earle, didn't care for what they felt was his condescending attitude toward them and the script. Van Wagenen then made an offer, upping the ante, and told them he wanted to produce it himself. He went to Redford and told him he had bought the movie as a Robert Redford Project, asking him if he would direct it; Redford agreed. But as time went by, Redford realized that Van Wagenen not only wanted to produce the movie, but had decided to direct it as well. "I was suddenly out of it and being asked to have my company make it," said Redford. Redford felt not only used, but bamboozled; it was only because his name was attached to the script that Van Wagenen had been able to get financing for the film in the first place. Now Bob was going to be shunted aside.

Still, Van Wagenen cast Redford as the villain of the piece. He got financing and decided to hire Vanessa Redgrave for the leading role. Then, according to him, "Bob pulled the plug." Others got on the bandwagon to denounce Redford, claiming that he wanted to keep Van Wagenen as his gofer and that he'd told Carolco the picture could never be made for the money they had set aside for it. In short, Redford was supposedly creating one obstacle after another. It was conveniently forgotten that Redford had been used, and he had never liked being used. Van Wagenen stayed on the board for the Sundance Institute for a few years but was replaced as director. Redford stopped taking his phone calls.

"There are two ways of looking at this," says a Sundance insider who spoke on condition of anonymity. "Sterling didn't understand that most movie stars have an absolute horror of being used, having their name used, bandied about just in order to get something for a third party. They feel *exploited*. On the other hand, Bob didn't understand that Sterling was simply looking for a chance to do something he'd always wanted to do, he was looking for his big break, you might say. It was only what Bob himself had been looking for, a way *in*, in the early days of his career. I don't think it's that Bob wanted Sterling to keep running things for him for the rest of his life, but he'd felt he'd given him a big chance when he made the appointment, and maybe he felt that Sterling had taken advantage of him."

Redford filled Van Wagenen's shoes with a man named Gary Beer, who became executive vice president. Beer rubbed some people the wrong way. One staffer suggested that judging from his expense account, Beer didn't seem to understand that he was working for a nonprofit organization. Others saw him as a yes man and toady who was bought and paid for by Robert Redford. Reportedly Redford cautioned Beer about "fat-cat behavior." Some people felt that much of the hostility toward Beer was created and confused because Sundance had multiple personalities—the resort, the institute, and the Sundance Group, whose purpose was to develop business opportunities for Redford. Beer was eventually transferred to this group, and Redford hired Tom Wilhite as Beer's replacement in 1988. Wilhite was in no way perceived as a yes man—which is why, it is theorized, he and Redford failed to bond and Wilhite didn't last long in his job.

Another bone of contention was the relationship between the Sundance Resort and the Sundance Institute. Redford had turned some of his acreage into the Sundance Resort, a ski and sun lodge whose profits were supposed to support the institute and its various programs. But the resort did not do as well as Redford hoped, and it turned out that the creation of the institute inadvertently helped keep the resort in business. The institute rented the resort's cottages for its indie filmmakers and the pros who helped them in the summer lab. All food for the lab and the institute came from the resort, even though it could have been bought from other vendors at cheaper prices.

In June 1981 Sundance held the first of its annual labs. At these labs independent filmmakers, raw new talent, worked on their scripts and the films that resulted. They were assisted by Hollywood professionals who were drafted for the cause by Redford. Seven scripts were chosen to receive the treatment, with the pros aiding, abetting, and critiquing the amateurs on every aspect of film production— from writing to directing to editing. In its first few years the lab had a definite road-show atmosphere, as the ski lodge's rooms were converted into makeshift stages and editing and screening rooms. Eventually these rough edges would be smoothed over. Despite the inevitable criticisms, many filmmakers were eternally grateful for the knowledge they acquired and the chances they were given at the Sundance Lab.

Redford was not always crazy about the types of scripts that were accepted into the lab. It was suggested that they would attract a higher quality of screenplay and even more gifted filmmakers if they could offer actual production. Redford was wary of this idea, especially of the staggering costs it would incur. They might have to go to the studios for financing, thus defeating the whole purpose of having an indie film lab. Redford at first wanted to avoid a commercial aspect at all costs. Then he thought it might be a good idea to emphasize that very aspect, figuring many aspiring filmmakers would have more enthusiasm if they felt their movie might actually get made.

What Redford didn't reckon with is that the type of indie filmmakers Sundance wanted to work with had absolutely no desire—then—to work on any project that might be deemed commercial, especially in Hollywood terms.

Nevertheless, a Production Assistance Fund was set up. Among the recipients of its largesse was a film entitled *Desert Bloom*, which was released theatrically in 1986 but started out as a Sundance Lab project three years earlier. The film was written by Linda Remy and Eugene Corr, who also directed. At first the filmmakers were thrilled, not only because of their treatment at Sundance but also because the institute opened doors that would otherwise have been closed to them, getting them in touch with important professionals. The magic words "Robert Redford" had opened those doors; but later, Remy and Corr charged that the actor also felt that it gave him the right to "meddle." Remy later claimed that although they were allowed to interview anyone they chose, Redford reserved the right to make the final choice. She also charged that Redford locked Corr out of the editing room and "took over" the film in a way that was every bit as pernicious as that of the studios. These and other charges against Redford may or may not be true; creative artists can be highly dramatic and self-serving in their selective memories, convinced their films are every bit as brilliant as *Citizen Kane*. In the end *Desert Bloom* opened to largely positive notices, apparently no worse for Redford's alleged interference.

But this was just the beginning of all the bitter squabbling and bickering, all of the accusations and recriminations, that would center on the Sundance Institute, the festival, and the lab in the years to come. And Redford—very reluctantly—was at center stage through it all.

O n June 14, 1949, a baseball player named Eddie Waitkus, an all-star first baseman with the Philadelphia Phillies, walked into a hotel room and was shot in the chest by a nineteen-year-old mentally disturbed typist named Ruth Steinhagen. Steinhagen later told reporters that she had been infatuated with Waitkus from afar for a couple of years and shot him in order to add some excitement to her dull life. This true-life story became the inspiration for author Bernard Malamud when he wrote his novel, *The Natural*.

Film rights to the novel were sold in 1976, and many different screenplays were written as a host of actors such as Michael Douglas, Nick Nolte, and Jon Voight became briefly attached to the project. A script by Roger Towne was sent to Redford, who agreed to do the movie; Redford, in turn, took the script to Barry Levinson (best known for *Diner*), who accepted the directorial assignment. The movie was filmed largely in Buffalo, New York, because it was there that the production company located a baseball stadium that most closely resembled the stadiums of the thirties and forties. (Redford had hoped to use Boston's Fenway Park, but officials there turned him down.) Plans to film many major sequences in Hollywood were scrapped when it was determined that everything could be done in Buffalo, and production offices were set up in the enormous Masten Street Armory. Much of the architecture of Buffalo had a 1930s look, and other sets were built right inside the armory. Some sequences, such as a carnival scene, were shot in nearby towns, and the few remaining bits were put together in Culver City, California, at Laird Studios.

In *The Natural* Redford plays Roy Hobbs, who leaves his home-town and childhood sweetheart, Iris (Glenn Close), to have a major career as a ballplayer. He has every intention of sending for Iris when he is settled, but on the way he encounters a disturbed woman (Barbara Hershey) who ends up shooting him. The story then moves forward sixteen years, when an older Roy Hobbs finally shows up to play for the New York Knights. Although everyone is skeptical about his abilities due to his age, Hobbs proves an outstanding hitter—until he becomes distracted by the sexy Memo (Kim Basinger). Eventually Iris comes back into his life, and he tries to explain how the catastrophic event of being shot derailed his life and left him demoralized. The team's owner doesn't want Hobbs to play, for unscrupulous reasons, and his doctor warns him that he could kill himself if he does; but Hobbs beats the odds and goes off with Iris and the son he never knew he had.

Despite a suspenseful climax and some interesting elements, *The Natural* is muddled and overlong, and it never really jells. A scene between Redford and the highly professional Glenn Close in a soda parlor is nicely acted, and Redford has a particularly good moment when Close's character, Iris, tells him that she has a son (he doesn't know it's his own child). He beautifully gets across Hobbs's perplexity, which he is too polite to express. Otherwise, Redford holds back far too often throughout the movie. When telling Close of his lost years and dreams, he is much too perfunctory in a scene that is pivotal to the story; and he has no reaction when Kim Basinger pulls a gun on him, even though he'd been shot by a crazy lady in the defining moment of his early life. When he first started making movies, Redford might have been afraid of acting too "large," or broadly, for the cameras—he understood that film acting had to be more subtle than acting on the stage—but throughout his career, he never really managed to achieve a happy medium.

The Natural (1984) grossed nearly $50 million, but the reviews were mixed. Redford was still very much considered a sex symbol, even though he was pushing fifty at the time. Only days after posters for *The Natural* went up in the subways in New York, the picture of Redford's face was "defaced" with the red imprints of kisses from his adoring female fans.

Redford's daughter Shauna was attending classes at the University of Colorado in Boulder and hanging out with her boyfriend, Sid Wells, a journalism major. Because Wells spent most of his time at Shauna's, he rented out his apartment—which was directly above Shauna's in a building his mother owned—to his roommate, Thayne Alan Smika, a college dropout. On August 1, 1983, Wells's brother Samuel went to the upstairs apartment and found his brother's body; he had been shot through the back of the head. Shauna, who had dated the twenty-two-year-old Wells for two years, was devastated by the news. Her father halted production of *The Natural* to attend Wells's funeral with his wife and Shauna. "It's upsetting, strange, sad news," Redford said. "He was very close to our family." Because of Wells's involvement with Robert Redford's daughter, the tragic case reached national prominence.

Although Wells was perceived as a clean-cut young man who never got into trouble, the police later found a letter from Shauna admonishing him for dealing cocaine and warning him that he was "getting in with some bad people." At first his death was suspected to be due to a drug deal gone sour, but eventually the authorities focused on his roommate. The murder occurred when Smika was scheduled to pay the victim rent money. Upon finding Smika at his mother's in Akron, Ohio, the police learned that he had just finished washing his clothes. In his mother's closet, they also found a 20-gauge shotgun with shells, which they thought might match the murder weapon. When it was determined, however, that this evidence might not be strong enough, District Attorney Alex Hunter decided not to file charges at that time. Three years later, a warrant was issued against Smika for a case of embezzlement. He then disappeared and was suspected of living in California under an assumed identity.

A few months after Wells's death, Shauna herself nearly died when she crashed her Ford Bronco outside Salt Lake City. The car wound up in the freezing waters of the Jordan River, from which a semiconscious Shauna was pulled by a local resident named Dorine Rivera. Rivera was invited to the premiere of *The Natural*, where a grateful father told her, "Saying thanks just isn't enough." Shauna eventually married a wealthy man named Eric Schlosser.

The United States Film Festival had been limping along for many years, presenting mostly low-budget, badly made, dull and inferior independent films. The films had little hope of finding a distributor, and they rarely did. Redford did not particularly care for festivals—all the hype and competitive nature turned him off—but he was reminded that the Sundance Institute had to go beyond its efforts to aid in the development of independent features and filmmakers. What about exhibiting these features, finding a way to market them and distribute them so that some genuinely fine pictures might actually be seen by a wider audience? Therefore, in 1985, the Sundance Institute took over the U.S. Film Festival, which eventually became known simply as the Sundance Festival. In 1989, the festival (still the U.S. Film Festival) presented Steven Soderbergh's *sex, lies, and videotape*—even Soderbergh thought it was overrated—which went on to have some considerable fame. Initially, Soderbergh saw Redford as some kind of hero; but the two would eventually have a bitter falling out over a subsequent project, one of Redford's best known and most successful.

Redford was soon coming under attack for not liking many of the films that premiered at the festival. He was seen as conservative, a slave to conventional taste (this despite his support for minority filmmakers), when independent films were—to some at least—supposed to be edgy and even subversive. Many of the films that were entered in the competition were sleazy, violent, dark and perverse, just too ugly for words—and they turned Redford's stomach. Redford saw no reason that an independent film couldn't have *class*. Many of the movies at the Sundance Festival seemed the products of immature minds, people out to shock or gross out viewers. Redford was not alone in thinking that while this kind of filmmaking might be visceral, that hardly made it great. The eventual director of such elegant, handsome, and tasteful films as *A River Runs Through It* and *The Horse Whisperer*—not to mention a sensitive near-masterpiece like *Ordinary People*—was not going to be impressed with the brains-on-the-back-seat-of-the-car nonsense of comparative schlock like *Pulp Fiction*.

In *Down and Dirty Pictures*, his book on the rise of independent film, Peter Biskind theorizes that "Redford's distaste for the pulpy tabloid underbelly of mass culture was probably a function of his own insecurities. A college drop-out, he suffered from the intellectual anxieties of the undereducated and consequently sought the imprimatur of literary or museum culture, which is why so many of the films he directed himself, with their lacquered veneer of exquisite pictorial beauty, are as lifeless as insects preserved in amber." Biskind seems to ignore the possibility that Redford, despite being a college dropout, could have become self-educated over the years. He may not be a true intellectual or renaissance man, but he has never been considered out-and-out stupid. It is also true that many well-educated and cultured people share a distaste for what Biskind describes as the "déclassé schlockmeisters Redford didn't get and didn't much like;" in fact, such people generally have more contempt for schlock than Redford has ever demonstrated.

In addition to criticisms of his taste, "Ordinary Bob" was not as well liked by the Sundance staff as he might have hoped, although he was never one to care that much about what people thought of him. Good thing, because some staffers came to think of his alleged "I'm just plain folks" routine as being a lot of bullshit. The typical remark about Redford was that "he wants to be seen as part of a group, but he's also the king." Well . . . duh! This is the way most if not all movie stars are, and it's amusing—or inexplicable—that anyone who worked with Redford would be surprised by it. As was once said of Al Pacino, who is *very* different from Robert Redford: "He wanted to be treated like a regular guy; on the other hand, if you didn't treat him like 'Al Pacino'—*fuck you!*" It's not just that movie stars can be egomaniacal assholes, but that they feel they've earned a certain respect, and they are sensitive to those people who may be envious or full of righteous indignation and who deliberately act like the star is nothing special as a way of putting them down or keeping them in their place. That's when the star stops being one of the guys and becomes The Star. In this Redford is no different. Plenty of people simply feel that Redford has a star attitude (especially if they have a disagreement with him), but there are also people who find him refreshingly down to earth—for a movie star.

The trouble was that Sundance needed Redford as a famous spokesman to attract people to the institute, but Redford was uncomfortable as a public person and even more ill at ease as a fund-raiser. Another problem with Redford as far as his staff was concerned was that he was hardly ever available; not only did he have family issues, but he had endless production meetings and script conferences for his own films, and he also needed free time to simply enjoy skiing and being at his ranch. Even when he did show up for a meeting, he was always late.

Then Redford simply flew off to Africa to make *Out of Africa*— when the staff desperately needed him to be in Utah.

Karen Blixen left Denmark at age twenty-seven for South Africa, where she married her Swedish cousin, the Baron Bror Blixen, and managed a four-thousand-acre coffee plantation even after separating from her husband. She cataloged the people she met, including natives she befriended, and recorded her adventures on the Dark Continent in her book, *Out of Africa*, which she penned under the pseudonym Isak Dinesen. Years later she did a follow-up entitled *Shadows on the Grass*.

Prestigious filmmakers, including Orson Welles and David Lean, had hoped to do an adaptation of Dinesen's stories. A screenwriter named Kurt Luedtke sent his friend, Sydney Pollack, a copy of his own adaptation of *Out of Africa*. Luedtke, who was hoping only for some constructive criticism, wound up making the film with Pollack. "I began, without knowing it, working on the picture," said Pollack. While exploring the logistics of making the picture on location, Pollack and Luedtke worked together on a number of drafts—by that time the screenplay had incorporated much material from Judith Thurman's biography, *Isak Dinesen: The Life of a Storyteller*. At the time of the film's release, Pollack said, "[*Out of Africa*] is a bit of a gamble . . . to do a $30 million picture that doesn't have a car chase, but with adults and an old-fashioned romance, is risk taking. . . . If this film is not successful, there won't be more films like it."

The film version of *Out of Africa* (1985) compressed and rearranged Blixen's journals and added a love affair between Karen and an adventurer named Denys to provide a romantic foundation for the story. It begins in 1913, when Karen is rejected by her lover in Denmark. Out of desperation, she asks his brother (played by Klaus Maria Brandauer) to marry her. After traveling to Africa, where the two run a farm in Kenya, she slowly adjusts to a very different and often difficult life. When her marriage falls apart, Karen is drawn to the dashing Denys, who loves her but can't commit. He wants a casual relationship with both free as the wind, and she longs for them to share eternal devotion. After episodes with wildlife and cultural exchanges with the natives, Karen's farm is destroyed; she loses everything. On top of this, Denys is killed when his plane crashes. Karen leaves Africa never to return. Taken as the story of a woman who loves and loses a man who cares for her deeply but, sadly, not quite enough, *Out of Africa* is very moving.

From the first, the actress who seemed perfect to play Blixen as a young woman was Meryl Streep. At the time she was seen as a star with character-actor ability, an actress who could do no wrong. Pollack had talked to some European actresses about the possibility of playing Blixen, but when it was decided to employ some star power, Streep's involvement was seen as crucial. "[Streep] is effortless to work with," said Pollack. "Reliable all the time, good-humored, always prepared, never lets narcissism stand in the way of her work. Of our 101 shooting days in Africa, she worked in 99, and never missed."

"Sydney is hugely manipulative," said Streep of Pollack as a director, "and the secret of his success is that he doesn't think he is. He makes you feel you did it. He keeps his ears open. He was directing and was writing it all as we were going along." Pollack also wanted his friend Bob Redford to play Blixen's love interest in the film—not her husband, but her friend Denys (pronounced "Dennis") Finch-Hatton, who in Dinesen's book was merely a loving friend. "After I got Meryl," said Pollack, "I needed someone equally strong who could make an immediate impression." Hence Redford. And therein lies the problem with *Out of Africa*, which is arguably Pollack's finest film. As more than one critic queried in astonishment, who would ever see the ultra-American, California boy Robert Redford as someone named Denys Finch-Hatton?

But Redford's participation was seen as essential if the film were to be made, let alone succeed. It was going to be a very expensive production, and the public might not readily flock to see a period piece set in Africa, especially if no big names were attached. Streep was a star, but of the second tier; she was not a superstar like Redford. Redford was attracted to the passionate sweep of the movie, the literate script by Kurt Luedtke, and a larger-than-life romantic part for himself—not to mention the way the film would explore other cultures and even make ecological statements, emerging in some ways as a paean to nature.

Finch-Hatton was described thusly by Blixen: "Denys should be set in an earlier English landscape, in the days of Queen Elizabeth. He could have walked arm in arm, there, with Sir Philip, or Francis Drake. And the people of Elizabeth's time might have held him dear because to them he would have suggested that Antiquity, the Athens, of which they dreamed and wrote. Denys could indeed have been placed harmoniously in any period of our civilization, *tout comme chez soi*, all up till the opening of the nineteenth century." Not exactly how one sees the very contemporary Robert Redford. On the other hand, Blixen also wrote of Finch-Hatton: "He could have cut a figure in any age, for he was an athlete, a musician, a lover of art and a fine sportsman. He did cut a figure in his own age, but it did not quite fit in anywhere." Since Redford had seen himself as an outsider in youth, and now measured himself in heroic terms, he thought the role would be a good fit. In some ways, it was. But he is still ludicrously miscast.

Sydney Pollack, however, claimed that Redford was the only one who could play the role, partly because Denys was "an optical illusion . . . enigmatic, elusive, private character who was wildly romanticized by women who wrote about him. . . . My task was not to present the literal truth about him but to present the truth as Dinesen saw it." He added: "I kept seeing Redford [in the role]. For me, Finch-Hatton was much more playable by Redford than anyone else because of all the roles Bob's played, and all we read about him as a man. He fits that persona, that sort of unobtainable, elusive figure."

We might wonder if it was really wise to have an actor who seems elusive play an elusive figure on screen when another actor could have truly fleshed out the character and made him real. In these statements, Pollack, of course, was trying to make it sound as if casting Redford were all part of a grand design and not just a sensible marketing ploy. Screenwriter Luedtke was nervous that Redford's participation would unbalance the film in favor of Denys when it was really Karen's story, but Redford reassured him and kept to his word. Redford is offscreen for much of the running time of *Out of Africa*.

Redford made no attempt at an accent for the film. There is an attempt in the film to explain this discrepancy with references to "America," but no one was fooled that the Oxford-educated Denys Finch-Hatton was anything but British. Streep, on the other hand, worked hard on her Danish accent and was quite successful at it, although some viewers found it annoying and others thought it was occasionally unintelligible. To many, the performances illustrated the difference between a movie star and a truly dedicated actor. More important, Streep creates a memorable, real character from the first, whereas Redford struggles throughout the movie to seem like something other than the mythic movie star in Africa. To be fair, the role of Blixen is much better developed; there's much more for Streep to work with. But another, preferably British actor might have imbued the male role with more substance and persuasiveness.

That said, Redford is hardly bad in the film. He and Streep actually play quite well together—such as in the first of two campfire scenes, when Blixen confesses she went away due to a touch of syphilis. Redford gets across his character's uneasiness over his developing feelings and his uncertainty at what her reaction will be when he asks Karen if he can move in with her. Redford is very good in the scene with his friend Berkeley (Michael Kitchen) when he learns that Berkeley is dying of black river fever. But he's generally unable to get across Denys's loneliness and world-weariness.

Ironically, Meryl Streep seems afflicted with Redford's minimalist approach in two key sequences: when she learns she has syphilis, a very big deal in that time period, and when she learns that Denys has died. Her odd nonreaction, especially in the latter scene, may be meant to indicate numbness or denial, but it just looks like massive underplaying—definitely the wrong way to go. Pollack, of course, allowed this and has to be held accountable for muffing a pivotal moment. (Undoubtedly influenced by Pollack's approach, Redford, when directing *A River Runs Through It*, also had his actors go for emotional detachment in a death revelation scene.) In real life, Blixen learned of Denys's death from a female friend after wondering why people she knew suddenly seemed to avoid talking to her; but in the movie, her ex-husband brings her the news. (And it is true that Denys bought Karen her gramophone; but he preferred modern music, not the Mozart he listens to in the movie.)

Redford can rarely show vulnerability, and never is this more apparent than in *Out of Africa*. Ever concerned with his image—the very image of being a man, albeit in an old-fashioned sense—Redford must always be seen as a "winner"; he can't allow any sign of weakness or insecurity beyond the vaguest glimmerings. It is hard to create a sympathetic figure with this attitude. Therefore, if the audience cries upon learning Denys has died, it is not so much because of his death, but because of its effect on the woman who loves him.

Despite these and other flaws, mostly structural, *Out of Africa* is a powerful experience. Pollack's direction keeps the long film flowing briskly; David Watkin's photography is exquisite; and John Barry composed one of his most opulent, memorable scores. It all comes together in the film's most magnificent sequence, when Denys takes Karen for a ride in his plane. We see a montage of stunning aerial shots of animals and rivers, a flock of flamingos taking flight, achingly gorgeous vistas, all drenched in Barry's intensely romantic and beautiful music. In her book, Blixen writes: "Where you are sitting in front of your pilot, with nothing but space before you, you feel that he is carrying you upon the outstretched palms of his hands, as the Djinn carried Prince Ali through the air, and that the wings that bear you onward are his." This feeling is captured by the movie as Karen ecstatically reaches her hand back for Denys to clasp it in his; the music fades, and we can hear only the sound of the engine and the air. This is what the movies are all about.

It is ironic, however, that a film starring a man so devoted to social causes was seen as oppressive by people in Nairobi. The *Kenya Times* charged that white extras in the film were paid more than blacks were. In an editorial, the paper argued that the government "should not allow foreign film firms to come here and insult us on our own soil just because some racist author wrote a racist book ages ago." Coproducer Terry Clegg admitted that there was a discrepancy in pay—whites received $25 a day; blacks received $9 unless they wore false ears or had their head shaved, in which case they received $15—but that his hands were tied. Clegg claimed that if whites were paid the same rate as blacks, it would have been impossible to recruit the hundreds who were needed for the film. He also felt that "it would cause a riot" if he offered $25 to blacks in a country where the average daily pay rate was much, much less. "We've been to the president's office, the ministries of information and labor and they can't solve the problem either," said Clegg.

While some of the blacks were fitted with artificial ears with wooden rings or bead work—the locals no longer stretched their ears and ornamented them the way they did in Blixen's day—several hundred white extras were given a trim so that they had a neat, clean Edwardian appearance. When the native lions proved a little too feral to safely interact with cast members, eight tame lions—better actors and less likely to eat an extra—were flown in from California.

Aside from a few deserved quibbles, the movie was praised to the skies and made money to boot. Knocking *Rocky IV* out of first place, it opened strong and earned $34 million in just the first month. In general, Redford did not fare well with the reviewers, however. Gene Siskel spoke for many when he wrote, "There is really only one thing wrong with Sydney Pollack's ambitious love story, *Out of Africa*. And that one thing can be summed up in two words—Robert Redford. . . . As I watched [Streep and Redford in] their scene together I saw Karen Blixen embracing Robert Redford and not the character of Denys Finch Hatton. . . . [Redford] seems distant to the point of distraction. He is not convincing in period outfits. He looks and acts as if he just walked out of the safari fitting room at Abercrombie & Fitch. He's not worthy of her interest, and so when the film builds to a climax of their relationship, after much screaming and debating about love and freedom, I sat there hoping that the fight would continue and that they would never achieve a single moment of passion." (Of course it must be remembered that intelligent women often fall for men who are "not worthy of their interest.") Siskel assured his readers that he didn't have a "knee-jerk negative reaction to Redford," that he had admired him in several previous films; but that in *Out of Africa*, "he seems so smug here that his every appearance is a royal pain in the eyes."

However, Jeff Millar in the *Houston Chronicle* lamented the absence of Redford in most of the first half of the film. Millar wrote, "When we do get a chance to evaluate his work, we find that it's excellent. There is no taciturn Hemingway rigidity to his great white hunter." Pollack, Luedtke, Watkin, and Barry all won well-deserved Oscars, and *Out of Africa* also won as Best Picture. Redford was not nominated.

The Hollywood community was rather startled in 1985 when it was announced that Robert and Lola Redford were getting a divorce. With their closed-in private lives and their retreat away from the world in Utah, they were seen as one of the few Hollywood marriage success stories. As Redford put it, "I never wanted to be one of those divorced show business casualties—so predictable. I wanted to prove that a marriage could last and prove the business wrong. But I couldn't." Lola and Redford had been separated for some time, although only their very closest friends knew about it.

Redford has never said much about his divorce, although he has at least intimated at an "official" reason for the breakup. "I spent so much energy trying to support Sundance that frankly I got a little lost." There is little doubt that Lola Redford felt as if she were living alone; her children were grown and living their own lives, and her husband was hardly ever around. Jeremy Larner, who wrote the screenplay for *The Candidate*, said, "[Redford] told me he was totally faithful to his wife. . . . They were very tight, they went through a lot of stuff together." According to one source, Lola simply outgrew her husband. "You have to remember that Bob was, after all, born in 1937, and he had a lot of those old-fashioned values and feelings about marriage and women's place." Now that her children were grown, Lola wanted to explore her options, and she didn't feel that Redford was always that supportive. Like many men of his generation, Redford wanted his wife home when he wanted her home, even though he was off doing a movie in Africa or in endless meetings about Sundance. When the children were little, Lola had plenty to occupy her time, but now she no longer felt as if she were sharing a life with Bob.

The source continues: "Just as Bob likes to have his own way as a movie star, he wanted his own way with his marriage. He's not mean or uncaring—not by a long shot—just set in his ways, the proverbial 300 pound gorilla. He couldn't understand that Lola now had her own needs and they didn't mesh with his. Lola not only wanted to explore all her options as a woman and a human being, but she also wanted to eventually find someone who could actually share quality time with her, and Bob was no longer that man. It was very sad really, because they still have deep feelings for one another."

According to Redford, the divorce "was mutual and it was right to move on." On another occasion he confessed, "I got married very young, at twenty-one. Obviously I don't want to denigrate the person I married, there were a lot of good reasons. . . . But when you ask me a question like why [the divorce], I have to say it was to save my life. That's what it felt like at the time." According to another source, Redford felt constantly pulled between the demands of his wife and the demands of his movie career and Sundance, that there just wasn't enough of him to go around: "Leaving his wife to go off somewhere created tremendous guilt in Bob, and when he was divorced, as bad as he felt, I think there was also this tremendous sense of relief."

Redford has remarked more than once than he never actually dated—or had to ask a woman out on a date—after his marriage. "It wasn't necessary," he said. "It just wasn't. It just happened naturally. It was evolutionary. It was natural evolution."

Apparently women had absolutely no problem asking Robert Redford out on a date. And many did, including his next costar, Debra Winger. Or rather, the two simply came together "naturally" during the course of filming.

Legal Eagles (1986) teamed Redford with Debra Winger, who at the time was hot; she had appeared previously in *An Officer and a Gentleman* and *Terms of Endearment*. Although Winger was the kinda, sort of, maybe/maybe not love interest for most of the movie—the two do finally realize their shared affection by movie's end—on-screen Redford sleeps with Daryl Hannah, who has a pivotal supporting part. Chelsea Dearden (Hannah) is being prosecuted by ADA Tom Logan (Redford) and defended by Laura Kelly (Winger) because Dearden tried to snatch back a painting given to her by her artist father when she was a child. Supposedly this painting, and many others done by Dearden, was destroyed the night a fire tore through their home and the artist was killed. Eventually Chelsea is suspected of murdering her former lover Taft (Terence Stamp), an art dealer who has the suspicious painting. Everywhere the lady goes a body turns up. At one point Logan and Kelly are nearly blown up by a bomb in a warehouse. Eventually the real killer is unmasked in another conflagration, Chelsea goes on her way with her painting, and Logan and Kelly seem to be planning a life together.

Legal Eagles is entertaining, if minor and occasionally illogical. It's a light suspense movie with a winning, very good performance from Redford, who is very assured—downright sparkling—and absolutely perfect in the breezy role of Tom Logan. Fans who'd been saying that he had a Cary Grant touch may have felt vindicated by this picture, although Redford is not really in Grant's league. Still, his charm carries the day, he displays insouciant conviction in the courtroom scenes, and he handles the moments of danger and action adroitly. He displays his sense of humor and fun as he tap dances to "Singing in the Rain." Winger is very appealing, and Hannah of the long head is oddly attractive if not exactly riveting as an actress. In his relatively chaste bedroom scene with Hannah, Redford reveals that he is rather hirsute, with a heavy thatch of chest hair (nowdays some macho men think it's obligatory to shave the hair off their chest and oil their pecs in a way that seems more feminine than masculine.) No particular sparks are struck in this bedroom scene. The Redford-Winger romance seems a little one-sided, with Winger giving with the wistful looks and Redford being indulgent (This was undoubtedly the case with their brief off-screen romance). They act well together, but their chemistry is not exactly combustible. Christine Baranski, who would later have wide exposure on television sitcoms, scored as Redford's secretary. John McMartin, who played Forrester, had earlier appeared with Redford in *Brubaker*.

Ivan Reitman, who directed *Legal Eagles*, said that if Clark Gable is king, then Robert Redford is president. He added, "Redford takes screen [*sic*] better than anyone I've ever seen. To go up against him on the screen you need someone of great substance. . . . I think Debra Winger has that kind of stuff." Reitman said an associate described Redford as a "work of art," and he could understand why. "The most amazing thing I ever saw was him walking in for his makeup test. I had by then seen him for a couple of months, was used to talking to him about the script. So some of my awe had worn off. And then I watched him walk into the light. And it was like, whoa! Oh, that's right, he's Robert Redford. And you see why. The light goes into his body and shines out."

Debra Winger had not been happy that she'd been "packaged"

with Redford by CAA (Creative Artists Agency) for *Legal Eagles*, which she had been told would be a kind of updated *Adam's Rib*. Despite Reitman's belief that Winger had the right stuff to work with Redford, Reitman and Winger did not get along as filming proceeded. Winger later charged that the film had been badly directed and execrably edited. She was probably also not happy that her off-set liaisons with Redford did not much continue after the movie was over.

For a while Redford was one of the chief Hollywood supporters of Colorado senator Gary Hart, who seemed to have a bright political future ahead of him. In 1987 Hart was seen as a prime contender for the Democratic presidential nomination. The married Hart was undone when he let a twenty-nine-year-old swimsuit model named Donna Rice sit on his lap during a cruise to Bimini on a yacht named *Monkey Business*; the photographs were published everywhere. Hart was said to have done himself no good by becoming friends with supporter Warren Beatty, who drew the senator into his libertine lifestyle the way Frank Sinatra had enveloped Jack Kennedy many years earlier. Redford opined that Hart should never have gotten entangled with "the Hollywood set." According to Redford, due to the influence of certain people, "he ended up thinking he was invincible." However, Beatty remained loyal to Hart even after the Rice scandal broke.

Despite his often debilitating health problems, Redford's son Jamie had managed to get his bachelor's degree at the University of Colorado, where his father had run wild so many years before. During a checkup, he discovered that he had a problem even worse than colitis; at twenty-five, he was diagnosed with PSC or primary sclerosing cholangitis. Although rare, this complication of colitis blocks the bile ducts of the liver and eventually causes deadly complications. Jamie was told that his liver would fail within five to ten years. "I took it as a death sentence," he recalled. But then, in denial, he decided that he would be okay, they'd come up with a cure in time, or it simply wouldn't happen. His girlfriend Kyle, who later married him, recalled the day he got the diagnosis as the worst day of their lives. Kyle and Jamie eventually married and had a baby son, Dylan—a few years later, a daughter Lena would come along—and hoped for the best. Redford was, of course, devastated by the news.

Although the film has its admirers, most agreed that *The Milagro Beanfield War*, Redford's directorial follow-up to *Ordinary People*, was a disappointment that was in no way in the same class as his directorial debut film. At the time Redford decided to make the movie, the script had been in development hell for thirteen years. The movie was based on a very long 1974 novel by John Nichols, and several writers—including Tracy Keenan Wynn, Leonard Gardner, and Nichols himself—labored to compress the book into a screenplay of reasonable length. Finally, David Ward seemed to come up with a script that worked.

The Milagro Beanfield War (1988) is in the category of the little guy versus the big guns, a genre that has been popular for as long as there have been movies. In his long book, John Nichols probably had the time to develop, and therefore interest the reader in, the many characters. With a running time of under two hours, however, Redford hadn't the same luxury, although the novel may never have been the best idea for adaptation to begin with. The movie deals with a poor New Mexican named Joe Moondragon (Chick Vennera), who uses water that he isn't supposed to use to irrigate his bean field. It's an act of defiance against developers who have come to town to take the land (he is one of the few who hasn't sold out to these people). Sonia Braga is a local activist who tells the neighbors that if they think they'll be hired by the development company during building or afterward, they're sadly mistaken; this prediction is borne out when Moondragon is denied a job. There's also a transplanted lawyer (John Heard), a young sociologist come to study the residents of Milagro (Daniel Stern), a young sympathetic sheriff (Ruben Blades), a law officer hired by the developers (Christopher Walken), and a crazy old coot who nearly drives a tractor over a cliff—not to mention the head developer, Mr. Devine (Richard Bradford), and his wife (Melanie Griffith).

The audience hardly gets to know or care about any of these peo-

ple; and the movie, meant to be wistful and poignant and life affirm-
ing, never catches fire. At one point Moondragon shoots an older
man in self-defense, and a posse is formed to bring him in. You'd
have thought Redford would have had enough of posses chasing after
the misunderstood after *The Chase* and *Tell Them Willie Boy Is Here*.
Mercifully, this subplot is resolved rather quickly. *The Milagro Beanfield War* is full of flavorful character actors and arid atmospheric
scenery and the occasional interesting detail, but it's practically still-
born. There is absolutely nothing new in the weak script—the meta-
phorical dramatic conflicts are easily resolved, the ending is pat and
abrupt. Everything is solved and summed up as in a sitcom, which
the movie resembles except it isn't very funny. Redford's direction
is perfectly professional and workmanlike but rarely inspired. The
situation is all black and white, superficial, the villain fat and smarmy
as expected, with the expected bimbo wife, the activist earnest, and
hero bravely impotent, the old folk with their rusty guns walking
clichés.

Although the film has a great many actors, it has no stars. The
actors playing the major characters are simply listed alphabetically
after the title. Completely unseen, Robert Redford is the star. If the
picture were meant as a reaction to Redford's battles with the developers who hung him in effigy, it certainly took many liberties. Joe
Moondragon is hardly Robert Redford, and Redford is hardly a poor
Native American New Mexican. But Developers versus the Rich and
Powerful Movie Star would hardly have made a good movie. Then
again, it might have been much more entertaining than *Milagro
Beanfield*, which is a distinctly minor picture. Without Redford appearing on-screen, the movie faded from memory almost the day it
was released. Some critics were kind to the film; some genuinely admired and liked it. Davie Grusin won an Oscar for his pleasant
music. Richard Bradford, who is solid in the role of developer Devine, had appeared years earlier in *The Chase*.

Originally *The Milagro Beanfield War* was to be filmed in the village of Chimayo, New Mexico, in the Sangre de Cristo mountain
range, which boasted an historic eighteenth-century plaza. But several Chimayo landowners, concerned that the town's peace and quiet
would be disrupted, got together to protest its invasion by the Hollywood interlopers. The whole thing began to strangely resemble the

situation in the movie itself, with the landowners the little guys and Redford the representative of uncaring big business. "I kind of admired it," Redford recalled, "because it was a stand against the obvious profit of a film company."

Redford and his cohorts tried to negotiate with the group, but as the weeks went by and the rainy season loomed closer and closer, they were forced to look elsewhere. The next best place was Truchas, a village farther up the mountainside. Although it was much less accessible and its weather was worse, Truchas had spectacular views—and more amenable residents. One big problem was the rain. Although it was not consistent, the precipitation meant that the all-important bean field was never as dry as it needed to be in the early scenes. Even in the later scenes, when the bean sprouts have appeared, the rubber stand-ins would be sucked up by an all-consuming mud. "The gods have had a lot of fun with this," Redford told one visitor to the location, "Right now I feel like I'm directing the weather."

There were other mishaps. Chick Vennera broke his fingers when he punched what he thought was a cardboard prop—it turned out to be a real brick wall. Vennera was impressed by the way Redford refused to be rattled by this or anything else. "He was as cool as a cucumber. This guy, I think, invented the word 'cool.'" Ruben Blades was impressed with the way Redford "doesn't force you to do exactly as he does. He lets you know what his ideas are and you are welcome to bring whatever you feel to the character."

Blades was surprised that Redford was so patient, and that he was "kind of invisible on the set. Oh, he's there, and he's in charge, but he's not flamboyant. If you just arrived and you'd never seen him, you would have a hard time pinpointing him." Redford was a far cry from such directors as William Friedkin, Peter Bogdanovich, Martin Scorsese, Francis Ford Coppola, and many others, who were infamous for their hysterical on-set blowups and their extremely neurotic and often pathological behavior while directing a film—especially when there were problems.

Redford developed a brief romantic relationship with Sonia Braga during and a while after the filming of the movie. But even she didn't get too close to Redford. She was grateful to have a director-actor "who understands all the psychological problems that can happen with an actor. He is trying . . . to solve these problems." But then she added, "But I am thinking not to talk too much about him, because when you talk about a person, people think you know who that person is." According to Melanie Griffith, Redford is "such a trip. He was so kind, so normal, even though he is Robert Redford. He's real patient, because he understands so well what it is to be an actor."

During filming, a group of Native Americans from Rancho de Taos came to the set and waited for several hours to show Redford a special concha belt they had made to register their protest over the strip mining of Chaco Canyon in New Mexico. Redford had suggested that he would talk to them, but when his schedule made this impossible, he had to tell them to be on their way.

A fresh and unexpected problem arose when Redford found out about a lawsuit that had been filed by a group of Hispanic filmmakers. The group charged that David Ward's script for *The Milagro Beanfield War* "bears a substantial similarity" to their own script, *King Tiger*, which was based on the life of New Mexico activist Reies Lopez Tijerina. In the 1960s, Tijerina had attempted to claim lands owned by the government by citing Spanish land grants. Tijerina was one of the plaintiffs, along with several men who had planned to produce the film version of his story, who claimed Columbia had ditched its plans to produce *King Tiger* after learning that Redford was doing *Milagro Beanfield*.

Redford was irked but basically unconcerned. "It happens on every film," he said. "Somebody comes out of the woodwork with their hand out." Both Ward and John Nichols denied that their work had anything to do with Tijerina. Further weakening Tijerina's claim, Nichols reported that in the twelve years since his book was published, Tijerina had claimed no connection between it and his life until he heard about the film adaptation. Attorneys for the plaintiffs said they would get an injunction to shut down the production of *Milago Beanfield War* if they found "sufficient comparisons" between the scripts. The suit never amounted to anything. Redford's biggest concerns were that the film was running many weeks behind schedule due to the weather and was way over its budget of $10 million.

"*The Milagro Beanfield War* is an enchanting blend of reality and fantasy, a movie where mortals walk arm-in-arm with angels, singing *Cielito Lindo* under a glorious New Mexican sunset," opined the *Van-*

couver Sun. On the other hand, the *Seattle Times* felt that the picture "hardly amounts to a hill of beans . . . in spite of the best of intentions and a good deal of intelligent, talented effort, less is less." The *Minneapolis Star Tribune* found some things to admire in the film, but thought it "loses much of its appeal owing to Redford's heavy-handed environmental politicizing. . . . Redford's opportunity to sway the audience is gone for good in a flood of melodrama."

This was a busy period for Redford, who was not only campaigning for Michael Dukakis on his presidential run, but preparing for a ten-day trip through the Soviet Union. He also kept busy with his activities at the Sundance Institute. Possibly as preparation for his starring role in *Havana*, Redford flew to Cuba and visited with Fidel Castro.

Not long after wrapping up *Milagro Beanfield*, Redford flew to Moscow to, as he put it, "show his films and to address the Soviet Academy of Sciences on ecology issues." On the way back home, he stopped at the Cannes Film Festival for the French premiere of his new movie. With Melanie Griffith and Sonia Braga at his side, he told a massive confluence of reporters that he had come only because "I was in the neighborhood." There was as much interest in his trip to Moscow as there was in *The Milagro Beanfield War*, if not more. When the reporters finally turned their attention back to the movie, Redford frankly told them, "Boy, this is really boring." The picture was well enough received at the festival, although the ecological message of the picture did not seem to particularly interest or absorb members of the French press. "I understand there are a group of citizens in Tierra Amarillo, New Mexico, who were inspired by *Milagro* to stand up to local developers," Redford proudly told the assemblage. Then someone asked about him and Sonia Braga, and he was gone.

As for Castro, Redford met him when he went to Havana, purportedly to attend a "script-writing workshop for women" in May of 1988. According to one insider, "The opportunity to meet Castro arose and Bob just couldn't resist meeting this famous individual. The political ramifications probably never even occurred to him. Bob was also into pushing his ecological agenda with world leaders, no matter what or who. Bob was too naive for it to occur to him that he might have been being used. He was 'Robert Redford,' after all, and could go anywhere."

In August of that year Redford received a letter from Richard Newcomb, director of the Treasury Enforcement Office in Washington, D.C. Newcomb wanted to know if Redford had paid his own expenses while in Havana, or if they had been paid by the Cuban government. This inquiry was due to the U.S. trade ban with Cuba, which prohibited "unlicensed economic transactions in which Cuba has an interest." Redford's Los Angeles lawyer, Vincent Chieffo, told the press, "I wouldn't even call it an investigation. They sent a letter and we told them the facts." Another of Redford's attorneys, Robert Gipson, said: "Our view of the federal regulations is there was no violation." Nothing ever came of the matter.

After *The Milagro Beanfield War*, it looked like Redford's next project might be an adaptation of Pat Conroy's novel *The Prince of Tides*. Barbra Streisand was very interested in directing and starring in the film, with her then lover Don Johnson in the role of Tom Wingo. But Redford acquired the property for his Wildwood Enterprises. He was going to star in and produce the picture for MGM/UA. When Streisand learned what had happened, she decided to call Redford and see if there was some way they could work on the project together. Redford and Streisand had several meetings, and they batted the director's job back and forth; first Bob said he would direct, and then Barbra said she would. Streisand had already proved her directorial ability with *Yentl*, and, of course, Redford had helmed *Ordinary People*.

When it was decided one way or another that Streisand would direct the film, Redford lost interest in playing Wingo. Although not necessarily a "control freak," Streisand was an auteur, like any number of directors from Hitchcock to Fellini, who liked any film she helmed to conform to her own artistic vision. Her ideas simply did not jell with Redford's. He took issue with the fact that every single scene of hers that was in the novel would be transferred to the screen, even if more essential sequences remained unfilmed. Redford was probably made acutely aware that Streisand was much more in love with this project than he was. He gave up the rights to the film, citing "artistic differences," and allowed Streisand to make the film she had always wanted to make. Her costar, however, was not to be Don Johnson but rather Nick Nolte.

In 1988 Sundance Institute executive Tom Wilhite came up with the idea of raising cash by holding a prestigious series of Great Movie Music concerts at Lincoln Center, and later at the Hollywood Bowl. He contacted film composer David Newman, who helped him plan the events, and in turn enlisted the services of such composers as Henry Mancini and Marvin Hamlisch. Tickets to the concerts sold briskly, and it was clear that the institute would raise some significant funds with the project ($600,000 was eventually realized).

Redford, however, wasn't entirely thrilled with the whole idea, or at least with the idea that his participation was practically mandated. *Robert Redford* and *Sundance* had become synonymous in the public's mind, and he was told that undoubtedly many people bought tickets just in the hopes of catching a glimpse of him. Redford never liked mingling with fans and would-be fans and the movers and shakers who wanted to meet a movie star; he hated that whole process. He even bitched about having to wear a tuxedo. He had told his people that he did not want the whole night to center around him, but it began to look as if it was shaping up in just that way. Snappish, he complained that Charlton Heston was coming to the event because of his involvement with the National Rifle Association. Staffers said Redford had known about Heston far in advance of the concert, but when he discovered he actually might have to shake hands with the man, he was nearly apoplectic. Redford spent most of the evening hiding out in one of the rehearsal halls, refusing to say hello even to important Sundance donors.

Still smarting from what he felt was the way he'd been hornswoggled into attending the Lincoln Center function, Redford decided to cancel the next Great Movie Music concert at the Hollywood Bowl in Los Angeles. The Bowl had already sold quite a number of tickets and threatened to sue him if he pulled out at such a late date, so he had no choice but to go ahead with it. Redford managed to cancel a third concert, scheduled for the Chicago Symphony; this move infuriated many staffers, who'd spent considerable time pulling the whole thing together. Many saw the cancellations as Redford's way of cutting off his nose to spite his face.

Havana (1990), which was actually shot in the Dominican Republic, was another collaboration between Redford and director Sydney Pollack. The film takes place in Cuba in 1958, when rebels are trying to overthrow the Batista government. Redford plays Jack Weil, who runs a high-stakes poker game for a mob-connected casino owner (Alan Arkin). He meets and is attracted to Roberta "Bobbi" Duran (Lena Olin), and helps her smuggle U.S. Signal Corps radios into Havana. Bobbi and her husband Arturo (Raul Julia), who are working with the rebels, are arrested and thrown in jail. Arturo's death is reported in the papers, and a smitten Weil pays for Bobbi's release. There follows an unconvincing romance between the two, which ends when they discover that Arturo is actually alive. The husband and wife are reunited as a sadder and wiser Weil moves on.

Havana is a long, meandering picture that holds the attention for a while—until the fake romance begins, and it becomes clear that there will be no real payoff for the audience. As some critics have noted, the picture isn't so much terrible as lackluster, mediocre, lacking in distinguishing features and truly great scenes. Pollack and company try hard, such as when Weil's vaguely sexy dalliance with two pretty tourists is intercut with the rebels being rounded up by the authorities, but not a single sequence is especially memorable or mesmerizing.

As previously noted, Redford is generally too civilized and gentlemanly to be entirely convincing as a kind of swaggering bad boy, but he's better than expected in *Havana*. In his youth he had to use his charm and tenacity to hustle for parts, convincing casting directors and others that he had what it takes, using sex appeal and flirtatiousness to create interest; in a role like that of Weil, he calls upon memories of those days to inform his performance. Still, Redford never strays far from the well-bred boy, even when he's asked to deliver lines such as "I'm gonna find the best fuck and the biggest game of my life," or must refer to another character as "a fake fairy." His aforementioned ménage à trois is intermixed with the rebel roundup and so darkly lit that it suggests sexiness without ever demonstrating it, as if Redford is simply too conservative to, say, show his bare ass on camera. One can't imagine any other major male star being quite so coy. Most actors, from Harrison Ford to Arnold Schwarzenegger to Al Pacino, would have used the sequence to cement their stud image and show off the good shape they're in. The threesome scene in *Havana* is so comparatively innocent (considering that the two women have clearly wanted to screw Weil since they were first introduced) that it almost seems as if it were lifted from an actual movie made in the fifties. Even homely, lisping Humphrey Bogart would have made it sexier. (Sydney Pollack has confessed his aversion for sex scenes, which is another reason that the ones in *Havana* are lustless as well as listless. Love scenes that work are "very hard to do," says Pollack.)

Jack Weil is meant to be the kind of essentially amoral adventurer with a heart who, for the love of a woman, becomes political and gets in over his head. In Hollywood's Golden Age, this character was frequently played by Gable, Bogart, and others. The roles were often under-written and then fleshed out by the actor. Redford has the charisma of these stars, but not the darkness; or at least he can't propel the darkness into his performance, good as it is.

Bobbi and Jack's romance, the cornerstone of the picture, doesn't really begin until the movie is half over. And their attraction is never believable, partly because of a weak script by Judith Rascoe and David Rayfield and partly because of the performances. Women who are grieving for their husbands may draw close to other men out of loneliness, but due to Lena Olin's massive and disastrous underplaying, Bobbi never seems especially distraught or desperate. She and Redford register little chemistry together, yet she and Raul Julia—who is wonderful as the handsome Arturo—seem right together. In a movie like this, the woman in the triangle must seem like a better match for the lover than for the husband if their affair is to be convincing.

Redford is, however, convincingly frightened in a scene when he's set upon and beaten by two thugs, registering the alarm and apprehension anyone suddenly attacked that way in real life would be feeling. This is superior to the Superman posturing of other macho actors, of the Golden Age and today, who feel that they and the characters they portray must never show fear. On the other hand, Redford shares with many actors over the decades a failing: he simply can't allow himself to become too emotional. At the finale, hiding behind his charm, he's much too offhand when declaring his love for the woman he's about to lose forever. No one expects Redford to be at the point of breaking into sobs, of course; but we've already seen that the insouciant Weil *does* have feelings, and this would be the perfect time, the pivotal time, to reveal them. It's hard to imagine an actor like Tom Hanks playing this scene without showing the depths of his emotion, but Hanks hasn't won two Oscars for holding back his feelings. Redford, as ever concerned with image, simply does not let himself go. But even if he had, it could not have saved *Havana* from tedium.

Although Redford and Olin don't exactly set the screen afire, there at least seemed to be something going on between them. According to Pollack, "I think she was unusual enough to make Redford the chaser instead of the chased. She has a European gravity and weight to her." Whatever Redford may have wanted, Olin denied that anything happened between the two offscreen, although she was scared when she first found out she'd be playing his leading lady. "Because he's a huge star," she said, "and by that time I had done American films and you hear so many things about American actors. But after spending two seconds with this extremely sweet person, that [feeling] went away. He very soon stopped being 'Robert Redford' to me." When he accompanied her to the premiere of *Havana*, she referred to him as "my mountain of security."

Lisa Cutter was chosen to play one of the outgoing lady tourists who hooks up with—and beds—Redford. "I was in orbit for three weeks after I got the part," she said, "but I was in orbit because of the role and because I was working with Sydney Pollack, not because of Robert Redford." Her mother and sister, however, were ecstatic. "They kept offering to put on wigs and take my place in the scene . . . they kept saying over and over again: 'you're going to kiss Robert Redford!'"

Havana got mostly negative notices and did not do well at the box office. Redford's name was not enough to bring people to the theaters. Olin's shot at major movie stardom was derailed by the film's failure, although she got much attention due to her splendid turn as Jennifer Garner's double-agent mother on ABC's *Alias* several years later. Randy Pitnam of *Library Journal* echoed most of the critics when he wrote that *Havana* was "a thoroughly professional if rather lifeless film . . . tiresomely predictable. Like many another 'big' picture before it, *Havana* scores admirably in its overall look (the set designs for 1958 Cuba are quite good), quality acting, and effective editing—while failing as a film. Watching it, one is neither moved to tears nor laughter. One is not moved, period—except to impatience, waiting for a 145-minute drama without dramatic impact to finally fizzle out." Another critic simply quipped, "Start the revolution without you."

To create widespread interest in the film, Redford did something he normally loathed, and that was to sit down for a television interview. The night before the film opened in theaters, NBC-TV ran a special program on Redford and Pollack and the many films they'd made together—culminating, of course, with *Havana*, which NBC obviously owned a piece of. Pollack also chose the release of *Havana* to defend charges that his leading man of choice was wooden on-screen. In interviews, he became an apologist for Redford.

"There's an interesting tension in [Redford] that exists between the golden-boy exterior and the complicated, darker interior," said Pollack. "And although we are as different as any two people could be in many respects, in the ones that are most important to collaboration, we are quite similar. That is in areas of taste. What we consider good acting is pretty congruent." Pressed by interviewers who talk about how wooden Redford can be, Pollack could only rejoin that he can't be that bad if the public enjoys the movie, citing *The Way We Were* and *Out of Africa*. "If they had all hated Bob and rejected that fantasy, it would not have worked."

Pollack feels Redford is not appreciated because of his "incredibly elegant understatement. It's easier for us to be impressed with acting where we see the effort. [Acting] is the ability to create truthful behavior within imaginary circumstances. You apply that, and Redford is an extraordinarily gifted actor. You may not like him, and you may want more effort in your acting, but I think he's quite gifted in that area." However, there has always been a general consensus that Pollack works with Redford so often not because of his great acting but because the two get along and because Redford is bankable.

Yet it is possible that Pollack really believes what he says about Redford. The two men come from the same generation and background, and both hold a now-passé belief that male actors (not to mention men in general) should leave the showing of emotion to the female of the species. Both men confuse understatement or subtlety with the withholding of emotion when that is not at all the case in truly first-class acting. In the film *Seven Thieves* (1960), as just one example, Joan Collins and Rod Steiger have a scene together in a car. Steiger's mentor, Edward G. Robinson, has just passed away, and Collins realizes that the older man was actually Steiger's father. Steiger has no dialogue; his facial expression shows his great depth of feeling, his eyes glimmer with tears. In no way does he chew the scenery, but he is beautifully and wonderfully emotional with a great economy in a way that Redford never is. Another example from the same film is an earlier scene in which Robinson feels utterly fulfilled and perfectly contented, and his face mirrors these emotions—again without dialogue or overstatement—with a sureness of technique that is breathtakingly simple but alive and highly expressive. Despite Pollack's comments, the simple truth is that as an actor, Robert Redford is just not in Steiger and Robinson's league. What some see as understatement may in reality be a limitation of range.

As for Redford, he says, "I like subtlety. Working with it is just enjoyable for me personally. But for other actors, subtlety can be missed. They work more overtly to make a point, more frontally than I have. I just prefer the other way." While he has said he feels underrated as an actor, he doesn't think it would be tasteful to whine about it. "Your work is either going to connect or it isn't." In all art forms, some people prefer subtlety to a more "frontal" approach, and it may be just a matter of taste. But it is also possible that Redford's need to be "subtle"—if that's what it is—has kept him from fulfilling his promise as an actor. The subtle approach is not always the way to go.

Pollack was angered by the way critics harped on Redford's age when they wrote about *Havana*. "All they talked about was what he looked like. 'How dare Bob Redford get old.' As though it was his own fault. The thing about Redford that I have always known and they should have known is that he was never, ever just another pretty face."

11

Steven Soderbergh was considered pretty hot after the success of his film *sex, lies, and videotape*, which had premiered at Sundance. Both Robert Redford and Sydney Pollack wanted to be involved with his next movie.

Redford had a meeting with the young director to discuss his film *King of the Hill*, for which Redford planned to be executive producer. Of Redford, Soderbergh recalled that "he's extremely smart and very candid, and I think we spent as much time talking about non-film related issues as we did about business." Soderbergh was also mulling over the option of doing another film, *Kafka*, with a different production team. On top of this Sydney Pollack had attached himself to a third Soderbergh project, *The Last Ship*. Reportedly Redford was put out when he learned that the director would be doing these other two projects before he would get to *King of the Hill*, which he might not even make at all. Apparently it irked Redford that Pollack had a firm deal with Soderbergh and he did not, because *sex, lies, and videotape* had premiered at "his" festival. If Redford did say this, it might have been more in jest than in earnest; he may have been more irritated with the delay than angry with either Soderbergh or Pollard. In any case, Pollack and Redford went off to make *Havana*, and Bob was incommunicado with the Sundance staff for many weeks. Soderbergh worked on *Kafka*.

When *Havana* was finished, Redford turned his attention to *King of the Hill*, which he owned the rights to after Soderbergh had brought the book to his attention. Redford requested a meeting with the director and said he was worried that Soderbergh was going to do the Pollack project before *King of the Hill*. Was Soderbergh really interested in doing the movie at all? Should he find someone else to make the movie with? Soderbergh got the impression of a veiled threat, real or imagined; he assured Redford that he was committed to the project, but couldn't say exactly when he'd begin work on it. Redford seemed satisfied.

Redford had hired Suzanne Weil, formerly of PBS, to replace Tom Wilhite as executive director of the Sundance Institute; but after returning from the *Havana* shoot, Redford fired her when he discovered that the institute's deficit had risen to the heights. It wasn't until six years later that he replaced Weil with Ken Brecher. Gary Beer was busy getting rid of many of the people who had been with Sundance from the first, including competition programmer Alberto Garcia. Tony Safford had been booted after the *Desert Bloom* brouhaha and replaced by Geoff Gilmore. Garcia bitterly assessed what had happened to Sundance, claiming that the bean counters—the very people the festival had never been intended to serve—had taken over. It also seemed as if the films that played at the Sundance Festival were no longer the product of regional filmmakers, but of people mostly from the media capitals of New York and Los Angeles. And there were many more criticisms.

For his part, Redford gave statements in which he wondered if his being involved with the festival at all was simply a liability. He explained that he seemed distant and uncommunicative because he wanted to step back, that people would take Sundance less seriously if they saw it as being the provenance of a "dilettante" using it for a "tax write-off." Redford actually got—and deserves—a lot of credit for sticking with Sundance when most actors, obsessed with their own careers, would have walked away after a couple of years.

There would be more headaches to come.

Sneakers (1992) is essentially the struggle between two childhood friends who are now middle-aged men. Twenty years earlier, Martin (Redford) and Cosmo (Ben Kingsley) pulled a computer prank that had serious consequences. "What if we get caught?" asks Cosmo. "We won't," replies Martin. Just after Martin leaves, the police show up. Cosmo does hard time in jail, while Martin (Redford) remains a fugitive, years later running a security business under a false name. When what Martin believes are government officials from the National Security Agency show up and ask him to take on a job in exchange for clemency, Martin's team reluctantly agrees to back him up.

The object they steal is a code breaker that can get past the encryption on any computer and theoretically learn any and all secrets. It turns out, however, that Martin wasn't hired by the government but by his old friend Cosmo, who isn't above a little killing and blackmailing. In order to make a deal with the real NSA, Martin and his crew steal the code breaker back in a series of complicated maneuvers. The title refers to the "sneaks," which is what Martin's group calls the jobs they do.

Although such heavy hitters as Ben Kingsley (marvelously sinister in a way that would appall Gandhi), James Earl Jones, Dan Aykroyd, and Sidney Poitier have roles in the film, Redford's is the only name above the title—a sure sign that he still had a certain industry clout. *Sneakers* is a light thriller on the border between caper and spy film. At times it's too "cute" for its own good, but it holds the attention in a minor way, has some effective scenes, and Redford is on top of it throughout. The film was competently if unexcitingly directed by coscripter Phil Alden Robinson. Sidney Poitier reported that neither he nor Redford, both of whom had directed features, interfered with Robinson—but perhaps they should have. Poitier found it refreshing that he didn't "have to carry the load," but remarked that he was "not a computer person. I have trouble with my VCR."

River Phoenix was cast in *Sneakers* as Carl. Phoenix had appeared in a few high-profile movies by that time (*Stand by Me*; *Indiana Jones and the Last Crusade*) and was considered a definite contender in Hollywood. In love with the script, Phoenix had gleefully auditioned for Redford's production of *A River Runs Through It* but lost the part to Brad Pitt. *Sneakers* was a much less exciting project, but Phoenix's agent suggested that it was the kind of commercial movie he needed to make to eventually command even higher fees. He also liked the idea of working with the sympathetic Redford. At the time, Phoenix was seen as a lot more bankable than Redford, because it was believed that younger people went to the movies more often than older ones did. Ironically, Phoenix hated the movie and saw it as "a degradation." He hated his character of "the cyberpunk nerd . . . the kind of guy you avoid playing if you want to walk with dignity at the premiere." Undoubtedly, the real problem was that Phoenix had hardly anything to do in the film, which did not showcase his abilities considering his role and limited screen time. Phoenix had difficulty concentrating on his lines because he was into serious use of hard drugs, and his performance is at times painfully obvious. In 1993, he would die of a drug overdose at the tragically early age of twenty-three.

A major change came over the Sundance Festival, and it was partly because of the scheduling and support of a movie called *Reservoir Dogs*, Quentin Tarantino's first feature. The film was brutal and ugly, rather kitschy, and featured an excruciating scene in which a man is tortured by having his ear cut off. *Reservoir Dogs* was only one of several ultraviolent films that premiered at the festival. "I could barely eat for twenty-four hours because they were so loaded with violence," said Redford. Responding to criticisms of the festival, as well as defending his own taste, Redford announced that he wanted to present films that were less commercial, that didn't contain so much "token violence." Ironically, Tarantino had gotten his start in one of the Sundance labs, an experience that he later praised to the skies.

Redford was seen as old-fashioned and stodgy by those who loved the edgy, gross, violent, campy cinema of Tarantino and others like him. Redford's own films may not always have been impeccably tasteful, but what he objected to about many of these other movies was that they strayed too far from his original vision. They were not the type of indies he wanted to champion; Redford wanted pictures that illuminated the human condition and elevated the spirit, although he was not necessarily turned off by films of darker intent. Worse, the films being produced by Tarantino and others were full of commercial elements; they reeked of Hollywood, with its continual appeal to the brain-dead minds of frat boys. It might be said that these films were doofus movies, calculated to appeal to boys of all ages who walked around with their baseball caps on backward. College dropout he may have been, but Redford was no doofus. He was a mature man with a (generally) mature mind, and he recognized that these frat-boy projects, whatever their merits or vitality, were—when you got right down to it—pretty mediocre. He wanted Sundance to stand for something better.

His attitude angered those who felt he had made some pretty bad and mindless movies himself. And there were those who thought that some of his tasteful, ennobling films were dull and lifeless, awash in their own brand of feel-good, greeting-card mediocrity.

Redford was still patiently waiting to begin *King of the Hill* with Steven Soderbergh. Soderbergh felt as if Redford was getting even with him for working with Pollack first by coming late or canceling meetings, but Redford was perennially late no matter who he met with. Redford called an associate of Soderbergh, but not the director himself. He made some decisions that Soderbergh disagreed with, but Soderbergh went ahead and finally shot the film. When it was done Redford asked to see it and, reportedly, didn't like it and asked to have his name removed. Soderbergh says he then told Redford he couldn't keep his fee if his name wasn't on it, if he did nothing for the film. Redford, according to Soderbergh, said he'd take the money and leave his name on the film. Soderbergh told him to forget it. There would be no name and no money, and he threatened to bring the whole unpleasant business to light if Redford didn't back off.

According to one source, "Redford was cast as the villain in this whole thing by Soderbergh but he has his side of it. Sure, Redford got impatient with the way he kept putting the movie off to make others, but to add insult to injury he just didn't like the damn thing. Redford felt he had done a lot to help the film get made; his name value alone helped to open doors. Soderbergh used all these connections from Sundance and Redford felt he should have given something back. It was also a simple personality clash. Redford just didn't like the guy. If he doesn't like you, and doesn't think you're fair or honorable, watch out!"

There would be further bad blood between the two men.

"If you want something very badly, set if free. If it comes back to you, it's yours forever. If it doesn't, it was never yours to begin with."

This is quoted by Demi Moore at the opening of *Indecent Proposal*, which was written by Amy Holden Jones.

Producer Sherry Lansing, a former starlet, had been the first female president of a Hollywood Studio, Twentieth Century Fox, in the 1980s. Later in the decade, Lansing and her partner Stanley Jaffe were producing such independent hits as *The Accused* with Jodie Foster and *Fatal Attraction* with Michael Douglas and Glenn Close. *Fatal Attraction* was directed by Adrian Lyne, who reteamed with Lansing for *Indecent Proposal*.

Indecent Proposal has a down-on-their-luck couple traveling to Las Vegas to try to parlay $5,000 into the $50,000 they need to hold onto their home. On the first night they win half of what they need, but the next day they are left with nothing. A wealthy man who is attracted to the wife asks her to help him play, just for luck, and he wins one million bucks. He offers the same amount to her and her husband if she agrees to spend one night with him. After some hesitation the couple agrees, and the wife and rich guy come together on his yacht while the husband, who regrets his decision, simmers. Later, the wife wants to forget the whole thing; but it nags and nags at the husband until his jealousy drives the woman right into the arms of the still-smitten billionaire. But in the end, she still loves her husband and returns to him.

Warren Beatty was first offered the part of the billionaire, John Gage. Lyne wanted Redford for the role because he thought it would be good to cast him against type; no one would expect *him* to make the pivotal plot pitch. Originally, according to Demi Moore, the part Redford played was conceived quite differently. "In the first script the Redford character was an ugly, stereotypical user, the rich guy without morals, values or ethics. In the rewrite, he became a handsome, charming guy, to whom challenging someone else's morals is a game. Then he falls in love with someone he can't have. It's much more multi-layered." Redford asked for these rewrites; had Beatty accepted the part, the character would have been much sleazier. Moore saw the film as a "morality play."

The prognathous Woody Harrelson was chosen for the part of the husband, right off his run as Woody the dopey bartender on the popular sitcom *Cheers*. "He was the kind of guy, an innocent, that audiences could forgive," Lyne explained. Unfortunately, Harrelson had already signed to do a film with Johnny Depp for MGM. They sued him, believing that he wanted out of the Depp film because *Indecent Proposal* would get more attention and make a lot more money. A settlement was arranged, and Harrelson was free to do the film.

For the movie, Lyne had not wanted to use Demi Moore, who was still married to Bruce Willis at the time. She had tested for every movie he made, and he had never called her back on any of them. He just didn't like her very much. But when she did a reading with a stand-in for Harrelson, something clicked, and he saw something in her that was right for the wife. She won the part over Nicole Kidman and a host of other actresses.

Lyne may have wished he had gone with Kidman, or anyone else, once filming began in the summer of 1992 on the Paramount lot and on location in Las Vegas. "Half the time I could have murdered her," he recalled. Moore said, "I don't want to say that Adrian's chauvinistic, but he has a more traditional sense of women. I just think it's how, out of his passion, he romanticizes [women]." The problem was that Lyne felt Moore's character should show more vulnerability while Moore wanted to make her stronger, even if it weakened the picture.

Many saw the film as a silly bit of exploitation, which "shocked and hurt" Lansing and got Lyne's dander up. "It was pure escapism, nothing more," he explained. Others saw *Indecent Proposal* as just another "production package" put together by cynical Hollywood power brokers who figured it couldn't hurt that Moore had just posed provocatively on the cover of *Vanity Fair*. The film's reviews were mostly excoriating. "So thoroughly implausible, all you can do is bow your head in astonishment," opined the *Los Angeles Times*. Although the film did not engender the interest or controversy of *Fatal Attraction*, a savvy marketing department encouraged talk shows and tabloids to do segments and features based on the premise of the film, along the lines of "What would you do if . . . ?"

Although the movie is on the superficial side, *Indecent Proposal* is a rather nice picture that will work for romantics and not work for just about everyone else. The sex scene between the billionaire Gage and the wife (Diana) is not shown, probably because only its repercussions mattered, and perhaps because Redford still had a prissy—or gentlemanly—terror of bare-ass bedroom scenes. The situation might have been more intense and believable had it been established that Gage and Diana already knew each other. The audience laughed in disbelief when the husband, David, after Diana has left him for Gage, arrives at a charity auction and bids away the entire one million dollars—on a hippo!—but this is his symbolic way of rejecting and apologizing for allowing his wife to be sold to Redford. (Still, most people in the audience, worrying about credit card debt and bills and everything else, would not simply throw away a *million* bucks for any reason). Redford is quite good in the film, playing a superficial man who is used to getting everything he wants. He has a nice moment when he sees Moore looking at Harrelson and realizes that he's lost her. "She never would have looked at me the way she did at him," he explains. To get her to go back to her husband, he pretends that she's only one of a dozen women he's "bought," although she realizes the truth. *Indecent Proposal* is one of those movies that's good enough that you wish it had been better. John Barry wraps it all in his usual sumptuous romantic score, which seems out of place at first but highly appropriate when the picture reaches its resolution.

Indecent Proposal was primarily seen as a vehicle for Demi Moore, who, incredibly, was at the time one of the top ten box-office stars of the decade. But the movie turned out to be one of Redford's more successful latter-day films and grossed over $200 million.

After *Indecent Proposal* came out, a radio interviewer mischievously asked guest Paul Newman if he would sleep with Redford for a million dollars. "For a million dollars I'd sleep with a gorilla," Newman said. When the radio jock asked, "A *male* gorilla," Newman shot back with "add ten percent." According to Newman, Redford's response to this exchange was that a million dollars wouldn't be enough to get *him* to sleep with Newman.

"I thought it was definitely a wonderful part," Redford said of his role in *Indecent Exposure*. "And since it didn't require that much time, it enabled me to edit *A River Runs Through It* [which was released after *Indecent Proposal*] simultaneously. I was very intrigued by working with a director with such a strong visual sense."

Redford undoubtedly thought that his other 1992 project, *Incident at Oglala*—for which he served as executive producer and narrator—

was far more important than *Indecent Proposal*. Directed by Michael Apted, the documentary (with some staged re-creations of events) advocated a new trial for Native American Leonard Peltier, who was convicted of the murder of two FBI agents in 1975. "This man has been railroaded," Redford said. "It adds up to an outrageous default in the American system of justice."

Peltier's supporters knew the one way that they could get Redford's support, and that was to play up the Indian angle, to tell him that supporting Peltier was a way of protesting the many injustices against Native Americans. Redford had gotten involved with the American Indian movement due to his interest in ecological causes. Also, Redford was first contacted by Peltier's supporters not long after making *Brubaker*, which dealt with assorted prison injustices. Once Redford became intrigued by Peltier's alleged plight, he called up Bob Woodward, whom he played in *All the President's Men*, and enlisted his aid in getting more information about the FBI case.

When Redford went to speak with Peltier at the federal penitentiary in Marion, Illinois, he made sure that the press was alerted. "I was extremely impressed by his stature and dignity and the kind of inner strength he had considering the pressure he was under," Redford said of Peltier. Originally Redford was going to use Peltier's story as the basis for a dramatic film, but he decided it would be better to do what he could to see that Peltier got a retrial, and for that purpose thought an advocacy documentary would be more appropriate.

The murders occurred on the Pine Ridge reservation in South Dakota. Pine Ridge was essentially a violent, crime-ridden slum, only it was in the open spaces instead of the inner cities. The area had a startlingly high murder rate; and for the most part, both the victims and their killers were Native Americans. Many of these killings came about due to a deadly feud between the Oglala traditionalists and nontraditionalist tribal government run by one Dick Wilson. In June of 1975, two FBI agents, Jack Coler and Ron Williams, drove onto the reservation and were never seen alive again. Peltier and two other men claimed the murders were in self-defense; but according to other reports, both agents were first badly wounded and then executed at contact range. In his autobiography, Peltier later claimed that the two agents were part of a massive paramilitary assault on the reservation, although there is absolutely no evidence to support this assertion. If it were true, the two agents would hardly have needed to make emergency radio calls for help. In his autobiography Peltier, a petty criminal and drifter, reinvented himself as a major force in AIM (the American Indian Movement) who had to be "taken care of" by the FBI.

That the FBI used to infiltrate and harass such "subversive" groups as AIM and various black and gay civil rights organizations is no big secret. But Redford refuses to look at the Peltier case on its own merits—he doesn't really care about Peltier's guilt or innocence—because, incredibly, he feels the deaths of the FBI agents were justified. In an interview in *Maclean's* that Redford gave to help publicize the movie, he said: "Even if he's guilty, he probably had good cause to do what he did, considering the abuse of these people by our government. There was intimidation. It was a war zone." But even *Incident at Oglala* makes clear that most of the murders on the reservation were committed not by FBI agents, but by natives murdering natives. The deaths of AIM members could just as easily—and more probably—have been attributed to gang violence as to the FBI. When the family of one AIM leader was killed in a fire not long after he gave a speech attacking the FBI, the feelings of paranoia proceeded at full throttle. The thought never occurred to anyone that the fire could have been a tragic accident, like tens of thousands of other house fires.

Despite his "difficult" childhood, Redford never really lived in a ghetto, certainly not anything like the inner cities of today or the Pine Ridge reservation, and he has no true understanding of their dynamics. With his distrust of authority, which became ingrained in him at an early age, he must believe in conspiracy theories and see the minority Peltier as a wronged victim—whether it's true or not. Therefore, the documentary focused on whether Peltier had received a fair trial, not on whether he was innocent or guilty. *Incident at Oglala* emerges as a well-crafted but highly biased piece that mentions the names of the murdered men only once and tells the viewer absolutely nothing else about them; we don't even learn if they have wives or children. (If they did, it's a good bet Redford never paid a call on any of them. Nor, we hope, would he say to their faces that the murders of the two agents were "justified.")

Incident at Oglala seems to indicate that the real killers of the two agents may have been acquitted, but it doesn't exactly clear Peltier of any wrongdoing. What it does make clear—inadvertently—is that many activists need to feel they are on the FBI's target list if for no other reason than to bolster their own sense of self-importance. Peltier's credibility goes completely out the window when he—and others—claim the real murderer is a mysterious man known only as "Mr. X." Peltier claims to know who Mr. X is, but he doesn't want to betray him by revealing his identity. Even his own daughter says on camera that she thinks Peltier is "stupid"—to put it mildly—to conceal the man's identity. Redford and other supporters want to believe that this only illustrates Peltier's "nobility," but the more objective viewer will understand that Peltier can't reveal the man's identity because Mr. X doesn't exist. Whether Peltier invented Mr. X in a misbegotten attempt to create a new suspect, as well as reasonable doubt, or if Mr. X is just a blatant device used by Peltier to sidestep his culpability, the mysterious figure only weakens—if not shatters—his case. Some critics felt that the (understandably) "stony defensiveness" of Peltier's accusers suggested his innocence. The sheer childishness of this reaction unfortunately suggests the quality of Peltier's defenders.

Incident at Oglala was seen by many of Redford's opponents, liberal as well as conservative, as proof of his bleeding-heart or "wacko" liberalism. That is, a liberal attitude undermined by paranoia, antiauthoritarian attitudes, immaturity, and an unwillingness to explore any other explanations but the one that puts the government in the worst possible light. This stance was seen as the left-wing answer to archconservatism, and just as extreme. As for Leonard Peltier, interested readers can make up their own minds not just by seeing the film, but by exploring the various pro and con websites devoted to the case.

By that point in his career, Redford seemed to have won out over his "rival," Warren Beatty. Redford was seen as a more serious and consistent filmmaker than Beatty. He generally chose his projects more carefully and was certainly seen on-screen more often than Beatty. Redford was still capable of playing romantic leads, which did not seem true for Beatty. Young, aspiring filmmakers look up to Redford as the founder of the Sundance Film Festival and, later, as a partner in Showtime's Sundance Channel; and they admire his campaigns for various social and environmental causes as president of the Sundance Institute. Beatty was seen as someone interested in flaunting his abilities in the bedroom more than anything else. Beatty has a solid foothold in Hollywood history due to *Bonnie and Clyde* and—most tellingly—the under-the-table blow job in *Shampoo*. It is also true, however, that Redford carefully guarded his on-screen image while Beatty took bigger risks. "Needless to say," Peter Bart wrote in *Gentleman's Quarterly*, "Beatty is a helluva lot more fun." Redford not only zealously guards his privacy, but hardly lets anyone into the inner reaches of his mind. More than one Hollywood insider has suggested that very few people even bother to pretend that they know Robert Redford. Redford keeps everyone at a distance.

Redford had apparently heard of Norman Maclean's autobiographical novella *A River Runs Through It* in 1983, when a producer named Annick Smith borrowed $15,000 from the Sundance Institute so she could option the book. Smith, fully hoping to make the movie herself, worked with a screenwriter and had talks with a director, Dick Pearce. But by 1987 her option ran out, and the movie had still not come together. The next thing she knew, Redford himself had approached Maclean. "When Redford gets control of a project, it's his project," she said, claiming that Redford took over and that was that. Redford may have felt that if Smith couldn't pull it together in four years, she never would. Dick Pearce was out in the cold, and he was very hurt by it, finding Redford's moves "Olympian." As a member of the American Rivers Association and a trustee of the National Resources Defense Council, Redford thought a film version of the novel could help win converts to his environmental causes. Later on, he responded on a more personal level to the story and characters.

Maclean had experienced some trouble in finding a major trade publisher for his book. But it was eventually picked up by a university press, became a cult item, and was nominated for a Pulitzer Prize in 1977 (the Pulitzer Advisory Board later overruled the nomination). The book was certainly not seen as a good bet for filming. Most agreed that its strength was in its prose style, which could not be translated to the screen. Moreover, there were no major female characters. Then there was Maclean's attitude; he didn't think much of Hollywood types. "Now there's a bunch that eats what they find run over on the road," he was heard to say.

A River Runs Through It (1992) takes place in Montana during the 1920s, when a stern Presbyterian minister (Tom Skerritt) and his wife are raising their two boys, Norman (Craig Sheffer) and Paul (Brad Pitt). The minister is addicted to fly fishing in the river, and his sons try to become as skillful as their father is. Norm goes off to college and seems to have his life in focus; Paul stays in Montana, gets a job as a reporter, but winds up getting in drunken trouble with the law time and again. Norman meets a girl and falls in love, while Paul seems to resist serious attachments. Finally Paul is beaten to death, his body dropped in an alley. Looking back on these events from old age, Norman realizes that there was much about his brother that remains an enigma, but he would always remember him as a wonderful fisherman.

Redford identified with the story, which dealt with a family like his own that was loving but unable to talk to one another about important things such as loss and grief. Redford saw himself as having been a lot like the wilder brother, Paul, in his younger days. "I was that son. I was that brother," he said. Richard Friedenberg, who wrote the screenplay for the film, came from an entirely different family: "Everybody talked and yelled about their feelings all the time." Friedenberg was originally reluctant to take on the project: "I can't do this film, Bob," he told Redford. "Jews don't fish."

Friedenberg was also concerned because there really wasn't a lot of dramatic incident in the movie. Much of it had to be invented. He and Redford decided they would have to research the life of Norman Maclean and ferret out more things that were true and that they could use in the movie. Maclean, by then a crusty and distrusting old-timer, was to be continually consulted. Friedenberg interviewed Maclean as the old man was trying to finish a new book despite assorted physical ailments. When the author didn't yield enough information, Friedenberg went through old newspaper clippings, Maclean's scrapbooks, and old yearbooks, and he talked to Maclean's family and friends. An incident when Paul and Norman ran the river at night in a duck boat and turned over in the rapids was turned into a much more dangerous—and much less believable—daytime episode for the film. Other scenes were painstakingly pieced together after months of research. A sequence in a gambling joint where Paul nearly gets into a fight was created for the movie. The biggest change from the novel was bringing in a love interest for Norman. In the book he's already married, but in the film, the story begins several years earlier so his courtship of the young lady can be included.

Maclean had no problem with the addition of the romantic subplot, but he was oddly reticent to talk in any serious way about his wayward late brother. It turned out that Maclean had fictionalized certain things about Paul in his novella. Paul had actually attended Dartmouth as Norman had, and he was not killed in Missoula due to alleged gambling debts but died years later in Chicago while, according to police reports, he was out one weekend evening spoiling for a fight. Maclean's novella presented a romanticized version of Paul, whose surface charm might well have covered a deeply flawed and unpleasant nature. Maclean didn't live to see the finished film. According to Redford, "I think he would have been pleased. But he was so tough and critical he might not be."

Missoula, Montana, where the story takes place, had grown too big since the 1930s to be used in the movie. Instead the cast and crew spent three months shooting the movie in the town of Livingston. False fronts and temporary second stories were erected on some of the buildings on East Callender Street, which was also made over by piling dirt and sand onto the too-modern surface of the road. Because the film began with period photographs of Missoula, the "on-location set" had to include buildings that would match. The fishing scenes were filmed two hundred miles away from Livingston on the Gallatin stream, a tributary of the Yellowstone River.

There were no sound stages in Livingston, so the sets for the Maclean house were constructed inside the civic center. A school was turned into a jail, a Lutheran church was redressed as Maclean's father's Presbyterian pastorate, and fascinated Livingstonians were drafted as extras. One lucky little boy got cast as Paul as a youngster. John Bailey, who owned a fishing store in Livingstone, was hired to teach the actors fly fishing—not an easy task. A 22-inch mechanical trout of fiberglass and lead was used for some sequences, and it proved a very adept little actor. When some shots proved too tough for the phony trout to handle, a milk carton slightly filled with pebbles was substituted and worked well as a thrashing fish.

As for the real trout, representatives of the Humane Society were there to assure the slimy critters were handled with care. Some of the trout were safely drugged to slow down their movements. No hooks could be used on the fish—ever—so a painless monofilament was attached to their jaws. The fish were delivered to the Gallatin from local hatcheries in containers of cool water. The "star" trout—the big one that Brad Pitt chases and finally lands near the end of the film—received special handling and was returned to its container of aerated water whenever it was tuckered out.

A River Runs Through It has many lovely things in it: exquisite photography by the Oscar-winning Philippe Rousselot, some nice performances, and some interesting vignettes and characters. Craig Sheffer and Brad Pitt are solid; although miscast as their father, Tom Skerritt makes a noble and sincere attempt. The religiosity of the piece is not overwhelming or oppressive, and Redford's direction is consistently assured. Some moments give one pause, however. In one fabricated scene, when the two boys disregard their friends' objections and crazily and deliberately ride their boat over a waterfall, they seem more imbecilic than brave and gutsy (and they aren't banged up very much). Similarly, the business with Norman's girlfriend Jessie (Emily Lloyd) driving her car on the train tracks with reckless disregard only makes her seem stupid while adding nothing to our understanding of her character—ironically, this actually happened in real life. A compelling Indian girl is brought in as Pitt's girlfriend—and for a touch of social conscience—but this very interesting character just drops out of the story line without a backward glance. Jessie's flamboyant brother Neal (Stephen Shellen) is introduced, and though we're given tantalizing hints about him, he goes back where he came from still sheathed in mystery. Worse, Paul remains as much an enigma to the audience as to his family, and his offscreen death is handled in an unemotional fashion that makes it hard to care about. It is, however, moving to see Norm as an old man looking back at his life after everyone he loves has died; but this takes place at the very end of the picture. Like Paul Newman, who directed several movies of his own, it seemed as though Redford felt if you moved an audience to tears, you were guilty of making a soap opera.

A River Runs Through It is a film you want very much to like; but for all its visual poetry, it lacks a strong story and dramatic thrust. Many sophisticated audience members could not get into fly fishing as a homey metaphor for the simple joys and perfections of life, although the fly-fishing scenes are filmed and edited to make them more interesting than you might expect. The movie can't quite overcome the fact that it keeps the audience at a distance from its characters. While many critics characterized the film as being "deliberately paced," it is not so much slow-paced but lacking in dramatic incident and tension. It spends two hours presumably building up to something, only to pull the rug out from under the audience by having the narrator, Norm as an old man (Redford), *tell* us what's happened to his brother.

Several reviewers felt that some aspects of *A River Runs Through It* were a lot of hooey. After describing Paul's remarkable skill at fly fishing in the movie—"a creature in the state of grace by virtue of the quantity and size of the trout he caught, and by the uniquely gorgeous way he cast for them"—John Simon writes, "Grace, apparently, is measured by such things. True, Paul casts with fioritura of an Italian operatic tenor or fencing master, but still, I ask, Grace? You might as soon judge a secretary's closeness to God by how many words she can type in a minute . . . the writing strikes me as no different from that in any commercial movie that makes the mistake of striving for art. . . . The fruitiest verbiage (Maclean's own) is reserved for the countless fly-fishing episodes, and it left me bemused, like a detailed account of the joys of sex from the lover of a woman I consider repellent." However, Simon also felt that Redford's voice as narrator was "a balm to the ear glutted with urban noise."

The film has no stars; the actors' names all come after the title, which comes after the words, "A Film by Robert Redford." A woman named Kathy O'Rear was costume designer for *A River Runs Through It* and other Redford films, and she became Redford's "steady" for several years. Redford's father died the year that *River* was released. Like everything else, Redford kept his relationship with his father very private, but the two got along much better once it was clear that Redford was hardly going to "amount to nothing." His father lived a quiet life, and his needs were attended to. Despite their early problems, Redford was very affected by the old man's death. Asked if his father might have been envious of his great success, Redford did not hesitate in saying no, but then added that he couldn't be that sure, "but that would take me into psychological areas I don't feel equipped to deal with."

After completing *A River Runs Through It,* Redford was again accused of snatching a project away from participants at Sundance. This time it was a script called *Quiz Show,* about the TV game show scandals of the 1950s. The project had first been offered to Steven Soderbergh of *sex, lies, and videotape* and *King of the Hill,* who'd crossed swords with Redford. Soderbergh spoke more than once to Richard Goodwin, who'd written the book on which the screenplay was based. Tim Robbins was penciled in as one of the leading real-life characters, Charles Van Doren.

Soderbergh was offered the assignment by Mark Johnson, who ran an outfit called Baltimore Pictures. Johnson's assistant was a woman named Gail Mutrux, who happened to be married to Tony Danz (the head of Wildwood, Redford's production company). Apparently, this is how Redford acquired a copy of the script for *Quiz Show.* Excited by the possibilities of the story, having lived in New York during the period covered by the movie, Redford decided *Quiz Show* would be the perfect basis for his fourth directorial project. Soderbergh was busy with postproduction of *King of the Hill,* and Baltimore officials evidently used that as an excuse to take the project away from him. Before he knew it, Soderbergh was out and Redford was in.

Soderbergh was enraged that Redford did not bother to call him and tell him the news himself; he had to hear it from others. Ingenuously, Redford replied that he didn't know Soderbergh "wanted" him to call him. Redford claims that he keeps his hands off of Sundance projects, that he knows it would not look good to raid the enterprises of other people—especially independent filmmakers. He maintains it's not his fault if he decides he would rather develop a particular project by himself, or with someone more appropriate; or if someone would rather make the film with him than with anyone else after learning of his interest. His opponents feel that Redford sticks to these rules only when it suits his purposes. "He wanted *Quiz Show* for himself," says one, "and he got it."

Whatever the ultimate truth, Soderbergh estranged himself from Sundance and boycotted the festival for several years, although in 1996 he submitted a new film that he had produced, Greg Mottola's *Daytrippers*. Predictably, the film was rejected by Sundance. He then submitted it to a new festival in Utah, called Slamdance—an obviously negative reference to Redford's festival. Slamdance hoped to show the films that Sundance was *supposed* to show. From the start, Redford was irritated with these interlopers, saying they were "parasitical." Slamdance ran *Daytrippers*. Ironically, Soderbergh dropped out of indie filmmaking for all intents and purposes and worked almost exclusively on big-budget, all-star Hollywood productions like *Ocean's Eleven* and other films starring George Clooney. Maybe Redford was right about him after all.

Regardless of its troubled preproduction history, *Quiz Show* (1994) is arguably Redford's finest achievement as a director, a film of which he can always be justifiably proud. The movie is based on the quiz show scandals of the 1950s. Herbert Stempel (John Turturro) is a Jewish schlump with a good memory for facts who has had a long winning streak on the NBC show *Twenty-One*. But the sponsor, Geritol, sees that the ratings have plateaued; Stempel is told he must take a dive by deliberately giving the wrong answer. The new champion is Waspy Charles Van Doren (Ralph Fiennes), a teacher from a distinguished family with little money of his own. It sticks in Stempel's craw that Van Doren is turned into a celebrity and matinee idol, and he goes to the district attorney to report what happened. Eventually the whole business is scrutinized by congressional investigator Richard Goodman (Rob Morrow), who suspects that Stempel is more than just a sore loser. Goodman becomes friends with Van Doren and tries to protect him (to no avail) when a special hearing is held and the truth comes out. It turns out that Stempel himself was fed the answers. Van Doren's career in teaching is destroyed.

The interesting thing about *Quiz Show* is how suspenseful and riveting it is, even though it is not about the fate of nations, mass murder, or heavy political matters. What's at stake is only the reputation of Charles Van Doren and the careers of many of the somewhat sleazy people involved with the production of *Twenty-One*. Yet we watch in fascination as the whole mess threatens to explode at any moment, inexorably moving toward a point where the Van Doren family will face an almost unendurable scandal.

Quiz Show benefits from the fact that its two main characters, Stempel and Van Doren, are both interesting shades of gray. Van Doren at first does the right thing and categorically rejects the producers' suggestion that he be fed the answers. In his first appearance on the show, however, Van Doren is blindsided by the producers, who give him questions that he has already answered correctly in their office. Trapped in a booth on live television, he is in an incredibly awkward position that few people would know how to handle. Should he come out and expose them on national television, or play along and deal with it later? He does the latter, although he never actually "deals" with it at all.

Stempel is a likable schnook; but like Van Doren, he isn't entirely sympathetic. It is clear that he has been a parasite on his mother-in-law, for whom he holds no sense of gratitude. At first you're rooting for him not to take a dive and answer the pivotal questions correctly, but when you learn that he was also given the answers, he ceases to be the nice little guy who was cast out of the limelight because he has a "face made for radio."

Redford's direction is adroit, with a fine eye for detail. He certainly brings out the best in his actors, all of whom are excellent. Turturro and Fiennes don't just play their characters, they *are* their characters. The actors turn in expert portrayals, right down to those with the smallest roles—for example, Allan Rich as the NBC guy, Robert Kintner. Redford also cast two well-known directors in minor parts: Barry Levinson plays the real-life talk-show host Dave Galloway, and Martin Scorsese proves surprisingly adept in the part of the somewhat sinister sponsor—or does Scorsese simply play him that way after years of making films about lowlifes? Perhaps the best performance in the film comes from Paul Scofield as the elder Van Doren. When he learns what his son has been accused of, he says, "Cheating on a quiz show is like plagiarizing a comic strip."

Not to quibble, but *Quiz Show* has some problems. The scene in which Charles Van Doren finally admits the truth to his father is well played, but moves much too fast to have the required impact. This is one of the movie's most important scenes, but it's over too soon. The business with Jack Barry, the host of *Twenty-One* (winningly played by Christopher McDonald), practicing how to say his name before show time smacks of dumbed-down comedy and is undeserving of this picture. *Twenty-One* had already been on the air for some time before the events of *Quiz Show*, so it makes little sense for Barry to rehearse lines he'd said a thousand times before. It's a sop to the uncultured audience that feels most comfortable with sitcom antics.

Quiz Show doesn't hit you over the head with it, but it has a subtext of the privileged versus the underprivileged, the Wasp against the Jew, the handsome athwart the homely, that resonates on a more subtle level. Hal Rubinstein in *Interview* made an interesting observation that may have been true for a large segment of the audience: "When we learn that both Stempel and Van Doren are cheating, we only want to forgive Van Doren."

Redford had seen the real Van Doren when he was actually appearing on *Twenty-One*. "I watched Van Doren because he was rising, rising, rising, and he had this kind of . . . there was an arrogance about him. Yet he feigned a kind of innocence. And as I watched him coming up with these incredible answers, the actor in me said: 'I don't buy it.' " Redford also meant for *Quiz Show* to examine the power that television has over the gullible masses. He recalled as a child seeing a TV set in a window and being fascinated by the fact that the man talking was miles away somewhere else but he could see him on the screen. "The idea was to set *Quiz Show* at this time of naive energy, when television's audience tended to believe what it saw as what really was."

The movie was also a reaction by Redford, who felt that "shame is pretty well gone out of our vocabulary." The TV people's lack of ethics, in his opinion, paved the way for the mind-set leading to the behavior of Richard Nixon, Senator Bob Packwood, and Oliver North. "I see the quiz show scandals as really the first in a series of downward steps to the loss of our innocence," said Redford, who believed those steps had continued with the assassinations of JFK, Bobby Kennedy, and Martin Luther King and led up to Watergate, Iran-Contra, and even O.J. Simpson. "I think people may look at this film and say, 'Well, as a scandal, big deal. But in a historical context, it's very much a big deal. This was the beginning of our letting things go. And what did we do about it? Kind of nothing, as long as we kept being entertained."

Redford also feels that the Van Doren scandal changed the way the American public looked at educators. "I have a theory," said Redford, "that Van Doren's collapse brought down with it the notion of academics as the people of the highest calling and that they never regained their place." Redford feels that in the past, members of academia were featured more frequently in the media, which is now undeniably dominated by movie stars. Redford would love for some sociohistorian to investigate his theory, which is compelling but may have flaws.

A lot of dramatic license was taken in *Quiz Show*, which brought Redford a great deal of criticism from those who charged that he messed with real lives and history because he used the real names of all the people embroiled in the farrago. In a *National Review* article Jeffrey Hart, who knew the Van Dorens, charged that Redford had the script altered to reflect his opinion that "Charles sought out the crooked world of TV and the quiz show because he sought revenge of some sort on his father's Olympian status. This strikes me as completely gratuitous. I saw no evidence of hostility between them, but rather an easy and thorough friendliness." Of course a lot of hostility can fester beneath a casual friendliness, and the movie really doesn't play up this aspect as much as Hart suggests.

However, Hart, who was at Columbia during the crucial period, claimed that rather than causing a sensation, Van Doren's performances on *Twenty-One* made few waves on campus. "My guess is that the real Charles tried out for the thing entirely as a lark, much as a group of young professors might go slumming at Atlantic City or seek out a really awful saloon." Columbia was not co-ed in 1956; so all the scenes of smitten girls going gaga over Van Doren, signing up for his classes, are entirely fictional. One critic commented that "any minute you expected to see Fiennes coming out of a classroom covered with dozens of lipstick marks like Bing Crosby in *The Big Broadcast*." Far from a matinee idol, the real Charles Van Doren was not that much better-looking than John Turturro, who plays Herb Stempel.

"I have to admit there's a little bit of a cheat going on," Redford explained, "and it was a tough one for me because I am among the minority of people not sympathetic to Van Doren." But this had nothing to do with the man's appearance. "He made his Faustian bargain," continued Redford, "but he made it much more clearly than I show. I made a choice to show the corruption of the innocent."

Hart was especially incensed with the way he felt Mark Van Doren was portrayed. "I began to see that Mr. Redford himself, unlike the Columbia students of the time, quite possibly thinks the real Mark Van Doren was . . . boring, that the real Columbia was snobbish and boring. I began to see that the real Robert Redford actually belongs to the ersatz world of *Twenty-One*." Redford was always drawn more to show business than he was to the world of academia; he never graduated from college. Then the daughter-in-law of the character played by Martin Scorsese joined the attack, stating that "I do not want the Robert Redford movie to become the 'textbook' on this period. I don't want the granddaughters of Edward Kletter to be ashamed of their grandfather."

Hart and others were appalled that even in the endnotes for the film, Redford fudged the truth "to give the movie a downbeat coda," as Hart puts it. Stemple did not work in the subways, but taught social studies. Charles *did* become a teacher as well as an author. Hart charged that due to "the process of distortion and falsification" in the movie, there was little difference between Robert Redford and the producer of *Twenty-One*, Dan Enright. "[Redford] seems to pride himself on his ideas, but they are crude, the ideas of a Beverly Hills virtue monger."

Another big difference between real life and the movie is that the man who uncovered the quiz show scandal was not Richard Goodwin but Joseph Stone, who ran the Manhattan district attorney's complaint bureau before becoming a judge. Stone was not pleased that his all-important role was completely left out of the motion picture. But since the film was based on a book by Richard Goodwin, the author was turned into an important participant of the drama. Redford wisely shows us the Goodwin character, well played by Rob Morrow, looking at an expensive car in a showroom during the credits, allowing the audience to have some familiarity with a character who actually doesn't get into the action until the movie is half over.

Redford had other reasons for doing this as well. "What is that man doing in that [show] room?" he said. "He has no business being there. So right away you're setting up that this is a very ambitious guy. The one thing all three characters—Goodwin, Stemple, and Van Doren—had in common was their greed, their ambition to make the myth real. And so the opening scene says right away how America was in a rush to act and think big."

Quiz Show was not the first, nor will it be the last, Hollywood movie to take liberties with history and the lives of real people. Redford might have avoided *some* of the criticism had he simply changed the names of the parties involved, made the film "inspired" by certain events; but he knew the picture would get more attention if it were presented as a "true story." As Max Frankel put it in a *New York Times Magazine* piece, "If license to fictionalize were all that [filmmakers] wanted, they would change the names of their protagonists and color them at will, leaving it to pedants to decipher each clef of the roman. Clearly, they want something more: to harness the power of history, to provoke the thrill that an audience feels when it thinks it's witnessing reality, and when it suspends the knowledge that the words and faces and scenes on screen are the creations of invisible hands."

But Redford had other things on his mind while he was making *Quiz Show*, and in retrospect it's a miracle that the movie turned out as well as it did. Just before shooting began, with everything in place to start and Redford anxious to proceed, he learned that a liver had been found for his son, Jamie. By that time, Redford's son was almost permanently ensconced at the University of Nebraska Medical Center, where he was the patient of one of the country's most respected transplant surgeons, Byers W. Shaw Jr., MD. Jamie's body was wracked with infections and high fevers, and the jaundice made his eyes and skin yellow. The liver came in the nick of time; tragically, it was from a twenty-nine-year-old man who had died of a brain aneurysm.

After Jamie called his father in New York, Redford shut down production of *Quiz Show* and flew to his son's bedside along with the rest of the family. The transplant proceeded and was deemed, with some reservations, a success. "I remember waking up, and my entire family was standing in a semicircle around my hospital bed, holding hands," recalled Jamie. "I will never forget it. In that instant, I realized the power of family—the power of family love."

Jamie seemed headed for a full recovery, but within a week it was clear that something was wrong. An ultrasound revealed a blood clot on the new liver. The doctors did what they could, but it was clearly only a matter of time before the new liver would fail. Within two months, Jamie was back in the hospital awaiting a new liver. "I was really starting to deteriorate," he remembers, "both physically and emotionally." Redford visited his son regularly; he told Jamie that he was going to completely shut down production on *Quiz Show* until the crisis had passed and do it the following year. Jamie told him that was crazy, that too many other people would be affected. Thereafter Redford would shoot *Quiz Show* from Monday to early Saturday and then fly Saturday afternoon to Omaha so that he could spend the rest of his weekend with his son. They watched footage of the movie and talked. "I really came to rely on this," recalled Jamie.

Jamie's mother was working on her dissertation for New York University, but she flew from Manhattan to Omaha to be at her son's side, or to babysit her grandson Dylan when required. Mutual love for their son overcame any tensions that they might otherwise have felt. "You're always going to be parents to the same children," Lola philosophized. "Bob and I really leaned on each other for a lot of emotional support." Redford himself recalled: "You want to reach down and make it all right and pick him out of his crib as you could do when he was little."

On his wife's birthday, July 7, Jamie learned that a new organ had been donated by the family of a nineteen-year-old man who'd died from a traumatic head injury. Within two weeks after the second transplant operation, young Redford was feeling well enough to be released from the hospital with a very good prognosis, and he remains healthy to this day. For a long time, Jamie felt guilty that someone had to die in order for his own life to be saved. "There's a constant darkness around it," he said. It took him awhile to accept that the sad fate of the donors wasn't tied to his own, that his need for a new liver didn't *cause* someone else to die.

The families of the young men who died did not want the organ recipients to know their names, but Jamie wrote letters and had them forwarded to each family. "I told them that I was going to do my best to honor their gift and live my life as well as I could," he said. He hoped they would understand that because of their selflessness, his wife would not be widowed and his son would not grow up without his father.

Two years after getting his life back, Jamie established the James Redford Institute for Transplant Awareness, which educates the public about some alarming statistics: that over 60,000 people in the United States alone await transplants, and twelve of those people will die each day because there aren't enough organs to go around. The nonprofit institute also answers any questions that potential organ donors might have. Jamie also produced a documentary, *The Kindness of Strangers*, which aired on HBO. The film profiled not only the patients who were waiting for transplants but also the families of those who died and donated organs. Jamie also produced a shorter film about organ donation that could be shown in high schools.

It wasn't long, of course, before Jamie was completely bitten by the movie bug, and he became a screenwriter for such movies as *The Acting Thing* (1996), *Cowboy Up* (2001), the telefilm *Skinwalkers* (2002)—with his father as executive producer—and *Spin* (2003), which Jamie also directed. Robert Redford has always said that his greatest achievement, without hesitation, is his children. "The hardest thing in the world is when your children have problems. There have been so many hits on our family that no one knows about, and I don't want them to, for my family's sake."

12

nother film that debuted the same year as *Quiz Show* was *Pulp Fiction*, Quentin Tarantino's follow-up to *Reservoir Dogs*. *Pulp Fiction* illustrated the big change that had come over independent filmmaking; and it wasn't just the increase in ugliness and violence, or that pandering to the frat-boy mentality by a filmmaker who in a sense was—and always would be—an overgrown frat boy. *Pulp Fiction* was completely indistinguishable from a Hollywood movie; it even had movie stars. True, John Travolta was practically a has-been before Tarantino resuscitated his career, and Bruce Willis's career was in a slump, but both men were still very well-known actors. *Pulp Fiction* also made a great deal of money, got a lot of attention, and was nominated for Oscars.

In fact, *Pulp Fiction* made well over $100 million, confirming that huge profits could be realized in independent film. Soon agents from multimillion-dollar distributing companies like Miramax were descending on the Sundance Festival with cell phones and sunglasses, attending screenings, hoping to find the next big winner, the next *Pulp Fiction*.

This whole development was galling to Redford on one hand and gratifying on the other. Galling, because Sundance was being blown out of proportion, its original purpose in aiding little films to find an audience lost in a sea of glitz and feverish bidding for distribution rights. Sundance filmmakers were more likely to be people who wanted to work *within* the system, to make commercial studio films and make millions, rather than work outside of it like true indie filmmakers. Infected with a corporate mentality, they were chasing the Hollywood Dream. (Ironically, Redford was the very image—the highly *successful* image—of the Hollywood Dream.) But Redford also found the situation gratifying, because Sundance was becoming the American version of Cannes. It was—in some ways—a smashing success that hardly had to beg for attention. Redford was only human, but he was also a movie star; and as much as he valued privacy, he also loved being part of—the very founder of—all this *excitement*. Whatever the vicissitudes of his acting career, he was still a major *player* and his festival was *hip*. (And with the growing attendance, which became huge, the resort cabins were sold out in no time.) He loved it; he hated it. Sundance had succeeded beyond anyone's wildest dreams—but it had also failed miserably, and Redford knew it. It was only going to get worse.

Many people were convinced Sundance had totally gone to the dogs by 1996, with the premiere at the festival of films directed by superstar Al Pacino, second-tier celebs Kenneth Branagh and Kevin Bacon, Gwyneth Paltrow's younger brother, and lesser names such as Stanley Tucci and Campbell Scott. These were people with connections, a far cry from the unknown filmmakers out there who had talent and a dream but weren't related to or acquainted with somebody famous. Reportedly even Redford was appalled at how the festival had "gone Hollywood," while his opponents suggested he secretly reveled in the attention and prestige garnered by the participation and attendance of stars of the first, second, and lower ranks.

Redford sounded arrogant and certainly didn't help matters when he complained that too many people at the festival were "not filmmakers. They are friends of, wannabes, would-bes, left turns, kookabees, people out on parole—everything is coming our way." One critic snapped: "As long as you're Al Pacino or Gwyneth Paltrow Redford wants you at the festival. If you have no pedigree or name you might as well just show your movie to your friends in your basement on Saturday night. Sundance has no place for you." Redford's people claimed he was referring to the large numbers of people attending the festival who had no films to present and who took up space at the screenings and parties; but it sounded, unfortunately, as if he were telling "would-bes" and "wannabes" that they were unwelcome at the festival, which had, after all, been created to help them.

Redford was continually perceived as being above it all, distancing himself from the festival he himself brought into being. "Does Bob

Redford really run this thing?" asked actor Dennis Leary. "I'm convinced he's not even connected. There's a blond guy who walks fifty yards away and waves at you." Apparently some minor-league celebrities got miffed because Redford didn't genuflect or pay homage to them. Redford said that he didn't mind criticism, but when "it starts to feel personal, it bothers me."

Stories came out of Sundance that Redford worked best with people who were content to operate in his shadow, who had no agendas—or great ambitions—of their own. But that works both ways. Why should Redford have had to put up with people who were less interested in serving Sundance than they were in having Sundance serve them? He hired people to work for Sundance because he knew he was too busy to run it and do it all himself. Of course he wanted people who shared his vision; of course he would become disenchanted with those who didn't. They were his surrogates, helping him fight the good fight, and it seems incredible that anyone who couldn't accept that would even want to work there.

Redford's employees began competing for his time, attention, and friendship—it was heady for some people to be friends with a major movie star, to say that Bob Redford was a "close personal friend" and not just someone who helped you pay your bills. They were frustrated when Redford couldn't find the time to attend a meeting or get back to them on some important item. Redford was frustrated because he expected to delegate, have people show initiative and think for themselves, but everyone wanted his approval. Says one Sundance staffer, "Redford doesn't suffer fools gladly. If he doesn't confront people it's because he doesn't like the ugliness of it. What would people prefer, somebody ranting and screaming and humiliating people all the time like [Miramax head] Harvey Weinstein? Bob acts like a gentleman and if that can be exasperating sometimes, so what? So he doesn't come right out and tell someone they suck. Once he realizes they're not doing their job he has a right to fire them and they're always so *surprised*, they thought he *loved* them and loved their work. Let me tell you, at Sundance there were and are a lot of incompetent people that Redford probably let stay a lot longer than he should have, but he'll never get credit for that, for giving them a chance to improve."

Still other Sundance staffers say that while supposedly Redford likes people to show initiative and act independently, especially while he's away for months doing movies, he gets flummoxed and irritated when he comes back and sees that they've done just that. Many, many people have characterized him as a "control freak"—or is he just trying to hold onto his vision even as he watches it slipping away, due partially to the actions of some of his employees? It all depends on who you talk to. The truth is that there is no easy truth.

After *Quiz Show*, Redford's next project was to be the film adaptation of Richard Preston's nonfiction book about the Ebola virus, *The Hot Zone*. Producer Linda Obst gathered together the screenwriter from *Quiz Show*, director Ridley (*Alien*) Scott, Jodie Foster as the female lead, and Redford for the leading role of virologist Karl Johnson. Not soon after everyone got on board, it was learned that a similar film or rip-off entitled *Outbreak* was going to be made—starring Redford's old friend and *All the President's Men* costar, Dustin Hoffman. It would now be a race to see whose picture would get into theaters first.

Disaster first struck Redford's project when Jodie Foster read the latest script, found that her part had been altered in ways not to her liking, and withdrew. Obst was frantic to find a new female lead. She then got a call from Redford's agent at CAA (Creative Artists Agency), who told her that *Outbreak*'s director, Wolfgang Peterson, and his screenwriter were going to fly to Sundance to talk to Redford. Obst was panic-stricken over this development until Redford gave her a call and told her, "I'm going to do your movie." Obst remembered that she "had to keep Redford in the movie at all costs—I believed in him; he had been so honorable to me and was so compelling a personality. Bob fell out after loyally hanging in there for eight, grueling, irrational months. For Bob, time had finally run out." *The Hot Zone* never did get made.

The American President was made, but with Michael Douglas in the title role and not Redford, who had been involved in discussions over the film for months. Apparently the filmmakers just did not see eye to eye with Redford on certain changes he was insisting that they make. After awhile Redford simply stopped taking their calls. "When stars are unhappy about something," says Peter Bart, "they rarely sit down for an earnest conference. Most often, they simply vaporize. Robert Redford has long been known by producers to be the kind who likes non-confrontation. If he's unhappy about a project, he'll simply disappear and not answer his phone."

Redford was also unhappy when he didn't receive an invitation to a Grand Canyon ceremony celebrating the creation of the 2,700-square-mile Grand Staircase–Escalante National Monument. He was especially ticked off because he had written to President Clinton, imploring that Clinton do what he could to prevent development in the region. The initiative to create the monument was labeled "stealth-like," designed to head off public hearings and a possible battle in Congress. Even the Republican governor of Utah was out of the loop; but Democratic supporters of Clinton, including Redford, were among those in the know. The hush-hush nature of the project was given as the reason that Redford's name was inadvertently left off the invitation list. Redford gave a call to Secretary of the Interior Bruce Babbitt, whereupon his invitation was immediately rushed over.

Up Close and Personal (1996) began life as *Golden Girl*, a biopic about the late newswoman, Jessica Savitch. According to screenwriter John Gregory Dunne, who worked on the script for *Golden Girl* with his wife Joan Didion, "[Savitch's] story was a perfect cautionary gloss on the perils of the counterculture—a small-town girl with more ambition than brains, an overactive libido, a sexual ambivalence, a tenuous hold on the truth, a taste for controlled substances, a longtime abusive Svengali relationship, a certain mental instability, a glamour job, and then in 1983 a final reckoning, at age thirty-five, that seemed ordained by the Fates—death by drowning with her last lover in three feet of Delaware Canal mud after a freak automobile accident." Redford and Michelle Pfeiffer were signed as stars, and Jon Avnet was hired as director.

The story of *Golden Girl*, if properly handled, surely would have made a compelling film. Rightly or wrongly Savitch became a symbol of the new TV journalism, in which promotions were based more on looks and personality than on long-time experience, thus setting up conflicts stemming from jealousy and righteous indignation. On the other hand, Savitch was seen as a hard worker and had undeniable flair on camera. She also had a severe drug problem, which affected her personality; a long-time relationship with an abusive man, also in TV news, who was in love/hate with her; a marriage of convenience to a wealthy older man whom she left disillusioned; and a second marriage to a bisexual doctor, who hung himself in the basement where Savitch was sure to find him. Her life provided enough material for several films, but in the end virtually all of it was scrapped for a brand-new storyline. Only a few elements of the original story would remain, in particular the long-time relationship between a man and woman who both work in a TV newsroom.

The film's executive producer was Ed Hookstratten, a TV news talent representative and former agent for such personalities as Tom Snyder and Tom Brokaw as well as Bryant Gumbel and others. Hookstratten had also been Jessica Savitch's agent, but he disliked the way he was portrayed in Alanna Nash's bio, *Golden Girl*. According to Hookstratten, it wasn't cocaine that caused Savitch's problems both on camera and behind the scenes, but the painkillers she was taking for a "serious deviated septum." (A deviated septum is generally a painless and quite common nasal condition.) To set the record straight, Hookstratten bought the rights to Nash's book, telling the author it would make a great movie. "The day we signed the contract," recalled Nash, "he told me that this movie was going to be about the Jessie *he* remembered, not the one with all the psychological problems. That's when I began to worry." Hookstratten, who had zero experience making movies, contacted his friend, the producer John Foreman, who became another executive producer on the film. It was Foreman who hired Dunne and Didion.

Years went by as the script languished in "development hell." Dunne and Didion were instructed to write one draft after another as the studio kept coming up with a new slant or direction. Different stars were attached to the picture: Kathleen Turner, Meg Ryan, and others. Directors were considered, ranging from Penny Marshall to John Schlesinger (*Midnight Cowboy*). Finally Redford became attached to the project, and it looked like a go. Pfeiffer was signed, and Jon Avnet was tapped to direct. It looked like it was all coming together, but this was only the beginning.

"I just thought it was a good, tough love story, a good dynamic of two raw characters," explained Redford. "I thought the collision of those two was interesting." After Redford finished making his fairly precise "suggestions," his character wasn't so "raw" anymore. Out was the man's alcoholism, and the same for his abusive qualities. (As previously noted, Redford would play only "cute" drunks, à la Sonny in *The Electric Horseman*, and never an out-and-out alcoholic.) Warren Justice was no longer a self-destructive figure. In contrast, Pfeiffer's agreeing to do the film also had a couple of conditions attached, but hers were much more practical. She could be on location for no more than four weeks, because she had just given birth to a son and had previously adopted a little girl who was then two. She was told that this would be no problem.

There were some problems between the director and his screenwriters, however. "It would be safe to say that we did not get along with Jon Avnet when we first met," Dunne remembered. "We had of course checked him out with people who had worked with him, and what they all said was that he did not suffer from an ego deficiency. Avnet liked long meetings, we liked short. He liked to talk, we did not like being talked at. He was a control freak, and we resisted being controlled . . . [it was] the worst working relationship with a director we had ever had." After fulfilling the terms of their contract, the Dunnes walked away from the movie, along with producer Scott Rudin.

"They'd send me the nastiest faxes," Avnet recalled. "I would ask them to try something, and they'd send back a fax with a note: 'This scene is dangerous to your health. It is inexorably cute." Despite describing his relationship with the Dunnes as "like oil and water," Avnet felt that "we ended up working together very well." He probably felt different after reading Dunne's book about the whole ordeal.

Jeffrey Katzenberg, studio chief of Disney, thought the movie was going to turn out to be much too depressing. He hated the idea of the leading lady dying at the end. Of course, it was the Disney studio that took the gritty story of a prostitute trying to start a new life against desperate odds and turned it into the mindless, cutesy crowd pleaser *Pretty Woman*. There are those at Disney who insisted it wasn't an objection to the darkness of the Savitch story that necessitated changes; rather, it was simply the new direction everyone decided to take.

A new script by Anthony Drazen, commissioned by Avnet, was

fashioned without the input of the Dunnes; it took the movie in very different directions. Redford wasn't happy with it, and neither was Michelle Pfeiffer. "Certain people felt the script needed more humor," she recalled, "but it was kind of scary because it was very close to shooting and Bob and I didn't like it." Things had not worked out for Redford on *The Hot Zone* or *The American President*, and he was anxious about having another big deal fall apart. Through their representatives, the two leads got in touch with the Dunnes and asked them to reinvolve themselves with the movie or it probably would never get made. Redford arranged for the Dunnes and Avnet to meet at his house in Connecticut to talk things over. "I think they were a little burned out from the futility of the exercise," Redford remembered. Ideas were hatched, dismissed, or taken up enthusiastically in a five-hour meeting, during which Redford occasionally popped in to make sure the screenwriters and director were not tearing each other's heads off.

"I have a hard time calling Robert Redford 'Bob,'" recalled Dunne. "He is younger than I am, and yet I would let his diminutive cross my lips only if I could not get his attention by catching his eye or clearing my throat.—'Bob' is somehow diminishing; it would be like calling Woodrow Wilson 'Woody.' . . . What [Redford] brings to the party is the power of his iconography, a presence that must be heeded. He is . . . a movie star with a mystery and an irony rarely seen onscreen anymore."

Redford told the little group that Michelle Pfeiffer thought the prison riot seemed too coincidental. He suggested that the sequence focus more on the two lead characters and not so much on the actual riot. Dunne was impressed with the quality of Redford's advice. "What was interesting about listening to Redford was that his remarks were always those of a director," Dunne recalled, "not an actor counting lines." Redford also suggested the inclusion of a love montage and felt there should be a much stronger ending.

During a first reading, it became apparent that much of the dialogue would have to be cut. Dunne was especially anxious that Redford's line "I've been to Havana" be cut; he was afraid it would solicit unintentional laughs from the audience because Redford's *Havana* had laid an egg at the box office. Oddly, they left in a line having

Redford's character say that he and his first wife lost a child—"she lived for one week and eight days."

By that time, *Golden Girl* had metamorphosed into *Up Close and Personal* and had nothing to do with Jessica Savitch. Everyone felt the film needed to be more upbeat and contemporary; Savitch's story took place during the seventies and eighties, when the news business, or so they reasoned, was somewhat different. Now the movie was a kind of journalistic *A Star Is Born*, with Redford the older mentor who falls in love with the beautiful younger woman played by Pfeiffer, and vice versa.

Redford said that he would have been far more interested in telling the real story of Jessica Savitch if he had been directing the movie. As an actor he felt there was little for him in the original *Golden Girl*, because Savitch had "like, five guys in her life when she died." (Actually, the role of the mentor with whom she had a long-term dysfunctional relationship would have been a wow of a part—for any actor but Redford.) Redford, however, was not thrilled when a scene during which he hauled off and slugged Pfeiffer—she then kneed him in the groin, which Redford loved—was cut from the script; he felt it was "absolutely quintessential to their characters."

For her part, Pfeiffer was discouraged by the way Avnet kept trying to turn it into a feel-good movie that made the material much lighter than she felt it needed to be. As Avnet sought the humor in each sequence, "we were kind of a weight dragging Jon down," she recalled. Avnet felt his decision to go "lite" was justified. "I have no interest in doing a biographical piece on a very self-destructive woman," he told writer Benjamin Svetkey. "You'd have to be a bit of a sadist to enjoy that sort of thing."

An unusual aspect about the shooting of *Up Close and Personal* is that the movie was filmed in sequence, which is almost unheard of. Avnet reasoned that doing so would make it easier for Pfeiffer to show the transition from the gawky girl who's rather gauche in front of the camera to the seasoned news professional. Therefore, she's much more awkward in the early scenes when her character is "on camera." For research, Pfeiffer sat at an anchor desk reading from a TelePrompTer and found the experience "humiliating. I didn't anticipate it being that difficult." She never felt she got good enough to do a stint as a real newscaster on network TV. Avnet often felt Pfeiffer wasn't exuding the proper energy or intensity in a scene, so his trick was to make her mad before actually shooting. When she realized what he had done, she only got madder, adding juice to the scene as Avnet intended.

Pfeiffer had always wanted to work with Redford, and though the two had discussed various projects over the years, nothing ever came of them. The part in *Up Front and Personal* appealed to her because she liked to play women "who pull themselves out of the rubble and overcome obstacles," as in her winning turn in Jonathan Demme's *Married to the Mob* (1988). She would tell reporters that she'd wanted to smooch with Redford since she first saw him in a movie when she was eight. She only had to wait about thirty years. Asked if perhaps her character was too dependent on a man, Pfeiffer said, "In the end she realizes she's not. It's her journey. Nobody's perfect. And a lot of women spend a whole lifetime realizing they don't have to be dependent on a man."

"There was very interesting stuff about Savitch that I would have loved to have kept," said Pfeiffer. "I probably would have liked for it to stay closer to her story. But I guess that would have been just *too* dark. We really wanted to make a love story." "This movie isn't *about* Jessica Savitch," Avnet ranted at reporters when the film was released. "This movie is *suggested* by Jessica Savitch." For his part, Redford recalled that although sometimes he really wanted to punch out Avnet, he generally found him "open and collaborative."

Kate Nelligan, who played Redford's ex-wife, enjoyed working with Redford. She also had admired the actor since watching him as a girl at her local movie house in Canada. "It's very hard when you don't act with the big, big movie stars every day," she recalled. "You come in and do your bit, you go away for a couple of weeks and you come back. So you never get over its being Robert Redford. It never becomes the guy that you go to work and see every day." Nelligan had trouble speaking to "Robert Redford" in the scenes when she says terrible things to him. "You can't do this, you can't say this to Robert Redford!" Jon Avnet reported that Redford liked the way Kate pushed him around and didn't hold back. "He responds very well to strong people, performers or otherwise. Redford's pretty tough."

Most of the reviews for *Up Close and Personal* were negative, citing the film's superficiality and predictability. Even the positive notices harped on those negative attributes, but felt that the film was full of some old-fashioned glamour, romance, and star power. The *New York Post* opined that the movie was "just as shallow and manipulative as that Barbra Streisand/Kris Kristofferson vehicle, but it won't jerk nearly as many tears from its audience. . . . One of the many problems with this movie is its uncritical endorsement of the style of advocacy journalism Justice [Redford] represents—in which a reporter injects his own opinion into a story and takes off to humiliate or destroy some powerful public figure. Innumerable recent surveys show that the public is understandably wary of this approach in which TV talking heads make themselves bigger than the stories they cover."

Some critics, many of them old enough to know better, made a big to-do about how much older Redford was than his costar. "Robert Redford sleeps with Michelle Pfeiffer and doesn't have to pay for it?" wrote the *New York Newsday* staff writer Jack Mathews, taking his cue from *Indecent Proposal*. "Things are definitely looking up for the aging Sundance Kid." Mathews also felt that "it is one of the ironies of Redford's long career that the only costar with whom he has managed a genuinely relaxed screen chemistry is Paul Newman. . . . Newman is his only costar with equal charisma." The *New York Post* felt that Redford and Pfeiffer generated "shockingly little chemistry with each other." The *New York Times* commented on "the cameraman who miraculously shoots edited scenes from two different angles—with a single camera—in the midst of a fast-breaking crisis. This is the magic of movies, if not of television news . . . but in *Up Close and Personal* it's the matinee idols who make the rules." (In the sequence referred to in the *Times* review, the camera *cuts* back and forth between Pfeiffer and the man she's interviewing when simply having the camera *swing* back and forth would have taken care of the problem.)

In interviews, Pfeiffer diplomatically pooh-poohed the idea that Redford was too old to be a leading man; it was something that had dogged him since *Havana*. "I think this movie will put that to rest," she said at the time of the film's release. "He's still every bit the leading man he's always been. . . . He's every bit as charming. Probably more so now that he has a little age on him. He was too handsome

when he was younger. He's more interesting now." The age difference between the characters is never referred to in the script itself.
The only age-related sequence is when Redford and a colleague
watch a Willard Scott type giving a birthday cake to an elderly
woman.

Asked if he doesn't think the sequence is cute, Redford responds:
"Do you think it's cute to be condescending to people just because
they happen to be older than you—when you're 98, fighting to hold
onto your dignity, and this 'Rob' comes out of the blue with some
cheap birthday cake calling you a 'beautiful youngster'?" The lines
may have been written by the middle-aged screenwriters; but Redford, no longer a youngster, could relate to them. Even he was occasionally victim of that type of age-related condescension.

Up Close and Personal is not really a bad movie; in fact, like *Indecent Proposal*, it's another one of those pictures that's just good
enough to make you wish it were better. Redford gives a perfectly
professional and very nice performance in the film. At times his underplaying is quite effective, especially in a scene when his boss (the
highly talented James Rebhorn) tells him off. Redford's quiet response contrasts vividly with Rebhorn's strongly played emotional
outburst. Pfeiffer is also effective, although—possibly influenced by
Avnet—she's a little too light when talking about her deceased husband, Redford, at the end of the film. A scene in a prison goes on too
long, but generally the film is fast-paced and fairly entertaining. A
nice, somber touch is applied when Pfeiffer, watching the TV screen,
sees Redford's body lying on the ground in the background after his
shooting death in Panama. It's highly ironic that after all the fuss
about the "downbeat" ending dealing with Jessica Savitch's death,
Up Close and Personal ends with the *hero's* demise.

Despite bad reviews, the picture opened strong (it was heavily promoted). It earned back its sixty-million-dollar costs and then some,
making the Disney studios a nice profit. But another irony is that
ABC Productions bought the rights to another bio of Savitch, *Almost
Golden*, and hired Sela Ward to play the real woman. The biopic
detailed all of the negative and "depressing" aspects of Savitch's life
and ended with her death as it happened in real life. Airing in September of 1995, *Almost Golden* scored extremely high ratings and became one of the most successful cable films ever made. It seems the

public could have handled the real story after all. If you doubt that this version would have been so successful at the theaters, remember that many other downbeat Hollywood biopics have been released and done very good business.

The same year that *Up Close and Personal* was released, Redford unveiled his latest Sundance conception: the Sundance Channel, which would run independent films twenty-four hours a day. The partners were Showtime and Polygram. A lot of the thunder was taken away by Bravo's Independent Film Channel (IFC), which had the same idea and got it on the air a lot sooner. "TV used to be exciting," Redford said. "Today, talk shows look like wrestling, and there's nothing equivalent to the dramas of the golden age. I'm hoping the channel will change that." Almost from the start, the Sundance Channel came under fire for hiring people who had no connection to the independent film movement. It seemed that Redford was damned if he did and damned if he didn't. The same people who accused him of running off for months and forgetting about Sundance now complained that he was spending too much time on all the minutiae of the Sundance Channel.

Redford was embroiled in a little embarrassment over a documentary called *American Movie*, which chronicled the efforts of an untalented, Ed Wood–type filmmaker to finish his wretched horror film. Scenes from the movie were going to be shown on the pilot episode of *Split Screen*, a show about the wild things filmmakers do to make their movies. Redford was considering the show for weekly airings on the Sundance Channel. Eventually Redford passed, with a note that "this is not the kind of filmmaker [the one featured in *American Movie*] we want to help promote." His decision should have come as no surprise to anyone who knew that Redford was looking for filmmakers of talent and intelligence, not schlockmeisters. But then the completed *American Movie* sneaked through the radar—at least Redford's radar—and wound up being shown at the Sundance Festival. "This was strictly to embarrass Bob," says one insider. "People were laughing about it."

Redford did not actually pick the films that played the festival. He could always try to veto the presentation of a particular film, and he reportedly had tried to do so more than once but was forced to back down. In any case, his hands were tied with *American Movie*. It would hardly be the first or last time that the festival premiered a picture that did not exactly meet with Redford's approval, or meet his criteria of what constituted a good independent film. According to another source, "The TV show would have promoted the filmmaker of the movie within the movie. The documentary was another matter. The filmmaker who was profiled in the documentary was an untalented person, but the documentarian was another matter. Therefore, it really wasn't so odd that they showed the finished film—the documentary that is—at Sundance."

Sometimes it was Redford's critics who were clueless, not Redford. While some people saw *American Movie* as a work that celebrated the spirit of independent filmmaking at all costs, the truth is it documented not an important, worthy piece of moviemaking and a talented director, but a piece of trash that didn't deserve to see the light of day.

As if the new Sundance Channel weren't enough to deal with, Redford decided to dabble in a new project, the Sundance Cinemas, in summer 1997. Redford made a deal with the General Cinema Corporation, which had theaters in fully half of the fifty states, to showcase independent movies in its theaters. It was an ambitious plan, but the problem was that the theaters were badly located and needed a lot of refurbishing, which Redford expected General Cinema to pay for. Redford was criticized for teaming with General Cinema in the first place, when many people felt it would have been better to go with Landmark Theaters because it was an art-house chain to begin with. Apparently Landmark had already been snapped up, and Sundance was left with General Cinema or nothing. People believed that Sundance was always a step behind in its dealings because Redford needed to go off to fulfill picture commitments at the worst possible times. Then Redford was excoriated for hiring an ex-jock and restaurateur to run the Sundance Cinemas instead of someone with experience in film distribution. Reconstruction began on a couple of movie houses, but eventually the whole thing fell apart and the work was never completed, at least not under Sundance's auspices. General Cinemas declared bankruptcy in 2001, effectively putting an end to all the plans for Sundance Cinemas. "I don't mind failing at something," Redford said. "But it's hard for me to let go of something that hasn't been tried. But I think that idea got away from itself."

Redford was said to be dissatisfied with the management of his Wildwood production company, which was run by Rachel Pfeffer and had offices in Santa Monica. Redford would show up late in the afternoon to find more people waiting to talk to him than a doctor with a thriving practice of hypochondriacs finds in his waiting room. Most of these people had little chance of getting any chance at Redford; even Pfeffer herself had to get past Redford's assistant, Donna Kail, in order to have just a few moments to speak with him. This situation had more to do with the demands on Redford's time than it did with any innate character flaws.

In July of 1997, Boulder police held a press conference announcing that they were reopening the investigation into the fourteen-year-old murder of Sidney Wells, Shauna Redford's boyfriend. Many people, including Wells's mother, found it interesting that this happened at the same time that the Boulder police were getting a lot of heat over the unsolved murder of little JonBenet Ramsey. Commander David Hayes of the Boulder police department commented that investigators were hoping that the new ballistics and blood DNA tests, which had not been available in 1983, would make all the difference in the Wells case. Hayes had waited two years for lab tests on shotgun pellets to be completed. An arrest warrant had not yet been made out for the still-missing suspect, Thayne Alan Smirka.

Meanwhile, at Creative Artists Management, agent Bob Bookman was orchestrating a campaign. Nicholas Evans was the essentially unknown author of "The Horse Whisperer," which at that point was only an uncompleted manuscript. Bookman's plan was to make it seem like "the book of the decade," which according to writer-producer Peter Bart meant Bookman could "auction it as though it were a Michael Crichton dinosaur book." The price for the film rights was set at three million; then Bookman offered five interested parties the right to talk to Evans on the phone and convince him why they should be the one to do the movie. The others who wanted to do the

film were mightily alarmed when they discovered that Redford was
one of the interested parties. When Redford offered to not only produce the film, but star in it and direct it, he effectively put everyone
else out of the running.

Michiko Kakutani's *New York Times* review of *The Horse Whisperer* was headlined: "A Load of Rehashed Horse Hockey." Kakutani
deemed the book "abysmal" and wrote, "About the only thing missing is a picture of Fabio on the cover." Redford was seen by many,
particularly among the literati, as one of the many purveyors of junk
books and junk cinema—movies and books cobbled together to
make big money and big deals—who were "dumbing down" litera-
ture and lowering the standards of art in general and cinematic art
in particular. His insistence that Sundance present films of class and
artistic merit seemed hypocritical, critics felt, if he was going to spend
so much time and money on Hollywood pabulum like *The Horse
Whisperer* instead of films of real depth and substance.

The Horse Whisperer (1998) deals with a rather cool New York editor named Annie (Kristin Scott Thomas), a Tina Brown type who
has an okay marriage and a daughter, Grace (Scarlett Johansson),
who loves riding on her horse, Pilgrim. One afternoon there is a terrible accident, and both horse and daughter are badly injured; the
girl loses her leg, and the horse is physically and "emotionally" traumatized. Annie is reluctant to have the horse put down; then she
hears of a "horse whisperer," Tom Booker (Redford), who lives in
Montana and can work wonders with horses. He refuses to come to
New York, so Annie packs up Grace and Pilgrim and drives all the
way to Montana to importune Booker to help. As weeks go by and
Booker begins to heal the horse, Grace and Annie bond with Tom's
brother, Frank (Chris Cooper), and Frank's wife (Dianne Wiest) and
their children. Grace comes out of her shell, and Annie and Tom
develop strong, loving feelings for one another. Annie's husband
(Sam Neill) comes to visit and realizes that he and Annie are at a
turning point. He goes home with Grace and leaves Annie to work
things out. In the end, a heartbroken Annie decides to return to her
husband.

Originally Natalie Portman was cast in the pivotal role of Grace,
but she had to bow out when offered the chance to make her Broadway debut in *The Diary of Anne Frank*. Filming on *The Horse Whis-*

perer had been delayed so, unfortunately, it would conflict with the Broadway run. Portman was a great admirer of Anne Frank, having read her diaries many times, and had also visited the home where Frank was hidden. It had always been her dream to play the girl, so the choice was an easy one for her to make. Redford was also disappointed when his first choice to play Annie, Emma Thompson, wisely passed on the role. Instead he offered it to a gal the British press call the "Ice Queen," Kristin Scott-Thomas.

Filming had to be delayed a year, because it was decided not to shoot during Montana's long, hard winter months. Despite the delay, bad weather frequently necessitated the postponement of filming for days at a time. The picture took over six months to complete, causing problems for many of the actors. "It was a hell of a lot longer than I thought," Kristin Scott-Thomas reported. "It was frustrating to wait for the rain to stop or the land to dry or the river to go down—it stopped being about work and became your life."

Then there were problems with the horses. Fake blood made some of the equines break out into hives. Then an animal chiropractor had to be flown in from Los Angeles on an emergency basis because one of the beasts threw its back out. Once more filming was delayed until the animal was ready, willing, and able to go through its paces. The original December release everyone had hoped for was pushed back to the following May. This gave Redford time to reshoot the accident sequence, which he had been dissatisfied with. (It still isn't perfect in the finished film.) The first cut of the picture was over four hours long. Redford spent much of the months before the May premiere choosing what to leave on the cutting-room floor; most agree he didn't leave enough.

When the final cut was put together, the film clocked in at two hours and forty-nine minutes, including the closing credits. Although some critics applauded Redford's decision to take his time—quite a bit of time—telling the story of *The Horse Whisperer*, the length works against the picture. *The Horse Whisperer* has a very slight, intimate story; much of the drama takes place internally. It's one thing for a movie like *The Godfather*, which is full of dozens of characters and incidents and a whole lot of action, to take three hours; but *The Horse Whisperer* hasn't a whole lot going on except in the characters' minds. Eugene O'Neill's *Long Day's Journey Into Night* is three hours long, but it is full of memorable, three-dimensional characters and has many strong dramatic confrontations—it is a work of depth. None of that can be said of the comparatively superficial *Horse Whisperer*. In the Golden Age of Hollywood and British filmmaking, plenty of films—*Brief Encounter* (1945) immediately comes to mind—could tell a story that was more romantic and powerful than *The Horse Whisperer*, and do it in half the time. *Brief Encounter* is only eighty-five minutes long, but it is much more effective movie-making than *The Horse Whisperer*.

The movie works on one level, and that is as Redford's personal statement, an explanation of why he loves the peace and beauty of open spaces. It is an evocation of the unspoiled West, functioning primarily as Redford's valentine to nature and the great outdoors, all captured with great beauty and precision by the cinematography of Robert Richardson. Richardson's work could have been dismissed as ordinary picture-postcard views were it not for its decidedly artistic elegance, which places it a notch above the standard. Some especially wonderful long shots are taken from high above as the truck and van holding the horse drive into the big country of Montana and we see the striking change in topography.

The Horse Whisperer is another fragile mood piece like *A River Runs Through It*, except that it has fewer characters and much less story to tell and is far more bloated. Far too much of it, as well, comes off as contrived and convenient. Like many movies, today or yesterday, it presents a rich person's fancy: ordinary people don't just drop everything they're doing to drive out West and find someone who can give aid and succor to either horse or daughter. But movie stars like Redford are entirely out of touch with "ordinary people." Some critics also found the movie antifeminist in that a woman who has mapped out a life and career for herself is willing to throw it all away for a man who would never, it is clear, do the same for her.

Some critics overpraised the film because it was seen as a "serious" movie in a day when explosions, car crashes, Arnold Schwarzenegger, and Jason Vorhees in a hockey mask taking an ax to teenagers were dominating the nation's screens. Because the Merchant-Ivory films also paid less heed to box-office receipts, they were similarly overpraised; in fact their deficiencies—inadequate scripting, James Ivory's insufficient direction—were almost gleefully overlooked. But even if some critics gave high marks to *The Horse Whisperer*, it is unlikely that it is a movie that they *enjoyed* all that much or would be in a rush to see again. We suspect that the typical admirers of *Horse Whisperer* were middle-aged women who loved horses and Robert Redford, but not necessarily in that order. They could cry along with Kristin Scott-Thomas as she tearfully drives back to New York because they, too, had to go home to their own husbands, who were undoubtedly in worse shape than Robert Redford and didn't look half as good as Sam Neill.

The movie taps into the peculiar connection that exists between some young girls and horses, although it is not a film that goes into analysis of this connection or of much else. There are scenes of Redford "working" with Pilgrim, pulling on ropes tied to the horse, letting him run, and so on; but we never really see him *doing* much of anything. Lovers of the outdoors and of horses may be mesmerized by the first two hours of the movie, but most people will find it becoming interesting only when it becomes apparent that Annie and Tom have fallen in love. And even then, nothing happens. Redford lets Thomas Newman's lovely score do a lot of the work.

Redford did bring out the best in his performers, however. Excellent work is done by Scarlett Johansson as the girl, Scott-Thomas as her mother, and Diane Wiest as the sister-in-law. The supporting cast is also uniformly fine, with very nice moments from the elderly Jeanette Nolan as Tom's mother and from little Ty Hillman as his nephew, Joe. Sam Neill was probably forced by Redford to employ Redford's usual "minimalist" approach in the scene when he has a serious talk with his wife. He and it are so devoid of emotion that the scene never rings true. Redford is aware that in real life people often hide their emotions, speaking with even voices and blank faces when discussing matters that weigh heavily on their souls; but movies *are not real life*, and they should not be.

Redford's own performance has a casual ease and charm that works for the most part, but he isn't on the level of the other actors, who simply *give* more of themselves. He falls back on being cutesy too often and is completely predictable, showing no real growth as an actor. When Tom tells Annie some details of his backstory, he seems uncomfortable. This is not to say that the *character* is uncomfortable discussing his personal life, and Redford gets that across, but rather that Redford's discomfit in talking of personal things—even when they're his character's and not his own—affects his performance. The climactic scene when Tom tells Annie that he loves her is almost comical; even Rock Hudson could have shown more passion, either on or off the screen, when telling a woman he loved her!

One scene in the movie works beautifully, however. When Tom and Annie dance together at the barn dance, the sequence is perfectly edited and features some wonderful pantomiming from the two actors. Redford's face is finally expressive, and for once you can believe what his supporters say about his getting across more with a look than other actors do with pages of dialogue. If the whole movie had been on this level, *The Horse Whisperer* would have been a much better picture.

But ultimately, *The Horse Whisperer* works for certain audience members only. As one reviewer put it, "Early in the film there is a horrendous accident in which two girls and two horses are hit by a truck, and horses' hooves are shown smashing through the windshield of the truck, apparently hitting the driver. If you find that you're concerned over what happened to the horses, you'll love this movie. If you're concerned about what happened to the little girls, you *might* like this movie. If you wonder what happened to the truck driver—we never do find out—then this movie is definitely not for you."

Along with the aforementioned positive notices, *The Horse Whisperer*—and Redford—also engendered some negative, occasionally smarmy, and even downright nasty reactions from reviewers. "*The Horse Whisperer* is based on the book by that British guy who wrote a book in order to get a movie based on it," quipped Mark Steyn in *The Spectator*. "[Redford has taken] some pulpy mush and turned it into a soft-focus valentine to himself. . . . Movie-goers accept the convention whereby Redford can never play opposite a woman his own age or, indeed, within 20 years of it. If Jane Fonda . . . or Katherine Ross . . . turned up in a Redford movie now, they'd be playing his mother. . . . But, in return, we're entitled to expect the guy to make a bit of an effort. There's no equivalent of the erotic tension Clint generates when he offers to help Meryl Streep in the kitchen. Instead there's absolutely zero chemistry between Rob and Kristin."

"In addition to Tom's love affair—consummated or not—with

Annie," wrote Gerald Kaufman in the *New Statesman*, "there is Redford's love affair with Redford. Seldom has any director set out so determinedly to mythologize his male star. Despite Redford's raddled right cheek, the man's features can still, if photographed appropriately, be made to look both pretty and rugged. So we are treated to lots of crinkly-eyed views of Redford, with the sun (or the lighting) haloing his golden locks . . . . Annie . . . replaces her east-coast power dressing with comfy western outfits (provided, of course, by Calvin Klein.).'' The critic also felt Johansson displayed a very limited acting range.

Many people felt Redford directed himself in *The Horse Whisperer* only because Clint Eastwood had directed himself in the adaptation of the bestseller *The Bridges of Madison County* three years earlier. Whether this is true or not, Eastwood certainly proved that it could be done (both films also have the same screenwriter). Redford said that he simply had a "feel for the material. This was probably the one film I could direct and act in."

One source insists that "Bob is very competitive. Of course he was competing with Eastwood, another Hollywood survivor. Maybe he started directing films originally to compete with Newman, who began directing years earlier. But he also wanted to do a long epic film because that's what his friend Sydney Pollack had done with *Out of Africa* and *Havana*, and he wanted to beat Pollack at his own game, prove he could do it just as well, if not better. Pollack and Bob have always been in competition with one another, but they've managed to keep their demons and jealousies suppressed for the most part. That's why Bob took up directing in the first place. There's no maliciousness in it—Bob just wants to do as well or better at everything as everyone else does. He has a movie star's need to be the best."

13

By 2000, Redford was reportedly getting a little irked that many of the films premiering at the Sundance Festival, films that actually began life in the Sundance Lab, would go on to win acclaim—*Boys Don't Cry* was one—and the Sundance Institute's role in the process would be virtually forgotten. He was also tired of seeing everyone else making a profit on these films except for Sundance. Another gnawing ache was that IFC, which had stolen some of the thunder from the Sundance Channel with its own cable channel of independent films, had gone into actual movie production. Redford decided it was time for Sundance to do the same.

His opponents charged that Sundance and all of its activities and divisions became more and more important to Redford as he grew older and his acting career flagged. Perhaps. But it could also be true that Redford wanted to continue nurturing—and now producing— the kinds of independent features that he had created Sundance for in the first place. Redford continued to act as executive producer on a number of other people's films, but there was only so much he could do himself. Jeff Kleeman from MGM was hired to head up the new Sundance Productions. This move turned out to be a bit premature.

Although he had hammered together a financing deal with Vulcan Ventures, which was headed by Paul Allen, Redford seemed reluctant to actually sign the papers that would begin the cash flow. (In return for money, Allen would be given a controlling interest in the Sundance cable channel.) Redford realized he might be going into business with Vulcan too quickly, that he needed to get to know the company and the man who ran it much better before he could proceed—so he simply stalled. As months went by, several employees were stolen away from other companies to work for Sundance Productions, and many interesting new projects were announced. Meanwhile Redford worked on *The Legend of Bagger Vance*, which interested him a lot more than business deals. He still hoped to work with Allen when he was through with the picture, however. But then—disaster: Universal, which had acquired Polygram's interest in the Sundance Channel, was bought by the French entertainment firm Vivendi, which had no intention of selling its interest in the channel to Allen, who was supposed to have bought out Redford's partners in the channel once the papers were signed. Now that would not be possible. Allen stopped returning Redford's phone calls, and Sundance Productions was effectively dead.

Gary Beer, Sundance's long-time chief operating officer, was fired by Redford around this time, supposedly for his role in some of these deals, although one source insists that is not the case at all. "Beer had absolutely nothing to do with the collapse of Sundance Productions, and Bob seemed perfectly happy with other deals he put together. I think it was more that Bob just didn't think he was always on top of things the way he had to be when Redford was preoccupied elsewhere. Let's just say they came to a *beating* of the minds and leave it at that." In an even more surprising move, Redford fired his long-time publicist, Lois Smith, a few months later. "It wasn't so much that she wasn't planting enough good stories about Redford," says one source, "but that she couldn't keep all the bad stories out of the papers."

Many of Redford's staffers and associates, most of whom conceded his "good intentions," saw Redford as someone who sort of wined and dined you, hung on your every word, when he needed your help and attention, but forgot you as soon as you were no longer needed. Unfortunately, Redford employed many people with fragile egos who couldn't seem to understand that they were not there to become his personal friend or lover—some female staffers had delusions along those lines—and that a man like Redford would inadvertently have his attention easily diverted by the next script, the next project, the next person in line. Some staffers made the mistake of thinking they were part of Redford's inner circle, his confidante, and they were hurt if not crushed upon finding they weren't. These people became especially bitter. Rather than being planets near the center of Redford's universe, they were only one of myriad atoms circulating around him. They didn't understand that anyone who had as many chestnuts in as many fires as Redford did couldn't become close friends with every single person he knew, worked, or associated with.

And then there was Sundance itself. Many films that would go on to be famous and successful and make lots of money and even win Oscars premiered at Sundance—*Memento, The Deep End, In the Bedroom*, among many others—but critics charged that Sundance was catering to Hollywood-type filmmakers whose films featured Hollywood stars. The institute was not benefiting the true independent filmmakers, especially those with little money or connections. On one hand, Sundance undeniably began and nurtured many careers, gave guidance and experience to many filmmakers, was in many ways a smashing success. On the other hand, many other filmmakers never got out of the starting gate. The original vision of Sundance seemed to have been lost, something mourned by many of the staffers who had been let go over the years as Sundance—and the vision—altered dramatically.

The Legend of Bagger Vance (2000) was based on a 1996 novel by Steven Pressfield. The novel's characters were the personification of Hindu and Indian concepts. Rannulph Junuh was an Indian warrior who receives spiritual guidance from Bagger Vance. Much of the book's spiritualism and symbolism were wisely jettisoned for the film version. Originally Redford was going to play Rannulph, with Morgan Freeman as Bagger, but it was eventually decided to go with younger and more bankable stars; Matt Damon as Rannulph and Will Smith as Bagger. Making the characters younger "made it better," Redford felt, "because it's more tragic for a young person."

"It's the classic journey of a hero who falls into darkness through some disconnect with his soul," said Redford, "and then of his coming back into the light with the help of a spiritual guide." Redford also wanted to make comments about the world of sports and how it has changed for the worse. "Today, sports is so much about money. The test is still there, but everything around it has made me pretty much lose interest in watching. I'm bored by all these guys on TV wearing insignias and endorsements. The skiers at the Olympics looked like the incredible tattooed men. What happened to the days when it was just the person out there doing it?"

In the film adaptation of the story, the decidedly nonethnic Rannulph Junuh (Damon) is so shattered by his experiences during the great war that it is years before he manages to return home or get in touch with his sweetheart, Adele (Charlize Theron). After her father dies, a financially strapped Adele comes up with a bold idea—a golf competition featuring (real-life) superstars Bobby Jones and Walter Hagen. She also enlists the returned vet Junuh, who was once a great golfer himself, to represent Savannah. Junuh is given great, if somewhat curious, encouragement by a mysteriously appearing black man (Bagger Vance), who asks to become his caddy, and the game proceeds. At first Junuh does not do very well; but as his confidence grows, his game improves, and it starts to look like he might have a chance after all.

"When Robert Redford calls you," remembered Smith, "you'll do anything. *Bagger Vance* was the first time I completely surrendered myself to the will of the director. I didn't let my ego scratch and claw for attention. I think we all felt a special trust in him because, being an actor himself, he's been in our shoes and knows what it is to create a performance." Smith wanted to do the film for another reason. "It's a movie full of white people, and the black guy gets to be God. I'm loving that one."

Matt Damon was a little nervous about playing a part that Redford had at first earmarked for himself, but remarked that the director "totally dispelled" that feeling. "I liked Matt," said Redford. "I didn't know him, but I thought he was a solid actor, intelligent, strong, with an All-American look that works for this character. And he hasn't been marked yet by life's 'stuff.'" Damon closely observed Redford in action, wanting to soak up all that he could about directing movies. One afternoon Redford joined in when Damon and his father, who was visiting the set, were playing catch. "I'm playing ball with Roy Hobbs [Redford's character in *The Natural*]!" the elder Damon remarked. According to Matt Damon, the Bagger shoot was "easygoing—not a pressure cooker."

Redford has been playing golf since he was eleven years old, when he used to sneak onto golf courses and hit a few balls until he heard some adults approaching, whereupon he would hide in the bushes.

Will Smith, who was already a golf fan, became "the ultimate golf junkie," as he described himself, after appearing in the movie. Damon had never played a game of golf in his life, which was problematic because he, not Smith, played the golf pro in the film. "I had to learn from ground zero," said Damon. "It was fortuitous that I hadn't played, because I undoubtedly would have picked up some bad habits." PGA pro Tim Moss was hired to work with Damon and turn him into a fairly credible golf player. Because Damon's character is off his game for much of the movie, his imperfections weren't much of a problem. Charlize Theron was not required to play golf, but she identified with her character because of the way Adele completes the work on her father's golf course; in South Africa, after Charlize's father died, her own mother rebuilt her husband's construction company.

Redford got a remarkable performance from a twelve-year-old actor named J. Michael Moncrief, who came from Belleville, Georgia, and attended a casting call his aunt saw announced in the local paper. More than 250 other boys auditioned, but Moncrief won the part of a boy who hero-worships Junuh. Little Moncrief had never seen a single movie either starring or directed by Robert Redford. "He told me to see *Butch Cassidy and the Sundance Kid*," said Moncrief, "but I slept through it." Dialect coach Elizabeth Himselstein used Moncrief's genuine Georgia accent to instruct the other actors in the film. At first Charlize Theron found the boy's accent impenetrable. "The language he speaks does not exist, let me tell you," she said.

The Legend of Bagger Vance shouldn't work at all, but it does, emerging as Redford's best directorial effort since *Quiz Show*. It's all too easy to pick apart the problems with *Legend* until one realizes and accepts that the movie is a *fable* and as such has to be taken on its own terms. Of course it's completely unrealistic for white characters to be so polite to a black man in the 1930s South; yes, we learn nothing about Bagger Vance's background; and the character, essentially a ghost, comes off as one of those all-knowing black stereotypes favored by Stephen King. It takes forever for Adele to tell off Junuh about just abandoning her after the war. The screenplay needs work; it should have fleshed out its characters beyond their use as symbols.

Yet *Legend* is a truly lovely movie that engrosses and moves the sympathetic viewer, making the playing of golf (!) seem not only sensuous, but sensual. This effect is primarily due to Redford's sensitive direction, although it is an understatement to say that the contributions of cinematographer Michael Ballhaus and composer Rachel Portman are also vastly important. As in the film *Strictly Ballroom*, the intensity and attention to detail makes you care about people and events that might not otherwise interest you in the least. *The Legend of Bagger Vance* is similar to *The Natural* in that it, too, is about a traumatized man who takes a long time to return to the woman and the sport he loves, but there the resemblance ends. Redford has taken his love of golf and turned it into a work of art.

Naturally, opponents of Redford and Sundance sniggered at *Legend*. Where were the ears being sliced off in close-up? How come nobody was getting his brains blown out in graphic realism? No screwed-up teenagers having sex in public restrooms? No grunge or hard rock or organs being disemboweled or displayed for the audience's edification? The poignant mood piece Redford had crafted made no impression on the trendoids or hipsters of all ages, and Redford could probably not have cared less. He was into class, not sleaze.

Once again, Redford's work engendered mixed reactions from the critics. "Redford lofts this heartfelt fantasy over the trap of banality to create a true sense of wonder," wrote Peter Travers in *Rolling Stone*. "Redford plays the game of filmmaking to reveal what he holds sacred: story, character, feeling, thoughtful pacing, and an alertness to nuances of honor and shame that most movies skip in the rush to the rush. In this new millennium, Redford's game couldn't be less trendy or more vitally alive." The *Austin American Statesman* declared that "Robert Redford's aggressively sentimental movie begs us to feel, but its cold calculation deflects emotional participation. Composed with Redford's characteristic care—he's a stellar craftsman—*Bagger Vance* is climate-controlled melodrama set at room temperature . . . And what of the big-grinnin' Bagger Vance? A benevolent black man doing good deeds for whites in the racist Old South is sheer white-liberal fantasy."

In 2000 the tabloids began running stories that Redford was planning on getting married for a second time. His bride? Attractive forty-two-year-old German artist Sibylle Szaggars, who had done some paintings of Native American life that Redford admired and bought for $16,000 a pop. Indians and art are two things that Redford and Szaggars have in common. The two did not get married. To this day they are an "item," staying together in Redford's various dwellings from Utah to Manhattan, although the official story is that they are not actually living together as such. Most of Redford's intimates feel that Redford is afraid to tie the knot because of all the pain engendered by his divorce. "He wants a woman in his life," says one insider, "but he doesn't want to recreate the situation where she feels she's second best because of all his assorted projects from Sundance to movies to the environment. It is unlikely that they will get married." Redford does his best to keep his relationship with Szaggars as private as everything else in his life, answering almost no questions about the woman, who is similarly coy with the press.

Redford was undoubtedly hoping to be cast in a hit movie when he made the mistake of signing up for *The Last Castle* (2001), which was directed by Rod Lurie. Redford was also intrigued with the idea of working with Lurie, "a staunch liberal who went to West Point," as Redford describes him. Lurie flew to London to meet with Redford; their first meeting lasted three hours, during which they mostly talked about *All the President's Men*. Lurie had been so impressed with that movie, he told Redford, that it inspired him to be a journalist as well as a filmmaker. "That movie changed my life," Lurie said. The two men had two more meetings before Redford would make a commitment.

In *The Last Castle*, Redford plays General Eugene Irwin. Through hubris, Irwin disobeyed a presidential order and disregarded reliable intelligence; his decision resulted in the deaths of eight men. After his court-martial, Irwin is sentenced to a military prison run by Colonel Winter (James Gandolfino), who has never seen combat. Winter admires Irwin; but when he learns that the general has only contempt for him, his attitude changes. The prisoners tell Irwin of injustices and ask him to help them, but Irwin only wants to serve his time without fuss. Gradually he comes to realize that Winter is inept and unworthy of his position and rallies the men to take over. Winter manages to take back the prison after a major struggle, and Irwin is killed.

Lurie had been warned that he might find Redford difficult to deal with, but instead found him to be "a piece of cake. He's a good guy. The best way to sum up my two actors is this: Between takes, Gandolfino would play chess. He must have played 200 chess games over the course of the shoot. Between takes, Redford would sit there and read the dictionary and quiz me on words." During the scene where Redford has to turn over all of his photographs to the prison clerk, the clerk picks up one snapshot and asks, "Is this your daughter?" Lurie substituted a head shot of Paul Newman for the actress who plays his daughter (Robin Wright Penn).

Lurie found Redford "very easy" to work with. "It's because he is a director and he realizes what it's like to direct a pain-in-the-butt actor. . . . We'd spend an hour or more in the trailer talking about his work. He never went to dailies because he knew that was unnerving. When he had advice, I'd take it."

The Last Castle has a fascinating premise that is almost completely muffed by a poor, contrived screenplay operating below the level of an old prison picture from the thirties. In *The Last Castle* virtually all of the prisoners—who undoubtedly have committed rapes, gay bashings, girlfriend beatings, and other heinous acts—are presented as good guys who just took a wrong step; the warden and *every single* guard are portrayed as sadistic thugs who are, incredibly, worse than their captives. Movies like this, of course, never show the prisoners' victims. In some ways *The Last Castle* is *Brubaker* redux, although it is much more simplistic—and simple-minded—than the earlier film.

The Last Castle, which battens on the soldiers-stick-together theme when Irwin and the prisoners bond and work together, simply and conveniently forgets that the warden and the guards—not to mention the soldiers who are called in to quell the rebellion—are *soldiers themselves*. It also forgets that the men in the prison are not the crème de la crème of the Army, but its fuckups. In one incredible sequence, a drug dealer working with Redford manages to jump into an Army helicopter that subsequently crashes after his struggle with the pilot. Redford rushes forward to pull the drug dealer to safety, but the pilot and the other soldier on board—innocent men just doing their job—*are completely forgotten*. As if that isn't enough, we're asked to believe that the oily drug dealer would turn down an offer from the warden to serve only a few weeks, instead of the several years remaining on his sentence, to work with Redford.

Stuff like *The Last Castle* appeals to Redford for two reasons. First, there is the hatred of authority that became ingrained in him when he was a youth rebelling against his father, his teachers, and the police. (We have to wonder what makes Redford feel that he was such a juvenile delinquent; were there more serious crimes in his past?) Apparently Redford lacks the emotional maturity to shrug off these antiauthority feelings as he gets older. Secondly, Redford is a limousine liberal who makes excuses for criminals because he truly believes that "there but for the grace of God go I." If Redford were a more introspective person, he might ask himself if he really would have turned into, say, a rapist or any kind of serious career criminal just because his acting career didn't take off. In addition, Redford clearly feels tremendous guilt over his success, which he does not really believe he deserves.

Movies like *The Last Castle* harken back to the days of Spencer Tracy as Father Flanagan in the *Boy's Town* movies. They promote the naive attitude that there are "no bad boys"—just boys in bad circumstances who have no other way to react. Most sophisticated people see this as an incredibly simplistic view of criminal behavior; but Redford is of the mind-set that sees all criminals as being somehow "victims of society" rather than people who must be held accountable for their own actions, which often hurt and destroy people whose "circumstances" are no better than their own.

Lurie attempted to justify the lack of balance in the movie by claiming that Leavenworth "is full of decent guys who have made one mistake and they're thrown into jail for it. There's not a single lifetime criminal in there." But he also admitted that "there's a fantastical element at work in the movie. Is it realistic? Maybe not. But it's a big old piece of entertainment that I tried to make as believable as I could."

In the film, Redford rattles off his lines with little conviction, feeling, or even aplomb; most of the time he seems bored. He's somewhat better in the scene where he's forced to move a pile of rocks while the inmates bet on him—a *Cool Hand Luke* kind of moment—and reveals that he's not in bad shape when he takes off his shirt. Some of the critics took ageist swipes at him, suggesting unfairly that he used a "body double" when there was no reason a man of his age couldn't simply exercise and stay in shape (probably better shape than the critics making fun of him). In the scene where Irwin's daughter comes to see him in prison, Redford demonstrates his wonderful ability to listen, but he doesn't react much to the very strong things the woman is saying in explaining that she doesn't really want a relationship with him. However, this scene works to the film's advantage, underlining the fact that Irwin is a law unto himself. If he ignored a presidential command, he's certainly not going to listen to a mere woman, even if she is his offspring. Still, Redford is too light and casual to make the scene convincing.

The Last Castle received mixed notices; many critics commented on its implausible moments and black-and-white characterizations. "The script turns the beleaguered prisoners into sympathetic victims of fate rather than the murderers and rapists and drug dealers they actually are," wrote the *Providence Journal*. "In order to sledgehammer home the point, Lurie and screenwriters David Scarpa and Graham Yost erect a Trojan horse of a plot device [stretching] the film's credibility until it snaps," opined the *Indiana Post-Tribune*. "Lurie's penchant for overstatement and windiness works against his message."

As usual, the critics were sharply divided over Redford's performance. "Redford seems to have wandered over from some educational-TV program," opined Moira Macdonald of the *Seattle Times*. "In scene after scene, he makes speeches about flags, or prison history, or leadership, or castles; it's all very noble and inspiring, but doesn't really disguise the fact that he's not actually doing anything. Redford's become such an icon that all he has to do is show up, recite lines in that laconic, all-American voice, and let the sunlight glint off his hair; no emoting seems necessary. 'He's become John Wayne,'" said my companion. . . . *The Last Castle* might have benefited from more pre-shooting talk about what makes an intriguing character— and what makes a star performance."

However, the *Belfast News Letter* felt that "Redford brings great humility to his role and is a striking physical presence, exuding the confidence and inner calm of a military leader." According to *Entertainment Weekly*, "Redford is impressively stoic and starched. But how did he ever get involved in such a simplistically heavy-handed salute to gentlemen warriors?"

By the time Redford and Brat Pitt reunited for *Spy Game* (2001), Pitt was every bit the megastar and sex symbol that Redford had been thirty years before. This was not a romantic picture (although a muted love story was at its core), but a suspense-action flick directed by Tony (*Top Gun*) Scott. Redford plays a CIA man named Nathan Muir, who is just about to retire when he learns the Chinese have captured his former protégé, Tom Bishop (Pitt), during a mission and will execute him in twenty-four hours. Muir expects his associates to do everything they can to get Bishop out, but political ramifications make his release a non-priority. Muir feels some responsibility for Bishop, and not just because he brought him into the CIA. He had ordered the kidnapping of a woman—a former girlfriend of Bishop's—who was involved in a bombing; not realizing the depth of Bishop's feelings for the woman, Muir planned to use her in an exchange with the Chinese government. Bishop has been captured while trying to rescue her. Without informing his superiors, Muir engineers the escape for Bishop and the woman he loves. As this story is played out, flashbacks show us how Muir and Bishop met and how they were involved with the woman Bishop falls for while on assignment.

In *Spy Game*, the direction is often electric; the camera rushes past things, zipping by buildings and balconies, in constant motion, which gives the film its style. The basic idea is not bad, although the music makes everything seem more significant than it actually is. Muir is not really a good role for Redford, who replaces the concern, anger, and intensity his character would be feeling with an almost breezy, devil-may-care attitude. Yes, Nathan does not want his superiors to have any inkling of what he's doing behind their backs, but Redford never *lets us in*—he might as well be back in a performance of *Barefoot in the Park* for all the emotional resonance he radiates. Pitt plays it relatively "light" as well but is more effective; *Spy Game* is more his meat and potatoes. But the odd-man-out quality of Redford's performance does serve, even if inadvertently, to set him apart from the smug or grouchy or deadly serious men he's interacting with as the story proceeds. Ultimately, whether by design or accident, Redford does not come off badly in the film at all; his star charisma is entirely intact.

There was concern on how to handle certain sequences in *Spy Game* after the attack on the twin towers on September 11th. "We had an internal screening at Universal with everyone who was involved," recalled Tony Scott, the film's director, "and then we had a public screening. A third of the movie is set in Beirut, and there's one sequence that involves a building blowing up. When you talk to everybody they've got images that stick with them—the papers falling, the fireball, the buildings dropping. In the end, all those things were brought to the table, but you can't just appease everybody."

Scott decided to recut the sequence so that it became "more linear and tighter. It's all seen from Brad's point of view. When we ran it with a public audience . . . [they] were sort of taken aback, but then it dissolved back inside Brad's character, and he took them through the rest of the journey." Scott said at the time, "You have to tread careful, but I think time heals. It [was] a tough call, but the movie is really a relationship movie."

Scott admired the work of his two stars. "It's hard for beautiful guys like Brad and Bob," he said. "They get pigeonholed and typecast into being the pretty boys, and people overlook them in terms of their ability." Scott noticed differences in their working styles while he helmed the picture. "Bob is so tight and so buttoned-up and knows exactly each moment how he wants that scene to play. He knows the interior of the scene, he knows the interior of the character, he knows the subtext. Where Brad is a lot more spontaneous. That can sometimes be a recipe for disaster, but in this case, it was good."

For Scott, Redford had always been an icon, and he was somewhat intimidated by the idea of directing him, especially because they have very different directorial styles. One afternoon Pitt and Redford shot a scene that takes place on a rooftop. Scott had cameras on the ground doing circular tracks even as a camera crew in a helicopter covered the action by flying around and around the roof. This was utterly baffling to Redford, who is far more interested in character and story than he is in fancy cinematic technique. "What the hell is he doing?" he asked Pitt, who could only shrug. Redford could not understand why such a simple scene couldn't be shot in a simple way. Why was it necessary to have so many cameras, to have them moving back and forth, let alone have a copter filming it all as it swung around the roof in circles? But later he said to Scott: "I don't understand why you're doing this, but I'm fascinated." Privately Redford may have thought it was a waste of film, but he decided not to protest. Scott found "laborious" the process of him and Redford discussing everything endlessly to make certain that they "were all on the right page." Scott also tried to get used to the many times Redford would shake his head and say, "Well, that's not how I would have done it." Redford felt out of control while making the film, which was the case right from the beginning of his career; the feeling only intensified once he became a director himself.

While filming scenes at Shepperton Studios in London, Redford agreed to talk to Jan Moir of the *London Daily Telegraph* during a break. The first thing he said when he came into the room was, "I'd rather lie down and go to sleep." Moir described the actor thusly: "He is of middling height and spare build, with a head that seems slightly too big for his compact frame. His hair, which undulates across that lollipop head in luxurious waves, is the colour of lightly-toasted bread and his complexion has been varnished with thick stage make-up; it looks like some tan-coloured concrete was poured on to his skin before he was baked in an oven for a couple of hours. If you rubbed his cheekbone, I suspect that it might crumble like an old biscuit. Heartthrob or not, in the workaday flesh he is an odd-looking creature—part Danish businessman, part Gordon Tracy from *Thunderbird 4*—but even in his glorious heyday Redford seemed oddly detached from his youthful, blond comeliness . . . in conversation he sounds like the wise old man on the mountain top and at all times he remains rather distant and self-absorbed."

Moir also noted that Redford seemed irritated when he was interrupted in his pontification by the interviewer having to change the tape in the recorder. "He exhibits the sonorousness of one who is never interrupted and does not want to be distracted when in full flow," said Moir. Others have observed this trait, although it is true of many, many people besides Redford. To be fair to the actor, Moir may not have quite understood that Redford, like any other movie star, knows that the reporter is there to find out about *him* and his projects, and therefore could hardly have been expected to start asking an interviewer about his own life, especially when there was so little time in which to answer questions. If Redford had taken the time to schmooze the reporter, he might have come off as more charming and less self-involved; but Moir probably wouldn't have liked it if he'd been called back to the soundstage before she got enough information for the profile.

In 2001, because he hadn't starred in a movie for a few years, Redford decided he would help publicize his two new features by giving an interview to *60 Minutes II*. His fans were shocked at how old and haggard he looked in the interview. In his films, like *Indecent Proposal* and *The Horse Whisperer*, Redford was covered with makeup and softly lit under the camera's glow. Interviewer Charlie Rose joked that in the following year, Redford would be eligible for social security, but Bob looked older than his years. A face that had been out in the sun too long and too often was prematurely dried out and wrinkled, especially around the lips; there were large, unsightly pouches under his eyes. Reportedly, Redford had some work done on the eyes after seeing himself on the program—or perhaps people's comments got back to him.

Redford has sharply criticized actors who go in for lots of cosmetic surgery, but he is one performer who could certainly benefit from it, if only to help repair years of sun and wind damage. "Everyone is getting pinched, lifted, and pulled," he said. "I'm looking weird because I'm not. But it just doesn't feel right for me to get surgery. I feel this obsession with plastic surgery is like chipping away at oneself. Everyone wants to preserve their time in history. I guess I'll just have to look for other ways." Redford joked to some colleagues that he's now "Brad Pitt's grandpa." Joan Rivers, who had drastic work done herself, attacked Redford for not admitting he'd had work done on his eyes. Redford's response was quite gentlemanly—merely that she was entitled to her opinion—considering most people think Rivers has turned herself into an unreal and vaguely grotesque wax dummy of decidedly feline cast.

Charlie Rose, a well-regarded reporter and television interviewer for *60 Minutes II*, was forced to put together a puff piece due to Redford's usual reticence about answering anything of depth in his private life. Rose, after reporting that Redford owned five thousand acres of land in Utah, expressed surprise that someone who used his clout to protect undeveloped land had now become a developer. "Development is a fact of life, sometimes too much so," said Redford, whose demeanor was entirely pleasant. He explained that he wanted to create a model of responsible preservation and development. "You can have it both ways in an equitable way," he said.

James Lipton also would have had a problem getting anything deep or new out of Redford when he appeared on *Inside the Actor's Studio* in 2005, except the program functioned more than anything else as a kind of worshipful *This Is Your Life*. Before an audience primarily consisting of young acting students and their teachers, Lipton talked of Redford's achievements and awards. By that time the actor had two Oscars, one for *Ordinary People* and a Lifetime Achievement Award (given in 2002), as well as the Lifetime Achievement Award from SAG (Screen Actors Guild) and the Cecil B. DeMille Award from the Golden Globes. Redford spoke like a great older statesman, and the audience punctuated his remarks with applause and ovations. Wearing glasses that gave him a professorial appearance and hid the bags under his eyes, Redford was pleasant but rather humorless throughout the proceedings. At one point he told Lipton that he hadn't wanted to do *The Way We Were* and had informed director Sydney Pollack that he didn't "want to just stand around being handsome." Lipton deadpanned: "That's a problem I've had all my life." Redford hardly cracked a smile and went right back to his story as if annoyed that he was briefly out of the spotlight. The rest of the time, he told the usual anecdotes but revealed absolutely nothing of the inner man. Sometimes Redford would be more revealing in private with certain skilled print journalists; but in front of an audience he was always Robert Redford the movie star, never Robert Redford the man.

By 2002 Redford's youngest child, Amy, who was then thirty-one, was beginning to draw a tiny bit of attention away from her father. In February of that year she starred as Catherine at the Players Theater in *Golden Ladder*, by Donna Spector. The play was billed as a "comic drama" in which Amy was a woman with a Jewish father and Christian mother. Conflicted and searching for answers, the young woman embarks on a "spiritual odyssey" with often humorous results. Reporters such as Patricia O'Haire of the *New York Daily News* were assigned to do feature stories on her, which undoubtedly would not have happened had her last name not been Redford.

Amy had not always welcomed this kind of attention. For years, the last thing she wanted anybody to know was that she was Robert Redford's daughter. At fourteen, during a rebellious stage, she shaved off all the hair on one side of her head. "Some people go inside themselves," she recalled. "I wasn't someone who liked to hide so I gave them something to look at. I just wanted room to become the person I was meant to be, not what was prescribed for me." She dropped out of the University of Colorado, as her father did, and adopted her grandmother's surname, Hart.

Robert Redford did not encourage Amy to become an actress. She got the call but wasn't certain the life was right for her until she went to the London Academy of Music and Dramatic Arts to study. "I knew then I was serious about it," she said. She registered under the name Amy Hart and used this as her stage name for quite a few years, admirably determined to make it on her own and not on the strength of her father's stardom. But as she approached thirty and major success seemed increasingly elusive, the Redford name didn't seem quite so bad.

An attractive, slender blond with blue eyes, Amy married photographer Mark Mann in 2001, and the two lived in downtown Manhattan. By that time Amy had resided all over the world, including Los Angeles, Paris, and London. "When I was growing up we lived on the East Side [of Manhattan]," she recalled, "but I never felt comfortable there. I love downtown, love walking the streets with my dog. I looked at a lot of different places before I realized the place I was born was the best place to be." In New York she gets fewer questions about her famous father than she does in LA—or in Park City, Utah. "People in this city are great. They take me for myself."

Amy also appeared in the play *Collected Stories*, by David Margulies, and she has done quite a few movies, including *Giving It Up* (1999), *Mergers and Acquisitions* (2001), and *Maid in Manhattan* (2002). In subsequent years she has done guest spots on *Sex and the City*, *The*

Sopranos, *Law and Order: Special Victims Unit*, and *Law and Order: Criminal Intent*. In 2005 she appeared in the films *Strike the Tent* and *The Music Inside*, among others. She also had a part in the play *Bhutan*, which was written by yet another celebrity offspring, playwright Horton Foote's daughter, Daisy.

Redford has always felt it is important for actors to have "another life" outside of acting. Although he has been very lucky, he knows that the business can often be, as he puts it, "cruel and brutal," which is why he did not encourage his children to become actors or even to enter the film business in any capacity. Still, it's in Amy's blood, and to a lesser extent in Jamie's. Redford's "other life" is his work at Sundance, not to mention his ranch.

Redford had often been criticized because he supposedly did not appear in independent films, even though his Sundance Festival was created to support "indie" production. Redford considered *Downhill Racer* and some of his other films to be independent films; he said they were at least "independent-natured" films, even though they had been "financed within the mainstream." But since the festival's inception (and before), the first real movie he had starred in that qualified for entry in Sundance was *The Clearing* (2004). Redford felt the studios financed some of his independent-natured films because he would do a big-budget, studio-type film beforehand, but it's hard to think of such films as *Ordinary People* or *Quiz Show* as being indies.

Sundance director Geoff Gilmore wanted to present *The Clearing* at the festival the moment he screened it, but Redford claimed to have reservations. "I was concerned about the appearance of being self-serving," he said. Gilmore won Redford over by pointing out that his being in the picture "basically says you're contributing to the very thing you created." Of course, the fact that something could be called an indie and yet star someone along the lines of Robert Redford and the very well-known Helen Mirren illustrated just how much the independent feature scene had changed over the years. *The Clearing* would not open wide, like most of Redford's studio films; following the typical indie path, it debuted in only a few cinemas before expanding outward.

As noted, Redford was teamed with the formidable Helen Mirren for *The Clearing*, in which they played a wealthy couple named Wayne and Eileen Hayes. Leaving his home one morning, Hayes is kidnapped by a strange man—Arnold, played by Willem Dafoe—who takes Hayes into the woods, saying his associates are waiting in a clearing. As they make the way into the forest and Hayes tries to bond with Arnold to get the better of him, the FBI consults with Eileen, who learns that her husband is still seeing the woman with whom he once had an affair. Eventually Eileen is instructed to deliver the ransom and manages to get away from her FBI followers; but once the money is dropped off, it becomes clear that an exchange is not going to be made. Arnold, who is captured through his sheer stupidity, was the only kidnapper; there were no associates and no clearing—Arnold simply murders Hayes deep in the woods. Eileen receives in the mail a letter from Hayes, which Arnold mailed for him after his death. In it, Hayes reaffirms his love for his wife.

As so often before, Redford portrays the character in this film as cool and controlled even when a man is holding a gun on him and he's being forced deeper and deeper into a situation that almost any man would find frightening. He never seems especially uneasy, which makes no sense, no matter how strong or tough Wayne Hayes may be in business. Talking to his captor, Redford is too often casual, offhand, almost playing it cute. If this was meant to show Hayes's disdain for Arnold, his belief that he will be able to best him in the end, it backfires. This is one reason for the lack of tension in the scenes between Redford and Dafoe; more suspense is generated by the scenes between Hayes's family and the FBI agent Fuller. Except for a couple of moments, *The Clearing* avoids painful emotion, and the death scene is completely muffed. It's shown in flashback—merely a glimpse of Redford's face, almost expressionless, then the flash and sound of the gun. The abrupt conclusion offers no revelations or mystery.

Redford still looks handsome on-screen, his voice as youthful as ever. He and Helen Mirren make a believable couple and have wonderful chemistry, although the picture gives them little real chance to act together. Mirren's strong emotional moments are played strictly to the camera. *The Clearing* holds the audience's attention long enough to convince them they might be witnessing something rare and powerful; but like Redford's performance, the movie itself is too cool and controlled, as if director Pieter Jan Brugge were afraid he'd be accused of helming a particularly melodramatic episode of *Days of Our Lives*. One can feel for Mirren's pain and loss, her mixed emotions and hurt over Hayes's infidelities, and the bit with the letter from a dead man is a poignant touch, but Hayes—because of the script and Redford's not-there performance—is such a shadowy figure that it's hard to be moved by his fate.

Reviews for *The Clearing* expressed admiration for some aspects of the production—mostly its reliance on middle-aged players in the middle of a Hollywood "youthquake"—but were generally negative. Wrote Todd McCarthy in *Variety*: "*The Clearing* tests the limits of how restrained a suspense film can be and still remain suspenseful. Classy, decorous and well acted . . . [it] is nicely crafted but too buttoned up to generate more than polite interest, much less the urgent excitement a kidnapping story might be expected to trigger. . . . [Brugge's] apparent urge to avoid genre clichés and audience pandering takes him too far in the opposite direction, as the picture resists every opportunity to quicken the viewer's pulse."

Lisa Schwarzbaum in *Entertainment Weekly* had reservations about the movie—"a foggy semi-thriller of inconsistent mood"—but seemed to admire Redford's performance: "*The Clearing* might well refer to those moments when one of the American cinema's most image-conscious celebrities drops his veil. The clouding might well refer to the rest of the picture." Referring to the scene when Redford tells Dafoe, "My wife doesn't look at me the way she did thirty years ago," Schwarzbaum writes: "For a moment we are so startled by the openness of the performance (from an actor used to feinting) that the rest of the story goes slack."

Brugge and Redford's miscalculations with their movie pretty much ensured an indifferent box office. The average episode of *Law and Order: Special Victims Unit* was more riveting than *The Clearing*, so why should people want to pay ten bucks when they could see something better—for free—on television?

Redford was back in Havana in early 2004, where he invited the family of Ernesto "Che" Guevara to a private screening of Walter Salles's *The Motorcycle Diaries* at the Cuban Institute of Film and

Art. The movie, for which Redford was executive producer, looked at the early years of the revolutionary traveling across Latin America before he joined up with Fidel Castro. Redford kept his remarks to reporters almost comically brief. "I've come to present the movie I've produced about Che," he said. "I'm very happy to be here."

He reserved his talking for his first-ever TV commercial, for United Airlines, intoning the phrase, "Where you go in life is up to you." Patricia Sellers of *Fortune* quipped: "Maybe this move is just another manifestation of Redford's desire to help the needy. United is, after all, in chapter 11." Redford also used his breath in railing against President George W. Bush and his environmental policies, saying that he would move to Ireland if Bush were reelected. When Bush won a second term, some Republican bloggers reminded Redford of his promise and took up a collection to buy him a ticket—coach only—to the Emerald Isle. Redford countered that he wasn't being literal. "I wouldn't waste my time on this administration," he said, "the dye is pretty well cast." Redford added that he wouldn't leave the country he loves just because of "some barking dog on TV."

Also in 2004, writer Peter Biskind (*Easy Riders, Raging Bulls*) came out with a follow-up tome entitled *Down and Dirty Pictures: Miramax, Sundance, and the Rise of Independent Film*, which focused primarily on Harvey Weinstein (and, to a lesser degree, his brother Bob) of Miramax and secondarily on Redford and the Sundance Institute. Although the book gave Redford his due as the instigator of the Sundance Lab and festivals and mentioned his commitment to independent filmmaking, it was largely a negative depiction, criticizing Redford for allowing Sundance to veer from its original purpose. It related deals that had allegedly gone astray because of Redford's procrastination and discussed his unfortunate (but entirely understandable, given his schedule and his dependence, after all, on a staff) habit of not being there to oversee things when it was most important that he do so. While the book was excellent in many ways, some critics noted that much of its criticism of Redford came from disgruntled former employees. Everyone with a grudge against Redford came out of the woodwork to sharpen their hatchets, especially those who felt he had "stolen" their projects away from them. "I regret that [Redford] didn't talk to me," said Biskind. "It would have benefited the book—and him—to see the world from his point of view." Biskind joked that he might do a book signing in Sundance, but only for an hour "before I get killed."

Redford was angry about being depicted in Biskind's book as a control freak infected with movie-star egomania (he didn't need to read the book; the reviews made clear what was in it). During the 2004 Sundance Festival, Redford let it be known that he would not be giving interviews; but then he reversed himself and spoke to the *Los Angeles Times.* Peter Bart, who'd worked with Redford on several movies, used the occasion to write his impressions of Redford in *Variety.* Over the years, Bart had frequently expressed his somewhat affectionate exasperation with the very private Redford.

In his new piece, Bart characterized Redford as a "thoughtful man," and cited Bob's concern for the environment and independent filmmakers. "I guess I can rightfully suggest that I know him," wrote Bart. "The trouble is, I don't. . . . He is a character in need of a rewrite. Not a total rewrite—just a touch of empathy here and there, a hint of passion, a willingness to confront people and ideas. But, of course, stars don't get rewritten." Bart suggested that "Redford Moments" kept getting in the way, and he gave an example. As Bart drove Redford to his home for dinner one night, Redford pointed at a house and said that his first girlfriend—at least he thought it was his first—used to live there. Bart waited for some elaboration, but none ever came. "A comment, an opening, and then nothing, no emotion, no subtext. . . . It was a Redford Moment." Of course it's just as likely that Redford was merely making strained small talk and had nothing else to say on the matter. He wasn't even certain it was the right house—or girlfriend. But when one becomes a movie star, every single phrase or pause becomes fraught with significance, even when it's an absent remark spoken to fill a silence or ease boredom.

In 2005 and since then, Redford has continued to be very busy. He reported that he and Paul Newman would definitely reunite for a new project—"We'd better hurry," both men quipped—possibly an adaptation of *A Walk in the Woods,* a book by Bill Bryson detailing the author's hikes through the American wilderness with a friend. Redford produced a new series on the Sundance Channel; entitled *Iconoclasts*, it features one well-known person interviewing another. In December Redford interviewed Paul Newman, discussing his charity work, race-car driving, and movie career. Along with old Broadway costar Julie Harris, singers Tony Bennett and Tina Turner, and ballet muse Suzanne Farrell, Redford was honored with a Kennedy Center award. Upon learning that he would be one of the five recipients, Redford said, "I have been blessed with a love for and ability in art, and it is a gift which I have attempted to make the most of. It is an honor to be recognized for this." Although many observers sensed the mixed emotions he felt, Redford managed a tactful and pleasant smile as he shook hands with President Bush.

Redford is remaining busy as an actor and director as well. In the fall of 2005 came the premiere of his thirty-eighth movie, *An Unfinished Life*. In this film Redford plays Einar Gilkyson, a recovering alcoholic and farmer. Einar lives with his best friend, Mitch (Morgan Freeman), who has been badly mauled by a bear. Einar's daughter-in-law, Jean (Jennifer Lopez), who's now running from her brutal boyfriend, shows up after disappearing twelve years earlier. She had left because Einar's son was killed in a car accident when she was driving. Einar's twelve-year-old granddaughter mistakenly assumes that Einar and Mitch are lovers. Both the bear and the beastly boyfriend show up to cause more trouble. "[You know] a film is in trouble when, despite the presence of an A list cast and a well-regarded director, the best thing in it is a partly digitized bear," opined *Variety*. "Redford, who seems to be putting his own laconic spin on a part that feels like it was written for Clint Eastwood, doesn't muster anything much more than dignity and manly grumpiness, but at least he can really throw a lasso."

Although it takes place in the American West, *An Unfinished Life* was actually filmed in Canada in 2003. In need of recutting and refocusing, it was held up for release for two years. "I can't even remember when we made it," said director Lasse Hallström. "One might think an old Swede like me would know very little about the American West, but I'm attracted to anything that has characters that leap off the page and come alive for me." Redford had higher hopes for his latest directorial project, *Aloft*, which deals with two men who track the flight of the peregrine falcon of North America.

With a woman to love and to love him back, films to make, children to care about—and who care about him—a solid career both behind and ahead of him, Redford is in a good place, growing old with grace and dignity, stepping back to make observations of life and show business that are often right on target. "Entertainment is a double-edged sword, frankly," he told the *New York Times*, "and it's kind of weird to be saying this because it's my day job. But I'm a little critical of how completely oppressive it's getting. Newspapers now have box office scores on the front page. The front page should be left for major issues that really affect us. And top 10 this, top 10 that—it's always changing. It's about as shallow and transitory as you can get."

As for himself, Redford has kept his sense of perspective and humor, a boon to all as they grow older in a world seemingly fixated on youth. "Nobody is swooning over someone my age," he says, "They see me, and they're more likely to say, 'Oh, is he still around?'"

FILMOGRAPHY

As Actor, Director, or Both

War Hunt (1962). Director: Denis Sanders. Redford plays soldier Roy Loomis in an underwritten Korean War drama starring John Saxon.

Situation Hopeless . . . But Not Serious (1965). Director: Gottfried Reinhardt. Redford plays World War II flier Hank, who is "captured" by a German shopkeeper and kept in his basement with another flier even after the war has ended, in a monumentally forgettable "comedy" with Alec Guinness.

Inside Daisy Clover (1965). Director: Robert Mulligan. This is Redford's first major Hollywood film, in which he plays bisexual actor Wade Lewis and Natalie Wood and Christopher Plummer star.

The Chase (1966). Director: Arthur Penn. Redford is the pivotal but hardly seen escaped convict Bubber Reeves in this overlong and overdrawn melodrama starring Marlon Brando.

This Property Is Condemned (1966). Director: Sydney Pollack. Redford plays Owen Legate, again the love interest of Natalie Wood, in a movie inspired by the work of Tennessee Williams but with none of his genius. The second directorial assignment for Pollack, who would work with Redford many times.

Barefoot in the Park (1967). Director: Gene Saks. Redford re-creates the role of newlywed Paul Bratter, married to slightly kooky and hysterical Jane Fonda in the film adaptation of Neil Simon's play.

Butch Cassidy and the Sundance Kid (1969). Director: George Roy Hill. Redford is the Sundance Kid in the film that turned him into a superstar and sex symbol supreme.

Downhill Racer (1969). Director: Michael Ritchie. Redford is David Chappellet in this overly low-key study of an egotistical skiing champ. First production of Redford's Wildwood International.

Tell Them Willie Boy Is Here (1969). Director: Abraham Polonsky. Redford is Sheriff Cooper in a dull chase film full of self-conscious political relevance.

Little Fauss and Big Halsy (1970). Director: Sidney J. Furie. Redford is Big Halsy in this weird little picture that seems to have even less to it than meets the eye.

The Hot Rock (1972). Director: Peter Yates. Redford is professional thief Dortmunder in one of his most entertaining movies.

The Candidate (1972). Director: Michael Ritchie. Redford runs for office as Bill McKay, a part that was tailor made for his image and talents.

Jeremiah Johnson (1972). Director: Sydney Pollack. Redford in the title role of a mountain man enduring and weathering assorted hardships and calamities in a beautiful frozen wilderness.

The Way We Were. (1973). Director: Sydney Pollack. Redford didn't really want to team with Barbra Streisand for this story of a star-crossed romance set in the McCarthy period, but it made a great deal of money. There was much talk of a sequel that never materialized.

The Sting (1973). Director: George Roy Hill. Lightweight if entertaining scam flick with Redford and Newman sauntering through and getting by on their charm. Another big hit.

The Great Gatsby (1974). Director: Jack Clayton. A miscast, much too reserved Redford makes little impression in this not terrible but not memorable version of Fitzgerald's famous novel.

The Great Waldo Pepper (1975). Director: George Roy Hill. Redford reteamed with the director of two of his biggest hits—sans Paul Newman—but this time lightning didn't strike at the box office or anywhere else.

Three Days of the Condor (1975). Director: Sydney Pollack. Redford and friend Pollack teamed yet again, this time for an insubstantial spy film that was virtually forgotten at the time of its release.

All the President's Men (1976) Director: Alan J. Pakula. The true events of Watergate turned into a top-notch suspense film with a very good performance from Redford.

A Bridge Too Far (1977). Director: Richard Attenborough. Redford got millions for a few days of work in this all-star, multimillion-dollar war flick from producer Joseph Levine.

The Electric Horseman (1979). Director: Sydney Pollack. One of the all-time worst Redford-Pollack combinations, it proves only that the road to hell is paved with good intentions. Slick, shrill, and empty despite its message, the film hardly works on any level.

Brubaker (1980). Director: Stuart Rosenberg. Redford stars as a new prison warden who is determined to make changes but comes up against corruption and indifference in this well-intentioned if imperfect drama.

Ordinary People (1980). Director: Robert Redford. Redford's directorial debut about a dysfunctional family and a deeply troubled young man garnered him a well-deserved Academy Award. It runs neck and neck with *Quiz Show* as his greatest achievement.

The Natural (1984). Director: Barry Levinson. Redford is a baseball player whose life is sidetracked by grotesque events in a story that intrigues but never quite jells.

Out of Africa (1985). Director: Sydney Pollack. Arguably Pollack's greatest film, most critics agreed that it would have been better if someone besides Redford had been cast as the male lead. The irony was that without Redford's participation, the noncommercial film—which actually did well at the box office—would probably never have been made.

Legal Eagles (1986). Director: Ivan Reitman. As district attorney Tom Logan, Redford gives a sharp performance while helping Laura Kelly (Debra Winger) to defend Chelsea Deardon (Daryl Hannah) against murder charges in this minor but entertaining thriller.

The Milagro Beanfield War (1988). Director: Robert Redford. Inspired by Redford's own problems with developers, this is a slight, obvious film about the war between a poor bean-field owner and some rich developers, but it was much admired in some quarters.

Havana (1990). Director: Sydney Pollack. A Redford and Pollack misfire placing Redford amidst rebels, gamblers, and gangsters in a volatile fifties Cuba and featuring an unconvincing romance with beautiful Lena Olin.

Sneakers (1992). Director: Phil Alden Robinson. Redford teams with such disparate players as Dan Aykroyd, River Phoenix, and Sidney Poitier in his first caper film since *The Hot Rock*, for mixed but generally fun results.

A River Runs Through It (1992). Director: Robert Redford. Redford turns in a solid directorial job in this handsome, well-acted if disappointing adaptation of the novella by Norman MacLean, set in Montana and focusing on the relationship between two brothers.

Indecent Proposal (1993). Director: Adrian Lyne. Although only in a supporting role as a billionaire who offers a struggling young couple a million dollars in order to sleep with the wife, Redford had one of his biggest latter-day hits.

Quiz Show (1994). Director: Robert Redford. Arguably Redford's finest filmic achievement, an incisive study of lives intersecting over the quiz show scandals of the 1950s and 1960s. Although Redford was criticized for the film's fictionalized aspects, the movie works beautifully on every level.

Up Close & Personal (1996). Director: Jon Avnet. The virtues of this not-bad movie starring Redford and Michelle Pfeiffer were pretty much lost when word got out that it had originally been intended to present the dramatic real-life story of newswoman Jessica Savitch.

The Horse Whisperer (1998). Director: Robert Redford. Redford directed himself in this mammoth adaptation of the novel. The film, a valentine to his beloved wide open spaces, was more often seen as Redford's valentine to himself.

The Legend of Bagger Vance (2000). Director: Robert Redford. Redford's superior direction and excellent performances triumph over an interesting if imperfect script in this unusual and rather charming evocation of a Southern fable about golf and life.

The Last Castle (2001). Director: Rod Lurie. Redford plays a court-martialed general incarcerated in a military prison in this action-drama whose compelling premise is completely undermined by an utterly contrived and often idiotic script.

Spy Game (2001). Director: Tony Scott. Redford reunited with megastar Brad Pitt—"the young Robert Redford"—in a slick, fast-paced, ultimately unsatisfying espionage thriller with a few twists and turns and whirling camera movements.

The Clearing (2004). Director: Pieter Jan Brugge. Redford plays Wayne Hayes, a kidnapped executive.

An Unfinished Life (2005). Director: Lasse Hallström.

Upcoming projects: *Aloft* (director); *Untitled Jackie Robinson Project* (as Branch Rickey); *Charlotte's Web* (as voice of Ike).

As Executive Producer

The Solar Film (1980)
Promised Land (1987)
Some Girls (1988)
The Dark Wind (1991)
Incident at Oglala (1992) Note: Redford also narrated.
Grand Avenue [TV] (1996)
She's the One (1996)
No Looking Back (1998)
Slums of Beverly Hills (1998)
How to Kill Your Neighbor's Dog (2002)
Love in the Time of Money (2002)
People I Know (2002)
Skinwalkers [TV] (2002)
Coyote Waits [TV] (2003)
The Motorcycle Diaries (2004)
A Thief of Time [TV] (2004)
Iconoclasts [TV series] (2005)

BIBLIOGRAPHY

Note: Most of the information in this book comes from many dozens of interviews conducted specifically for this book or on the set of various Robert Redford films, or with those who have known and worked with Redford over a period of years, as well as interviews with Redford himself. The following books have been consulted to double-check information or to provide leads for further research.

Alexander, Jane. *Command Performance: An Actress in the Theater of Politics.* New York: Public Affairs, 2000.

Amburn, Ellis. *The Sexiest Man Alive: A Biography of Warren Beatty.* New York: HarperEntertainment, 2002.

Auster, Bruce B., and Michael Satchell. "Did Redford Know the Secret?" *U.S. News and World Report,* May 12, 1997.

Bart, Peter. *Who Killed Hollywood . . . and Put the Tarnish on Tinseltown?* Los Angeles: Renaissance, 1999.

———. "Redford's Sounds of Silence." *Variety,* January 19, 2004.

———, and Peter Guber. *Shoot Out: Surviving Fame and Misfortune in Hollywood.* New York: Putnam, 2002.

Billen, Andrew. "The Real Redford." *London Evening Standard,* August 5, 1998.

Biskind, Peter. *Easy Riders, Raging Bulls: How the Sex-Drugs-and-Rock 'n' Roll Generation Saved Hollywood.* New York: Simon & Schuster, 1998.

———. *Down and Dirty Pictures: Miramax, Sundance, and the Rise of Independent Film.* New York: Simon & Schuster, 2004.

Brown, Jared. *Zero Mostel: A Biography.* New York: Atheneum, 1989.

Buhle, Paul, and Dave Wagner. *Hide in Plain Sight: The Hollywood Blacklistees in Film and Television, 1950–2002.* New York: Palgrave Macmillan, 2003.

Callan, Michael Feeney. *Sean Connery.* New York: Stein & Day, 1983.

Callow, Simon. *Charles Laughton: A Difficult Actor.* New York: Grove Press, 1987.

Carr, Jay. "Out of Africa." *Boston Globe,* December 18, 1985.

Chamberlain, Richard. *Shattered Love: A Memoir.* New York: ReganBooks, 2003.

Davidson, Bill. *Jane Fonda: An Intimate Biography.* New York: Dutton, 1990.

Dillman, Bradford. *Are You Anybody? An Actor's Life.* Santa Barbara: Fithian Press, 1997.

Dinesen, Isak. *Out of Africa* and *Shadows on the Grass.* New York: Random House, 1937.

Dougan, Andy. *Actor's Director: Richard Attenborough Behind the Camera.* London: Mainstream, 1995.

Douglas, Melvyn, and Tom Arthur. *See You at the Movies: The Autobiography of Melvyn Douglas.* Lanham, MD: University Press of America, 1986.

Dunaway, Faye, with Betsy Sharkey. *Looking for Gatsby: My Life.* New York: Simon & Schuster, 1995.

Dunne, John Gregory. *Monster: Living Off the Big Screen.* New York: Random House, 1997.

Edelman, Rob, and Audrey Kupferberg. *Matthau: A Life.* Lanham, MD: Taylor, 2002.

Ehrlich, Gretel. *The Horse Whisperer: An Illustrated Companion to the Major Motion Picture.* New York: Dell, 1998.

Evans, Nicholas. *The Horse Whisperer.* New York: Dell, 1995.

Farrow, Mia. *What Falls Away: A Memoir.* New York: Doubleday, 1997.

Finstad, Suzanne. *Natasha: The Biography of Natalie Wood.* New York: Harmony, 2001.

Fiori, Pamela. "The Natural." *Town and Country*, November 20, 2002.

Fonda, Jane. *My Life So Far.* New York: Random House, 2005.

Foote, Timothy. "A New Film about Fly Fishing—and Much, Much More." *Smithsonian*, September 1992.

Glatt, John. *Lost in Hollywood: The Fast Times and Short Life of River Phoenix.* New York: Primus / Donald Fine, 1995.

Goldman, William. *Adventures in the Screen Trade.* New York: Warner, 1983.

Goodall, Nigel. *Demi Moore: The Most Powerful Woman in Hollywood.* London: Mainstream, 2000.

Griscom, Amanda. "The Outsider." *Sunday New York Times Magazine*, December 8, 2002.

Hackett, Larry, with Todd Gold, Ken Baker, Cathy Free, and Danielle Morton. "The Eclectic Horseman." *People*, June 8, 1998.

Hart, Jeffrey. "Van Doren and Redford." *National Review*, 1994.

Hinson, Hal. "A Pretty Boy No More." *Chicago Sun-Times,* January 1, 1991.

Huisman, Mark J. "Sundance's Lavender Screen." *The Advocate*, February 4, 1997.

Hunter, Allan. *Gene Hackman.* New York: St. Martin's Press, 1987.

Johnson, Brian D. "Verdict on Trial." *MacLean's*, July 27, 1992.

Kearney, Jill. "No More Playing It Safe." *San Francisco Chronicle*, March 27, 1988.

Kilday, Gregg. "Secrets and Buys." *Entertainment Weekly*, February 7, 1997.

Leff, Leonard. "The Elusive Gatsby." *Opera News*, December 1999.

Lenburg, Jeff. *Dustin Hoffman: Hollywood's Antihero.* New York: St. Martin's, 1983.

Lindfors, Viveca. *Viveka . . . Viveca.* New York: Everest House, 1981.

Mackenzie, Suzie. "American Dreamer." *The Guardian*, August 14, 2004.

Maclean, Norman. *A River Runs Through It.* Chicago: University of Chicago Press, 1976.

Manso, Peter. *Brando: The Biography.* New York: Hyperion, 1994.

Moir, Jan. "Interview." *Daily Telegraph*, March 1, 2001.

Moore, Mary Tyler. *After All.* New York: Putnam, 1995.

Munn, Michael. *Gene Hackman.* London: Robert Hale, 1997.

Murphy, Mary. "The Sundance King." *TV Guide*, January 12, 2002.

Nash, Alanna. *Golden Girl: The Story of Jessica Savitch.* New York: Dutton, 1988.

Obst, Linda. *Hello, He Lied and Other Truths from the Hollywood Trenches.* Boston: Little, Brown, 1996.

Phillips, Julia. *You'll Never Eat Lunch in This Town Again.* New York: Random House, 1991.

Pringle, Gill. "Be My Guest." *Sunday Mirror*, 1998.

Quirk, Lawrence J. *Paul Newman.* Dallas: Taylor, 1996.

Riese, Randall. *Her Name Is Barbra.* New York: Birch Lane, 1993.

Robb, Brian J. *Brad Pitt: The Rise to Stardom.* London: Plexus, 2002.

Rubinstein, Hal. "Interview with Robert Redford." *Interview*, September 1994.

Ryan, Tom. "The Way He Is." *Sydney Morning Herald*, November 27, 2004.

Sandford, Christopher. *McQueen: The Biography.* New York: Taylor, 2001.

Schoell, William. *The Films of Al Pacino*. New York: Carol Publishing, 1995.

Simon, Neil. *The Play Goes On: A Memoir*. New York: Simon & Schuster, 1999.

Spada, James. *The Films of Robert Redford*. Secaucus, NJ: Citadel Press, 1977.

St. Michel, Carrie. "The Redford Family's Private Crisis." *Good Housekeeping*, September 1999.

Stack, Robert with Mark Evans. *Straight Shooting*. New York: Macmillan, 1980.

Svetky, Benjamin. "Not Necessarily the News," *Entertainment Weekly*, March 8, 1996.

Taylor, William R. *Sydney Pollack*. Boston: Twayne, 1981.

Thomson, David. "The Sundance Kid No More." *The London Independent*, October 2, 2005.

Websites

http://highandlowny.tripod.com
http://quirksreviews.tripod.com
www.imdb.com
www.msnbc.com
www.noparolepeltier.com
www.washingtonpost.com

INDEX

About the Authors

Lawrence J. Quirk is one of the country's foremost film historians. He is the author of over thirty-five books on the cinema and film stars, including the national best sellers *Fasten Your Seat Belts: The Passionate Life of Bette Davis*; *James Stewart: Behind the Scenes of a Wonderful Life*; and *Bob Hope: The Road Well Traveled*. He is editor emeritus of the online classic film website *Quirk's Reviews Online* (http://quirksreviews.tripod.com).

William Schoell is the author of such novels as *The Dragon, Fatal Beauty*, and *The Pact*, as well as numerous books on films, celebrities, and the performing arts. He is coauthor (with Lawrence J. Quirk) of the national best seller *The Rat Pack: Neon Nights with the Kings of Cool*, and he has written well-received biographies of Dean Martin, Al Pacino, Edgar Allan Poe, and H. P. Lovecraft. He is executive editor of the entertainment and performing arts e-zine, *High and Low NY* (http://highandlowny.tripod.com).